PLATE I

By courtesy of]

[E. Pollard & Co., Ltd.

A MODERN TAILORING DEPARTMENT.

Neatness and simplicity characterise this well-furnished interior.

THE MODERN TAILOR, OUTFITTER
AND CLOTHIER

THE
MODERN TAILOR
OUTFITTER AND
CLOTHIER

GENERAL EDITOR

A. S. BRIDGLAND, M.J.I.

EDITOR OF "THE TAILOR AND CUTTER"

VOLUME II

CONTENTS

VOL. II

CHAPTER I

CHAPTER II

CHAPTER III

CHAPTER IV

CHAPTER V

CHAPTER VI

CHAPTER XV

CHAPTER XVI

CHAPTER XVII

CHAPTER XVIII

LIST OF PLATES

VOL. II

THE MODERN TAILOR, OUTFITTER, AND CLOTHIER

VOL. II

CHAPTER I

THE WHOLESALE TRADE

By G. W. SUMPTER

(Head Cutter and Designer, John Shannon & Son, Ltd., Walsall. Late with John Barran & Sons, Ltd., Leeds)

IN the tailoring trade, as in every other branch of industry, the last few years have seen many and very varied changes.

The wonderful mechanical appliances, which the brains of our engineers have put forward, are equal in their effectiveness to anything in operation in other trades.

Along with the assistance of such machinery, organisation has devised methods of utilising to its full all the possibilities of such labour-saving devices. The combination of units of machinery, and application of power for driving same, have brought into being the establishment known as the " factory." Along with this have come into existence methods of production known as the " wholesale," whereby goods are produced in quantities, and by combination of effort are put forward at keen competitive prices.

Power looms produce the cloth, and power-driven machinery, in the hands of experienced operators, converts this into garments. It is a state of modern business that one finds in every quarter. Our trade is affected no less than any other in this direction. The particular features of hand-craft, slow and expensive, were not standard and definite or speedy enough for modern requirements. Glorious examples cling to our memory, as does also the speculative chance of goods produced by those methods.

Products that are dominated by the human element have not always been ideal. Productions from the factory may lack much, but they also possess features of excellence due to the highly specialised process, and its expert operators.

The wholesale branch of the tailoring business is growing by leaps and bounds, and is continually encroaching upon the hand-craft tailor. One almost dares to wonder if the complete craftsman, who can cut and make a garment throughout, will soon be non-existent. In a large measure the success which has come to the wholesale branch of the trade may be traced to a lack of properly trained labour. Ours is a highly skilled business, and one in which much patience is necessary to become an efficient craftsman.

For many reasons the trade has not attracted those apprentices who were essential if hand-craft methods were to survive ; for instance, the long hours and the uncertainty of such a seasonal trade.

Then there is the nature of the trade. It is quite to be understood that the average highly spirited boy was not attracted to a calling where he would be required to sit crosslegged for many long and weary hours.

Then, again, the status of our craft has not been of the highest, and very many who came into the business did not keep it up, or drifted away in the slack periods. Thus it will be seen that the wholesale became essential to provide the demand for clothing in sufficient quantities. Also the regular employment with its reasonable hours has become attractive to a far greater degree than the old-time craft methods. Our object here is not to join in the chorus of lament so frequently heard anent the decline of hand-craft, but to set out for the reader's interest an outline showing the activities and methods of the Wholesale Tailoring Trade in all its branches.

To study this branch of the trade to-day we must dismiss from mind the crude and ill-fitting efforts of earlier days. When first this method of production came into being it was employed principally towards the production of working-class garments, where strength was more important than elegance. By a gradual process, due in a measure to the introduction of much skilled labour from hand-craft quarters, and by much diligent study and experiment, a class of production is available that is equal to, if not better than, much of the alleged hand-craft goods. It is a side of the business that must be considered entirely without prejudice, and must be judged on merit. Methods that are speedy are not necessarily inefficient, and

PLATE II

By courtesy of The Marsden Press Matter Co., Ltd. Wigan.

MARSDEN PERFORATED LAYS IN USE FOR THE MARKING OUT OF MEN'S CLOTHING.

efforts that are unorthodox may yet be worthy. Achievement is the object of all effort, and the method by which results are obtained is not too essential.

I write as one knowing both sides of the trade, hand-craft and machine-craft, and assert that skill is required in the latter in but little less degree than the former.

The prime object before the wholesale manufacturer is bulk orders, standard details, and quantity of output. Orders in bulk are much less in evidence to-day than formerly. The variations in style offered in the wholesale production, the many cross-fittings, and the very extensive ranges of cloths, have caused the retailer to buy more piecemeal, with a view to making his stock as varied as possible. The standard details are set out under the headings of model numbers, and many aids are provided to maintain a particular design. Quantity of output is assisted by such means as cutting out with the band knife machine, the electric cutter, and also still in many cases by the use of the old-fashioned " bucky " knife.

Another very valuable help towards the speedy output are the Marsden lays. These consist of pattern outlines marked on to a glazed paper, after which they are perforated. Powder is applied to the lay, with the result that on the removal of the lay marked-out garments remain on the cloth. This is a very valued advantage to the wholesaler, as it maintains a standard of quantity of material used, and if the lays are first planned very, very carefully they will remain in use until the particular model is revised.

Then also in the factory are lifts, conveyors, and many other helps that materially contribute towards speedy handling and quantity of output.

But, to start at the beginning, let us first consider the question of cutting for this branch. This calls for a particular study, and a very definite subject to cater for. The average figure, not too erect, moderately muscular, demands reasonable ease, and sufficient size to allow of generous underwear and free filling of pockets.

One has always to bear in mind that the productions in the wholesale are distributed in all quarters, and must be of such proportion as to find acceptance among the many different classes amongst whom they circulate. It is advisable that the figure chosen for model should be rather inclined to head forward, and to have those particular traits of figure suitable to a sedentary occupation. He should be 5′ 8″ in height, 38″

chest, 32½″ sleeve. Such a figure would represent the generally accepted basis for a regular fitting 38 size, or to the old time sizing—size 5. This is the class, size, and type upon which most wholesale houses base their sample productions.

Having got our figure duly impressed on our mind, we will review the particular features to be incorporated into our pattern. The back balance must be long, going fairly high into the neck, the back stretch must be easy in size, the cut must be rather deep in the scye for ease in slipping the coat on. Buyers for Ready-for-Service garments require these to be such that they can be slipped on with free ease and will readily fall into place on the figure. The shoulders and neck must be cut to get a good clipping collar, for this is a point in particular. The collar must lie snug to the neck, high at the side, and nicely control the lapel. These points present but little difficulty where skilled workers are at hand to carry out the requirements, but with the wholesale the cut must be such that manipulation is reduced to the minimum. All parts must go together with ease, and without the assistance of stretching and shrinking, and those many points infused in the handcraft production.

In the past it was generally considered to be quite impossible to produce a good fitting garment without these many aids, but the designers and pattern cutters for the wholesale have had to find an outline of garment that can be put together by young and not very experienced labour, with but little assistance from men. Such garments must be sound in fit, and not without reasonable style. To the hand-craft operator this would appear to be well-nigh impossible, but the many productions that are finding favour and meeting with support from a fastidious as well as a casual class go to prove that our efforts have not been wasted.

We live in an age when price counts for so very much, and where change is so much desired. The man in the street does not care to be known by the suit he continually wears, hence his desire for a generous change of raiment. Under the old method of production this was only possible among the wealthy, and those comfortably off, owing to the price; but now, thanks to the keen prices and quality of garment produced by the factory, it is possible for even a working man to enjoy a free change, and with it a feeling of increased self-respect. It is easily possible to buy two suits for the price of one produced by the old methods, and this, with such extras as flannel trousers and sports coat, makes for the better dressing so very notice-able among the men of to-day. Walk through the popular thoroughfares of any of our industrial cities and towns and see the working man out with his family. He may very well mix freely, and feel at his ease, for the factory has provided him with a respectability within his means, and of a class that does him credit.

Much time and testing have been given to the establishment of a size card such as will give the best proportion to the largest possible number. This is most important, and. it is probable that much of the success of this branch of the trade is due to offering such a sound basis of fitting. First place is taken with standard sizes, which come under the heading of " Regulars." Then there are the " Shorts," a fitting that has very strong sales, and one that probably many buyers would do well to stock in larger proportions. Then there are the " Longs," not quite so much in demand. In addition we have the disproportions under the heading of " Stouts " and " Short Stouts." Regular fittings are based upon a figure whose height is approximately 5′ 8″ ; Shorts on a figure 5′ 6″ ; Longs on a figure 5′ 11″. Stouts are sizes where the waist is equal to the chest, and are applied to both the regular and short patterns. A complete size card I illustrate elsewhere, with the necessary treatment for the special fittings. From this it may readily be judged that stock fittings are available for almost all requirements. Their adaptability is surprising to many critics, and they fit quite pleasingly on figures one could not truly call good.

Then there is that class demanding personal attention, and preferring to have the tape put around them, which insists on a suit being made to their particular measures. Here again the factory offers service, with an organisation specially arranged to deal with this class of trade, and very big things are being done. A special staff of cutters known as " measure " cutters (as distinct from " stock " cutters) deal with these. Each cutter is provided with sound sets of block patterns marked up into sizes. To these are applied the measures sent in with the order, the particulars of pockets and details are noted, and special care taken to express these requests in the cut-out garments. These cutters are trained in the correct treatment of figures requiring long and short back balance, head forward, stooping, etc., etc. They are also experienced in interpreting the wishes and giving effect to many very scantily expressed orders. They meet with considerable success, where the measures are accurately taken and the particular figures correctly described. What failures there are can usually be traced to badly taken measures and exaggerated or omitted particulars and measures. Measure cutters have also to be trained to observe any inconsistent measures, and to use reasonable discretion in dealing with same. Many little points of guidance are prepared for them, such, for instance, as the comparisons of leg and sleeve, length, back width, etc. To this also is added an understanding of the particular requirements of different districts, such as very muscular figures, etc.

Generally speaking, measure cutting is on a par with the cutting for the retail side of the business. When one considers the number of cutters who cut from a set of block patterns (or gods) one can well define the duties of a measure cutter. This bespoke side of the wholesale also calls for baste-ups for those who require to be fitted on. A special staff prepares these, and after fitting they are marked up by the most experienced men, usually those who have had considerable practice in trying on, and can the more readily judge what is required.

The staff in a wholesale factory cutting room contains workers under many different headings, and much care is needed to frame up an organisation where goods pass along freely and there is no bottle-neck to deter. Speed is the prime object, without which cutting costs would rule against the trade.

The progress of a measure department is through the following sections : Receiving the order ; passing it into work ; cutting the required length of cloth to execute same ; cutting the outsides with a complete set of rough outfittings. Trimming up by the outsides ; and from this to the fitting-up room, where thread marks are put in. Linings and fittings are accurately cut, and the garments are then booked into their respective departments of factory for making.

The progress of all stock goods is through the following hands : Putting the orders into work, and sorting the various orders over to secure the thickest possible cutting lays. These are then marked out on the most suitable cloth by hand, or a Marsden Lay. They vary in thickness according to the orders available and the width of the cloth. In good quality material it will pay to re-mark a lay, where the cloth is an extra width, but in low quality goods this may not be considered advisable. The comparison of time spent, as against cloth saved, must be taken into keen consideration. Stock patterns comprise a complete outfit, facings cut to accurate fittings in a width according to the grade of the trade, flaps, welts, facings, flys, etc. ; all must be to size and accurate. Lays are then folded up according to the class and thickness of the cloth—suiting materials up to as much as 30 thick ; overcoatings (light), 30 ; overcoatings (heavy), 12 to 20 thick. While this is in progress a junior will be engaged laying up Italian cloth, Silesia, fancy Silesia, canvas, and stays. These are laid up in the same order with the colours to correspond with the cloth lay. This facilitates dividing to assure that the coloured shades are correct and that the various cuttings are correctly matched. Fitters-up work in conjunction with the cutting machine, as also do the dividers. The fitters put in the thread marks, cut the flaps to match each forepart, should there be a check or stripe. Flaps and welts are tacked or pinned to their respective portions, size tabs and markings are then put into the bundles, and away they go into the factory for making up. Great care must be exercised to see the sizes do not get crossed, and to this end many firms adopt some system of notches denoting size, and also make free use of gum tabs. The fitters also mark freely on the wrong side a (X) or some other such indication of the wrong side of the material. This is very helpful where the light is defective, and it greatly facilitates the machining. All things must be done to assist the operator to go full steam ahead and to be free from any doubt.

The makers' work tickets will tell him or her how it is to be stitched, and the condition of the garment or bundle must be such that machinery can be kept running and not idle while the operator is enquiring about something or other.

The amount of material taken by the cutters in a factory does not differ very much from the quantity required in the retail bespoke. This is owing to the better facings and fittings generally ; but with stock sizes economies can be effected to a very considerable degree by cutting two or more sizes together ; also, in many cases, by opening out the material to the full single width. This is usually most effective when applied to overcoats ; trousers also lay up better in this way. The cutting of trimmings in bulk manner is also particularly effective, and it is in this direction that economies are most successful.

DIAGRAMS

The diagrams that support these notes are intended as a suitable outline of what is produced in the better class wholesale trade.

They are of proportions accepted by many of the leading and largest buyers of ready-for-service goods. These gentlemen are not concerned generally with exaggerated style; their main stock is safe, and will appeal to the average man. Exaggerated degrees of fitting, and of style, are usually bought as a separate side line. These are produced from special patterns and designs, and are not to be confused with general stock orders, the demand of the average man.

BASIS OF THE DIAGRAMS

It is always refreshing and most interesting to produce goods known as "something snappy"—outlines that catch the eye; but be it always remembered that a designer's success is the amount of turnover that his firm has, and snappy goods with scanty sales do not cut much ice for him.

How often we designers have produced goods to meet the request for "something new." The reception of these productions has probably been very pleasing, complimentary, and has created a keen interest; but how often, with doubt and fear, have we been asked : " Will it sell ? "

Men are so conservative in the matter of dress that one is very limited in scope, and there is not much chance for a " creation."

I mention these points in defence of the diagrams I have drawn. We of the wholesale deal principally with safe, well-balanced garments, neat and moderate in style. The aim should be to produce what a gentleman may wear.

NON-PRODUCTIVE POSITIONS

Visitors to our factories ofttimes pass comments upon the numbers employed, and the people they see about other than those actually engaged in production.

This can be readily understood when it is realised that a cutter's duty is to cut, machinist to machine, tacker, etc. etc. ; each has to keep to a particular, well-defined task. And hence many incidental duties, such as making out of the tickets, scaling of sizes, dealing with the cloth, trimmings, etc. etc., must of necessity employ considerable staff, if the organisation is to be efficient. The keeping down of these non-productive positions is a point to which good management devotes much watchfulness and care.

Again, in the factory there are many posts quite essential, but not included in the actual production costs, e.g. bookers-in and out of trade, keepers of wages books, order seekers, listers, mechanics, etc. Whereas many firms, undoubtedly, try to run their works without an adequate staff employed on these demonstrative duties, others overdo it, and carry far too many, thus creating a very heavy load, which must be recognised as a direct burden on production.

Modern business methods appear to devote very much interest to its administrative side, e.g. costing clerks, clerks working out the percentage of the quantities under different grades, and under different prices of materials used, etc. These grow and multiply by leaps and bounds; and though, undoubtedly, many valuable data are obtained, one must still bear in mind that it is " merchandise that counts." I mention this in passing, for it is well to understand that the clerical side, with its alleged attainments and its lofty ideals, does not always harmonise with the practical side. Both sides play their part in the conduct of a business, but your buyer only judges your goods, the results of your practical side. Modern methods appear to willingly spend shillings to see that the pence do not go astray.

Then in addition there is the selling side. This again can quite easily be a source of considerable outgoing, and is a department that must be given consideration in all matters appertaining to costings.

I mention these points, for it is well that we should realise a side other than the practical.

MAKING-UP

Our next consideration, and a very important one too, is the actual making-up of our garments.

In the first place, it would be well to consider the lay-out of an up-to-date workroom, specially designed for the manufacture of a medium and better class man's lounge coat. It has always been a case of " many men, many methods," and it is not surprising to find in workrooms almost as great a diversity of procedure, as cutters with systems. However, the main point and object should be time-saving, and efficient workers on garments through their various stages of development.

Very often in the lay-out or plan of a workroom we find

gross anomalies, such as work going backwards and forwards, instead of being constantly progressive. This can and must be eliminated, if we are to produce a good garment at low cost.

The plan of a workroom must vary according to the system of manufacture.

Of these systems we might mention sub-divisional and semi-divisional. The machinery required is very much the same for all, viz., sewing machines, blind stitch, sleeving, padding, button-holing, etc. The division of labour, and the allocation of the different parts, call for expert knowledge on the part of the supervisor, or foreman, as he is generally called. He must be a man of expert knowledge and capability, for, not only does his job include tailoring, but he must be somewhat of a psychologist, as the human element is so great a factor in all specialised jobs. Often we find the staff jerky and ill-balanced, largely due to bad judgment and, perhaps, inconsiderate treatment of those in charge

A foreman should always remember that his staff is there to produce, and he is there to see that they do produce, and anything which interferes must be ruthlessly cut out.

By the divisional system we mean that the various parts of the garment are made by different workers, and are gradually assembled in progress of manufacture, passing on to the next process in their correct order.

One of the great advantages of this system is the low cost of teaching labour, and the good results that may be quickly achieved.

Again, a quick and inexpensive system is always desirable where female workers are concerned, as the problem of good labour—an ever-present bogey to the supervisor—is a constant source of anxiety. The majority of girls leave after a few years' service to get married, and the wedding bells have often tolled the passing of an expert. The workrooms should be so designed that the work, when passed in from the cutting and fitting-up rooms, is directly ready on the first table to be given out to the machinist.

Regarding the vexed question of the ideal speed of sewing machines, it has been our experience, having regard to all points, wear and tear, etc., to be 2,700 to 3,000 stitches per minute. This works out well in actual progress.

Taking the sub-divisional system first, the following is the order usually taken for lounge coats.

Pockets.
Coat linings.
Join collar and canvas.
Mastel pad collar.
Machine canvas.
Mastel pad lapel.
Join up.
Under press collar seams and lining.
Machine bridle.
Tape edge.
Fasten tape.
Pare collar canvas.
Baste edges, facings on, and out.
Pare scye.
Pare bottom, vents, etc.
Sew in sleeves.
Press edges.
Stitch edges.
Button holes and felling.
Press off, button, and overlook.

All these processes are completed by different workers, and the ratio of time taken by each determines the factor of how many are required to balance the staff. The supervisor will make innumerable motion studies before he gets the correct balance, and will find liberal use of a stop-watch desirable.

One of the failings of the system is absentees, which means much duplication of workers, and, consequently, frequent " drags."

To identify the various sizes, and prevent crossing, notches are put in in the various parts by the fitter and cutter. Given a long run of the same class of garments on bulk this system answers very well, but where any odd garments are required, and garments varied in style, it is generally a failure.

We shall now consider what is known as the semi-divisional method. This consists of grouping various processes of the sub-divisional under one heading, and it answers equally well for bulk orders or singles. The machinist is given a coat with all in that is required for the machining and basting. Pockets are put in, linings and sleeves made, coat joined up. This is about equal to the first seven processes of the sub-divisional.

Passing on to the under presser, all seams are opened and the whole coat, linings and sleeves, handed to the baster. After basting on canvas, collar creased by presser, and pared by shaper, the facings are basted on, and a machinist in close proximity to the baster runs the facings on. After basting, the coat is edged, pressed, stitched, and sleeved, when it is ready for button-holing and finishing. The finishing, pressing and buttoning occupy a portion of the room to themselves. Finally, a brush over, and a general overlook. This system requires a good deal of thought in points such as the placing of padding machine, pressing tables, etc., etc., to save time in handling. We put this system forward as one used by some of the best houses in the trade, with excellent results, both in time-saving and to avoid what is generally known as "hopeless mix-up."

A man's lounge coat made on this system will cost, or may cost, under piece-work rates, something as under :

		d.
Machine .	. . . .	11½
Baste	. . . .	11
Under pressing	. . . . . .	3½
Edge pressing .	. . . . . .	3½
Collar and lapel padding .	. . . . .	1
Running on and sleeving .	. . . . .	2½
Pressing off	. . . .	8
Buttoning	. . . .	1

(A basis set)

Add to this the cost of supervision by workers, etc.

Nothing is required for carrying garments from one part of the room to the other, as the individual worker passes the work on when their process is completed to the next one. Much depends on the supervision, and the standard of efficiency will be no more, either in speed or quality, than the supervision.

"A stream can rise no higher than its source," was never more true than in a clothing factory workroom.

BOYS' AND YOUTHS' SUITS

Sizes	ooo	oo	o	1	2	3	4	5	6	7	8	9	10	11	12	13
Age		3	4	5	6	7	8	9½	11		12	13	14	15	16	17	18	19
Breast	.	22	22½	23	23½	24	25	26	27	28	29	30	31	32	33	34	35
Sleeve	.	16½	17½	18½	19½	20¾	22	23½	24¾	26	27	28	29	30	30½	31	31½
Waist .	.	—	—	—	—	—	—	—	—	27	27½	28	28½	29	29½	30	31
Leg .	.	—	—	—	—	—	—	—	—	25½	27	28	29	30	30½	31	31½

P.T.U. trousers will be 1½″ shorter.

BOYS' AND YOUTHS' OVERCOATS

Breast on vest same sizes as suits. Sleeves ¼″ longer than suits ooo to 6.
Sleeves 1″ longer than suits 7 to 13.

KNICKERS (Scotch Shorts)

Sizes	000	00	0	1	2	3	4	5	6	7	8	9	10
Age	3	4	5	6	7	8	9½	11	12	13	14	15	16
Length in leg	4	4½	5	6	6½	7	8	8½	9	10	11	12	12½

MEN'S SUITS

Stock Sizes

Sizes	3	4	5	6	7
Breast	34	36	38	40	42
Sleeve	31	31½	32½	33	33½
Trousers waist	31	33	35	38	40
Trousers leg	31	31½	32½	32½	32¾

P.T.U. will be 1½" shorter.

MEN'S OVERCOATS

Breast on vest, same sizes as suits. Sleeves 1" longer than suits.

MEN'S SUITS

Regular Sizes

Sizes	33	34	35	36	37	38	39	40	41	42	44	46
Breast	33	34	35	36	37	38	39	40	41	42	44	46
Sleeve	30½	31	31½	31½	32	32½	32½	33	33	33½	33½	33½
Waist	30	31	32	33	34	35	36	38	39	40	42	44
Leg	30½	31	31½	31½	32½	32½	32½	32½	32½	32¾	33	33

P.T.U. trousers will be 1½" shorter.

LONG SIZES

Sizes	33	34	35	36	37	38	39	40	41	42	44	46
Breast	33	34	35	36	37	38	39	40	41	42	44	46
Sleeve	31½	32	32½	32½	33	33½	33½	34	34	34½	34½	34½
Waist	30	31	31½	32½	33	34	35	36	38	39	41	43
Leg	32	32	32½	33	33½	34	34	34	34	34	34	34

P.T.U. trousers will be 1½" shorter.

SHORT SIZES

Sizes	34	35	36	37	38	39	40	41	42	43	44	46
Breast	34	35	36	37	38	39	40	41	42	43	44	46
Sleeve	30	30	30½	31	31¼	31½	31¾	32	32	32½	32½	32½
Waist	32	33	34	35	36	37	39	40	41	42	43	45
Leg	29½	29½	29½	30	30½	31	31½	31½	31	31	30½	30½

P.T.U. trousers will be 1½" shorter.

Sizes				36	37	38	39	40	41	42	43	44	45	46
Breast	.	.	.	36	37	38	39	40	41	42	43	44	45	46
Sleeve	.	.	.	30½	31	31¼	31½	32	32½	32½	32½	32½	32½	32½
Waist	.	.	.	35	36	38	39	40	41	42	43	44	45	46
Leg	.	.	.	30	31	31	31½	31½	31½	31	31	31	31	31

P.T.U. trousers will be 1¼″ shorter.

VESTS

The making of men's vests on the semi-divisional system has proved its value as a quick and efficient method of production.

The usual procedure being :

> Pockets ⎫
> Linings ⎬ First machinist.
> Making back ⎭
> Under press.
> Baste facings.
> Run-on facings.
> Baste out.
> Edge press.
> Edge stitch.
> Backing.
> Finishing.
> Buttonholing.
> Press off.
> Buttoning.
> Passing.

This will progress much the same as the man's lounge coat already described, due regard having been paid to the proper disposition of staff, and special attention paid to reserves, particularly for " backing " or " bagging," a term very largely used in the trade.

The approximate cost for making a garment of the medium to better class S.B. fronts, four pockets, would be approximately as follows :

					d.
First machinist	.	.	.	.	7½
Basting	.	.	.	.	2
Under pressing	.	.	.	.	¾
Stitching and bagging	.	.	.	.	1¾
Finishing	.	.	.	.	½
Press off	.	.	.	.	1½
Buttoning	.	.	.	.	1

TROUSERS

An extensive trade has been built up of late by the increased demand for odd trousers, as apart from the ordinary trousers of suits. In consequence much competition has arisen. Methods and organisation which a few years ago seemed everything that could be desired have been scrapped and superseded by up-to-date machinery, and well-thought-out procedure. Everything that tends to cheapen making costs, or improve appearance without incurring extra cost, is eagerly sought for. One would have thought that the last word had been said in machine-made trousers, but that is not so. Steady research in methods and operations has frequently revealed waste. It is to-day possible for trousers to be well made at a speed and price quite unheard of a few years ago.

A tribute must be paid to the up-to-date cutter, who, in collaboration with the supervisor of the workroom, arranges that each bundle of work is tied up in such a manner that when the string is cut by the machinist every part of the garment to be made is in certain order and sequence.

This may appear to many to be undue elaboration, but a trial will soon convince and prove its value.

With the making of single trousers the divisional system is not an ideal one, and is generally voted a failure. The amount of marking and notches, etc., creates operations and extra handling at increased cost, and hinders output.

With bulk trade the semi-divisional system of machining trousers is again the best. The first consideration is the lay-out of the machine bench, which should contain up-to-date machinery, buttonhole machine, felling machine, serging machine, buttoning machine, and triple lock-stitching machine. The procedure and progress of work should be as follows :

Putting in pockets.
Sewing of fly lining, and making buttonhole fly.
Joining up.
Canvas tops.
Under pressing.
Fell bottom by machine.
Button fly and tops.
Felling waistband and finishing.
Pressing off.
Passing.

The Hoffman Press will be found a great asset in these days

of creased trousers. Taken on the semi-divisional method the first three operations are done by the same machinist. Tops and canvas stitching by another.

The basic price for a medium to better class trousers with hip pocket and raised side-seam should be approximately :

					d.
First machinist	.	.	.	.	. 11
Second machinist		.	.	.	. 1
Under pressing	.	.	.	.	. 1
Buttonholing	.	.	.	.	. ½
Bottom felling	.	.	.	.	. ½
Buttoning	.	.	.	.	. ¼
Finishing	.	.	.	.	. 4
Press off by Hoffman	.	.	.	.	1½

Although, of course, this may be varied very largely up or down, it can be taken as a basis, and the quality of work turned out will be just as much improved as waste is eliminated.

PLATE III

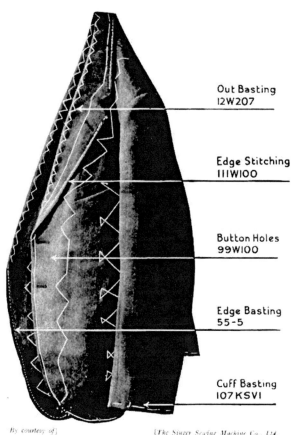

Out Basting
12W207

Edge Stitching
111W100

Button Holes
99W100

Edge Basting
55-5

Cuff Basting
107KSVI

By courtesy of] *[The Singer Sewing Machine Co., Ltd.*

EXAMPLE OF MACHINE STITCHING.

PLATE IV

Lock
Stitching
96K12

Lock
Stitching
96K12

Overseam
Stitching
107W3

Lock
Stitching
96K12

Basting
Stitching
55-5

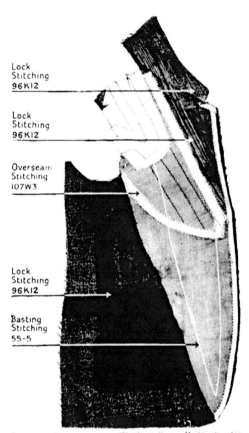

By courtesy of   The Singer Sewing Machine Co. Ltd.

EXAMPLE OF MACHINE STITCHING.

PLATE V

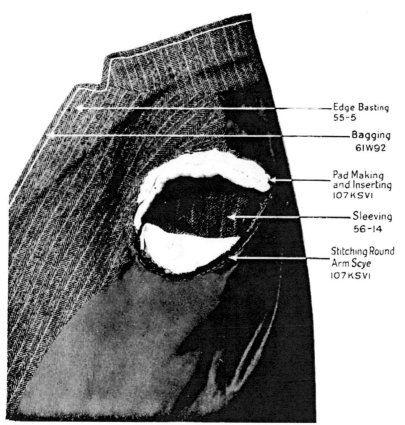

Edge Basting
55-5

Bagging
61W92

Pad Making
and Inserting
107 KSVI

Sleeving
56-14

Stitching Round
Arm Scye
107 KSVI

EXAMPLE OF MACHINE STITCHING.

PLATE VI

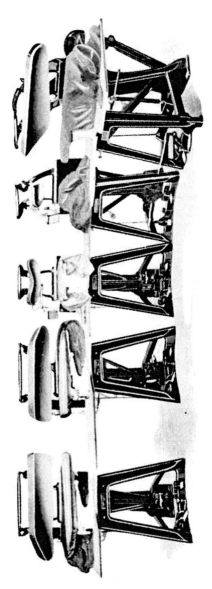

By courtesy of James Armstrong & Co., Ltd., 151, Queen Victoria Street, E.C.4.

THE PROSPERITY "FORMIREST" BATTERY.

CHAPTER II

THE WHOLESALE TRADE

By G. W. SUMPTER

(Head Cutter and Designer, John Shannon & Son, Ltd., Walsall. Late with John Barran & Sons, Ltd., Leeds)

MAN'S LOUNGE JACKET

THE style of lounge jacket illustrated by this draft is one that has had quite a long run. It has been popular now for very many seasons. This type of garment does not vary to any drastic extent as the seasons come and go, but, like "Charley's Aunt," is still running. The chief variations are a lesser or greater degree of shapeliness at waist ; longer or shorter waist line ; varying run of fronts, which may be more round ; the buttons set to carry the higher lapel ; also the angle of lapels and the length of collar. This last is probably the most variable point of style. The other parts I have mentioned are slight variations, not to a very marked degree, but just enough to mark one season's productions from the last.

The model I have put down is snug-fitting, with a high waist line, and bold about the front ; with broad effect, generous fitting in every section, excepting the hips, which clip closely to the figure.

The drafting lines by which this drawing is produced I do not claim to be either elaborate or highly systematised, but rather to be the structural draft, giving all those essential points, after which the designer gives play to the model and style he is producing. Certain points we must have on which to build up our design, but after these points are produced the skill and ability of the designer show themselves in the outline produced. This draft carries the high shoulder seam, and broad lines in the upper part of back, high at the waist, and snugly defined. It is intended for a regular 38 chest size, and suitable for the average type of figure referred to in my comments upon cutting for the wholesale. A figure of 5′ 8″ in height, not too erect, but of such proportions as those created by the numerous sedentary occupations of so many of our clients.

T. II—2   17

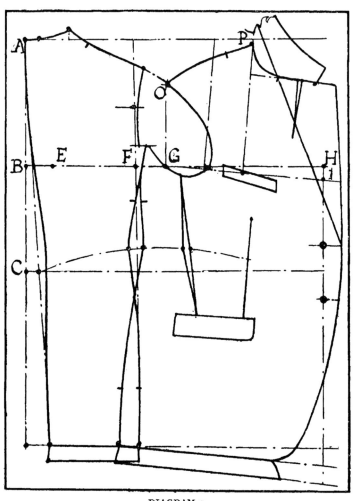

DIAGRAM 1.

Diagram 1

DRAFTING THE LOUNGE COAT

The points set out in the foregoing are the essentials, without which we cannot hope to produce a well-proportioned garment. Those sections of the draft for which I have not quoted quantities are those features purely dependent upon the style of the moment, or the desire of the designer.

The Scale is Half Chest Size

A to B ⅓ scale, plus 3″ for depth of scye.

A to C waist length 17″ and on to full length 29″.

Come in from C 1″ and rule through from A, after which shape in the centre seam ½″.

B to E is 2″ always.

E to F is ⅓ scale.

F to G is ⅓ scale.

G to H is ½ scale, plus 2½″.

Drop the breast line ¾″ at point " I " from " H " and then divide.

The neck-point is mid-way G–I.

Front of scye is mid-way G and neck-point line.

Rule up to " P " ⅓ of scale, plus 3″.

G up to O for shoulder slope is ⅓ scale.

The width at back neck is ⅓ scale, plus 1″ and raised ¾″.

For the centre line of fronts add 1⅜″.

To the points produced by the above construction outline, apply the style of outline you are setting about to produce.

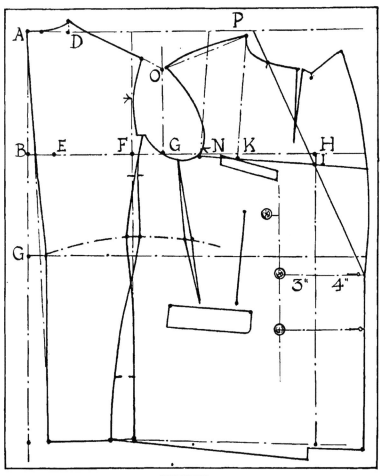

DIAGRAM 2.

Diagram 2

D.B. REEFER COAT

The points to be found to produce this garment are exactly similar to those of the S.B. lounge, with the following exceptions: For the centre line add the quantity required for D.B. fronts according to the degree of boldness required. Whatever amount is added over, come back this amount less 1" for the line and position of buttons. This drawing has 4" over the centre line, 3" back for the button line, which in the completed garment would allow of a button distance of $6\frac{1}{4}$". This after deducting the make-up of the front edge, and the distance of the buttonhole from this edge. Such quantity gives a very bold front so much in vogue at present. Phoney buttons are placed $\frac{3}{4}$" further back, purely for ornamental style effect.

Diagram 3

VEST

To produce the vest proceed in a similar fashion to that of the lounge coat, excepting the depth of scye, which is $\frac{1}{3}$rd plus $3\frac{1}{2}$", or $\frac{1}{2}$" deeper than in the lounge.

Come in at C 2".

Advance the neck-point forward from point " P " 1" for the stand of neck.

The back of this drawing is cut to carry a cloth neck piece, but, of course, this can be altered by raising back neck 1" for a " grown-on " stand, without cloth neck bits. This latter finish is the more general in the better grade of garment.

The model put down has breast cuts, and is not intended to button on the lower bottom button. The measure-up allowance for cutting Italian back is $2\frac{3}{4}$" over the half chest, $2\frac{1}{2}$" over the half waist.

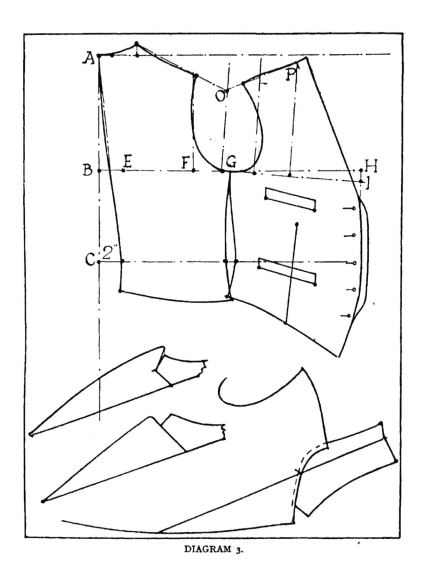

DIAGRAM 3.

Diagram 4

SLEEVE DRAFTING

With this subject I have put down two outlines for sleeve drafting.

One drafted into the scye, and one drafted separate.

We will deal with the latter first.

C is the starting point.

Measure up to B the height of back sleeve pitch above the breast line, plus $\frac{1}{2}''$.

To obtain height of crown, point A, draw a line connecting O O at the shoulder ends on the coat draft.

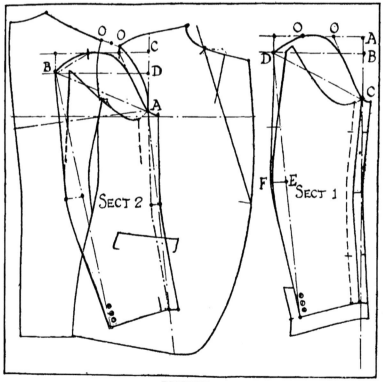

DIAGRAM 4.

The height of the sleeve crown is obtained by making point A 1″ less than the height of this point from the breast line.

As an example. Midway O O may be 7¼″ up from breast line, the height of the crown will be 1″ less, thus 6¼″.

Now for the distance between the front and back points of the top side sleeve.

To provide this quantity measure on the coat the distance between the pitches in a direct line.

Measure up from back pitch to " O " and then from " O " on the forepart to " A."

This quantity—10″—apply to C–D.

Next divide the " A " line on sleeve crown height in three divisions, and complete the sleeve crown as diagram.

Check the length of sleeve, make the cuff 6½″ wide, or to the style required, and then connect with point " D."

From elbow at point " E " give 1½″ spring for point " F."

For the under side sleeve see that the run corresponds with the under run of scye. If a false forearm is required add ¾″ to top side, and deduct ¾″ from under side.

This will produce a very satisfactory good-hanging modern sleeve, not possibly quite so easy as the old-time " flat " model, but a sleeve of good appearance and character.

To draft the sleeve into the scye we proceed in a similar way to the above, with the exception that to find the sleeve hang we draw a line at two-thirds of the pocket mouth forward, and then proceed on the lines of the above, by this means assuring ourselves of a hang of sleeve according to our wish.

Diagram 5

FITTING OVERCOATS

This is a style of overcoat very much favoured among the more dressy end of the trade, and a model which has brought very much business to the wholesale producers.

It is drafted out by exactly the same procedure as that of the lounge coat.

It must, of course, be cut up at least 2" in size, or 1" in scale, and even more than this if intended for heavy weight materials.

All first-class wholesale houses carry among their sets of patterns light and heavy for use according to the character of the cloth employed.

Point " P " is $\frac{1}{2}$" longer than on a lounge, to allow of the extra for covering the thickness of the undercoat, and the back neck is $\frac{1}{8}$ plus $1\frac{1}{2}$", and raised 1".

The method of allowing the front over-lap is exactly similar to that employed in the D.B. reefer jacket.

Diagram 6

ULSTER COAT

This again may be produced as the foregoing, on the same procedure as the lounge, but it must be produced very large in size, the whole character of this garment being one of ample and generous proportions. This is a very fine model, always in demand, with but little variations as the seasons come and go. The type of pocket, the placement of the buttons, and the choice of stitching and finishing of the edges and seams, are about the only features of variation.

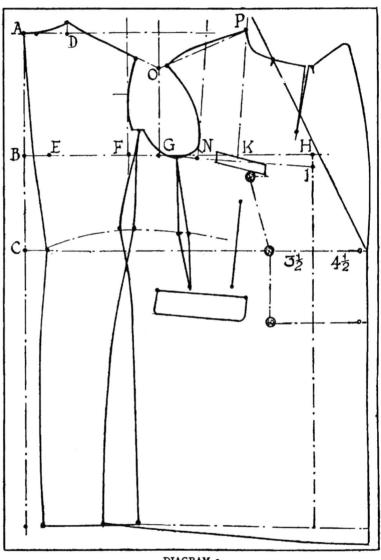

DIAGRAM 5.

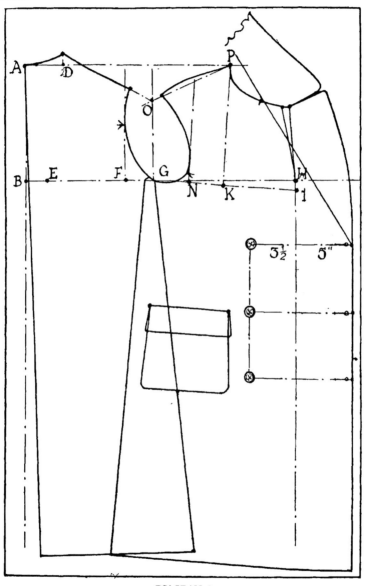

DIAGRAM 6.

Diagram 7

Interlinings

We who are engaged in the wholesale devote very much attention to the interlinings. We consider these the foundation of the coat, and it is essential that they should mould to the form, produce ease where required, and be such that shaped Hoffman presses may produce worthy results. They are also a means of helping the coat to retain its form and shape for a long period.

We spend quite a lot of money in the production of interlinings and careful shaping of same after they have been made.

In the U.S.A. this branch of the business is quite distinct, and a really first-class speciality.

No. 1.—This is a simple and exceedingly effective method of cutting the interlinings. I design this for ease over the shoulders, and to produce a concave form. One of the particular features of this method is that it avoids weakening the strands in the haircloth and hair-canvas.

Point C is found at approximately one-third of the shoulder width.

Overlap ¾″ at point " A," and ⅜″ at point " B."

The smaller sketch shows the result.

The lower section you will note is straight across, and the spring is put on to the upper portion. This is a type of interlining with which I have had very excellent and satisfactory results.

No. 2.—This is an outline intended as a foundation for a very full-chested model, one that carries a breast dart, and with which much shape is required. A glance at the diagram will make this self-explanatory.

No. 3.—This again is a very simple model. A section is cut out as depicted on the drawing.

This section about 6″ deep is 1″ wide at the bottom, tapering to nothing at point " A."

Into this a section strip as mark " C " is put, thus opening out point " A " and creating a very desirable spring in the upper portion, to give the hollow shapely shoulder. The cut across the breast will produce form, and a clinging effect.

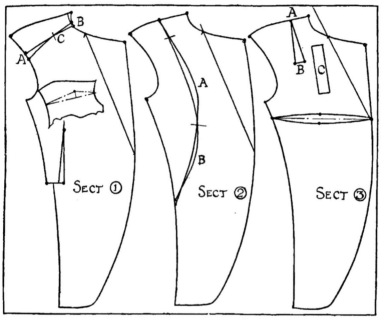

DIAGRAM 7.

Diagram 8

TROUSERS

THE subject of trouser cutting is one worthy of far more attention than is usually bestowed upon it.

A clean-hanging pair of trousers is as much a work of art as any other garment. There are business houses whose reputation for trousers has been the foundation upon which has been built a large and successful business. It behoves every cutter to give careful study to this subject, and not dismiss it as a junior qualification.

The outline I have put down in my diagrams is such as used in the wholesale.

For the better class grade of goods—super suits, dress and worsted trousers, it is close in the legs, and of good free hang.

For a lower grade of production a somewhat different outline is required to meet the requirements of extra ease. More stoop and stride are required in these lower end goods, and in addition extra ease is allowed for the seat and throughout.

TOPSIDES

A to C	Is side seam plus $\frac{3}{4}$".
B from C	Is the leg, plus $\frac{1}{2}$".
N	Is midway C–B plus 2" from C.
C–D	At bottom is $\frac{1}{8}$th scale (seat size).
B–E	Is $\frac{1}{8}$th scale. Divide the bottom equal half each side of D. Connect O–E, after which spring out 1" to F.
H	Is $3\frac{1}{2}$" from B.
H–I	Is $\frac{1}{4}$ seat.
M from K	$\frac{1}{4}$ waist, plus $\frac{1}{2}$".

UNDERSIDES

G from F	Is $\frac{1}{8}$th scale for underside fork.

Allow $1\frac{1}{2}$" through leg seam of underside for seams.

For seat angle pivot Z–F, and find point V.

Z is $\frac{1}{6}$ scale from I.

Measure up waist, plus $1\frac{1}{2}$", or $2\frac{1}{2}$" if a waist cut is taken out.

Measure up seat plus $2\frac{1}{4}$".

5" is allowed at bottom to produce 2" cuffs.

NOTES

For a lower grade production these points of difference must be noted.

Make C–D $\frac{1}{8}$th, NOT $\frac{1}{8}$th.

For seat angle pivot Z–E for point V, but connect seat line with F.

In this grade of goods measure up seat size plus 3".

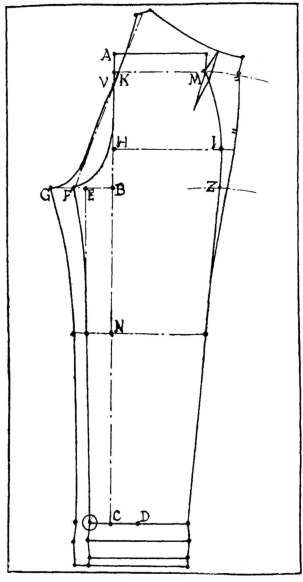

DIAGRAM 8.

Diagram 9

BREECHES

QUITE a considerable business is done in breeches in our factories to-day, and among them some very good class trade.

The style I have drawn in the diagram is one that meets with generous sales, and commands excellent prices, carried out in some of the best breeches materials produced to-day.

The style is full and generous, and of proportions accepted by those whose judgment of breeches is most severe.

The essential points are on similar lines to the trouser outline.

The following are the salient points of difference.

TOPSIDES

B to H Is half the leg, less ½".
H to I Is 2½" for small.
I to K 4" for calf.
B to C Is 1" and rule through to A.
C to D Is ⅓th.
        From D rule through H to point I at small.
I to M Is ¼ small, plus 1".
H to O Is ¼ knee, plus 1½".
        Connect O–M to bottom.
B to F Is ¼ seat, then to G, plus 2".

UNDERSIDES

D to E Is ⅓th for underside.
        1" is allowed through E–P to bottom.
For seat angle pivot F–D to find V.
        This gives a moderately crooked seat, not so intensely angled as some advocate.
Measure up knee, small, calf, plus 1", or according to the elasticity of the material employed.
Take out under the small 1".
Be sure to check that the side seam harmonises in length with the top side, so that there is no contraction when the breeches are closed.

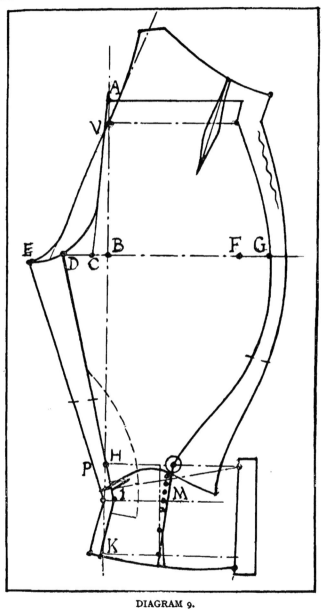

DIAGRAM 9.

Diagram 10

PLUS FOURS

N O study of models would be complete these days without the inclusion of plus fours.

A very popular garment, which if produced with a good balance and hang is very pleasing.

There are many degrees of fullness and fall-over, and several ways of finishing the bottom.

The style put down is fairly full and generous in fall, and represents the more popular idea of a satisfactory knicker.

These may be finished with 3 or 4 button continuation, but the wide strap and buckle as depicted in the diagram is by far the most popular.

The tops are finished with a straight waistband, and usually two pleats.

The finish at the bottoms I have put a " V " cut out of top and underside.

Where the material is of a soft nature, these may be fulled into the band or strap.

A small open vent is made at the side seam, which is cut 1″ longer than the leg seam.

Proceed as for trousers.

B to C	Is ½ leg, then allow 5″ to 8″ for fall-over. In this case I have allowed 7″.
C to D	Is ⅛th seat. Divide the width of knee equally each side. These are 28″ knee.

	Proportion may vary from say 24″ to 30″.
B to E	Is 1″. Carry this through to top of fly.
E to F	Is ⅛th.
F to G	Is ⅛th for underside.
B to M	Is half seat, plus 2″.

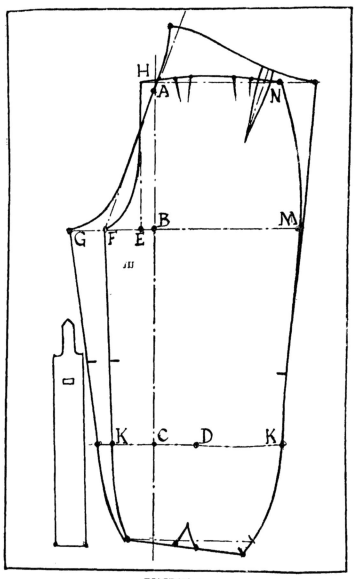

DIAGRAM 10.

CHAPTER III

GRADING FOR THE WHOLESALE TRADE

By REUBEN SYTNER

IN the wholesale branch of the tailoring trade the production of patterns is most carefully studied. Not only are they cut in 1″ sizes, but also in sets covering the various types of figures (except deformities), such as regular, long, short, stout, corpulent, long stout and short stout, etc., etc. When one has to cut a set of fifteen 1″ patterns in each of the above-mentioned types, it will be seen how well " covered " are the various sizes and types of figures.

When grading from the 36″ pattern, it is not advisable to go beyond the 42″, using the amounts laid down for depths, as these do not increase in the same ratio above 42″ chest.

SECTION 1

One method of grading is to cut two patterns—a 36″ and a 42″ chest—and grade between them. Mark the 42″ back pattern on a piece of paper, then place the 36″ chest pattern on the sheet, both chest lines and centre of back lines together, and mark round it.

Connect all points together by drawing lines through them ; divide all lines drawn between the points into equal parts according to the sizes desired—2″ ; 1½″ ; or 1″. In this case it is divided into 2″ sizes. From the 36″ chest following the lines drawn through all points we can now also produce sizes down to 32″ chest, since 2″ sizes have been produced between 36″ and 42″ ; therefore in all cases come in from 36″ to 32″ two-thirds of the distance between the 36″ and 42″ patterns as in diagram.

The same procedure is followed in the forepart, Section 5 ;

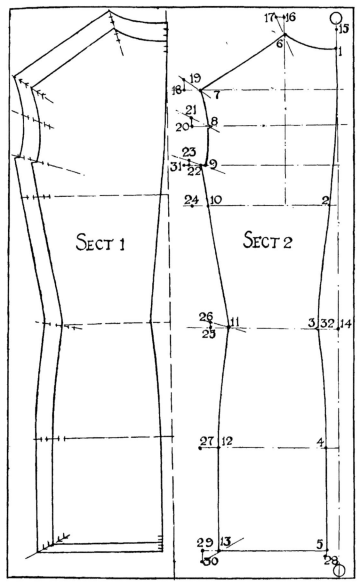

DIAGRAM 11.

top-sleeve, Section 10 ; under-sleeve, Section 12, and collar, Section 8.
This method of grading is true in principle, but is very rarely used, most designers grading from one pattern.
Whilst a 36" chest pattern has been used to grade from, a 38" pattern may be used equally well, providing two-thirds of the amounts laid down are used. For instance : 15 from 1 is $\frac{2}{3}$" ; 16 from 6 is $\frac{2}{3}$" ; 17 from 16 is $\frac{2}{3}$", and so on.

GRADING THE BACK

SECTION 2

Place the back pattern on a sheet of paper and mark it in. Also mark :
The scye depth line : 2–10.;
The waist line : 3–11 ;
The seat line : 4–12.
From 3 at the waist go out to 14, the amount the centre of back waist has been suppressed, and draw the back construction line " o–o " (in the same way that the pattern has been produced).
By the back construction line o–o.
Square across through 7, at the shoulder ;
Square across through 8, at the back pitch ;
Square across through 9, at the top of side seam ;
Square across through 10, at the scye line ;
Square across through 11, at the waist line ;
Square across through 12, at the seat line ;
Square across through 13, at the bottom.
15 from 1 is 1".
By the scye line 2–10 square up through 6 to 16 ;
16 from 6 is 1", the same as 15 from 1.
Square across from 16 towards 17.
17 from 16 is $\frac{1}{8}$" ; draw a line from 17 through 6.
18 from 7 is 1" ; square up from 18 to 19 ;
19 from 18 is $\frac{3}{4}$" ; draw a line from 19 through 7 ;
20 from 8 is 1" ; square up from 20 to 21 ;
21 from 20 is $\frac{1}{2}$" ; draw a line from 21 through 8 ;
22 from 9 is 1" ; square up from 22 to 23 ;

23 from 22 is $\frac{1}{4}$" ; draw a line from 23 through 9 ;
24 from 10 is 1" ;
25 from 11 is 1" ; square up from 25 to 26 ;
26 from 25 is $\frac{1}{4}$" ; draw a line from 26 through 11 ;
27 from 12 is 1" ;
28 from 5 is $\frac{1}{2}$" ;
29 from 13 is 1"   square down from 29 to 30 ;
30 from 29 is $\frac{1}{4}$" ; draw a line from 13 through 30 ;
31 is $\frac{1}{4}$" beyond 22 (a seam width).
We now have the outline of the 42" chest back ; the centre of back seam from 15 to 28 ; the back neck from 15 to 17 ; the shoulder seam from 17 to 19 ; the back scye seam from 19 through 21 to 23 ; the side seam from 31 through 24, 26, 27 to 30 at the bottom, and the bottom from 30 to 28.
In some systems of grading, all neck and shoulder lines from 6–7–8–9 are drawn into a position at or near to 2, the centre of back on the scye depth line. This method would be correct if all patterns were drafted alike, and all points lay in a given ratio to 1–2 the scye depth, but since cutters vary the distance from 1 to 2, it may be anything from 9" to 9$\frac{3}{4}$" ; then again, some cutters vary the back neck width from 2$\frac{1}{4}$" to 3$\frac{1}{4}$", as they also vary the shoulder seam, back pitch, etc., as well as back width. Therefore one can see how difficult it will be to fix a point on the centre of back that will give the same increase per size for all back patterns ; the same reasoning applies to all parts of the pattern, unless one bears in mind the relation of width to depth, or vice versa.

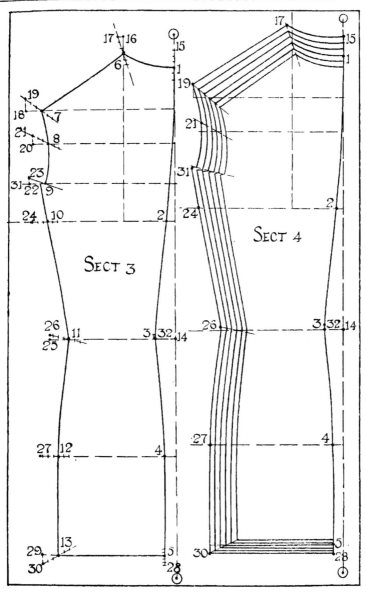

DIAGRAM 12.

SECTION 3

Take the 36″ back pattern and connect up :

15 to 17, the back neck ;
17 to 19, the shoulder seam ;
19 through 21 to 23, the back scye seam ;
31 through 24, 26, 27 to 30, the side seam ;
28 to 30 the bottom ;
32 is ¼″ above 3, the centre of back waist.

We are now ready to divide the space between all points according to the patterns desired. For instance, if 2″ patterns are wanted, all spaces are divided into 3 equal parts. We thus obtain 36″–38″–40″–42″.

If 1½″ patterns are wanted, all spaces are divided into 4 equal parts. We thus obtain 36″–37½″–39″–40½″–42″.

If 1″ patterns are wanted, all spaces are divided into 6 equal parts. We thus obtain 36″–37″–38″–39″–40″–41″–42″.

SECTION 4

To make the grading and dividing clear to those who have never graded patterns before, I have divided all spaces into 3 equal parts for 2″ patterns, it being quite evident that a greater number of divisions on a scale-drawing, such as this diagram must be, does not show out as clearly and is liable to make the grade appear difficult to follow and copy.

To produce patterns down to 32″ chest all that is necessary is to come in from 36″ to 32″ two-thirds of the distance between 36 and 42, or if a 38″ pattern is used to grade from, then come in from 38″ to 32″, 1½ times the distance from 38″ to 42″ ; then divide this distance into the sizes desired. Should one work to 1½″ sizes, then it will be necessary to decide whether to work down to 33″ or 31½″ and use the proportion of the increase. For instance, if one wants patterns only down to 33″ chest, then come in from 36″ one-half of the amount from 36″ to 42″ ; or if 31½″ is desired, then come in from 36″, three-quarters of the amount from 36″ to 42″.

GRADING THE FOREPART
SECTION 5

Follow the same procedure by marking it on a sheet of paper ; marking also the breast, waist and seat lines, and the pockets.

1 is on the scye line ;
2 from 1 is 1½" ;
3 is on the waist line ;
4 from 3 is 1¾", square up from 4 to 5 ;
5 from 4 is ¼", the same as 25 to 26 of back ;
Draw a line from 5 through 3, and 5 to 2 ;
6 is on the seat line ;
7 from 6 is 1¾", the same as 4 from 3 ;
8 is on the scye line ;
9 from 8 is ½" ;
10 is on the waist line ;
11 from 10 is ½", if there is no under-arm cut ; or if the under-arm cut is a small one then 11 from 10 is ⅜ths ;
Square up from 11 to 12 ;
12 from 11 is ¼", the same as 5 from 4 at front waist ;
Draw a line from 12 through 10 ;
13 is on the seat line ;
14 from 13 is ½" ;
15 is at the bottom ;
16 is squared down and is ¼" from 15 ;
17 from 16 is ¼", the same as 30 from 29 of back ;
From 17 draw a line parallel with the bottom ;
18 is at the top of side seam ;
19 from 18 is ¼" ;
Square up from 19 to 20 ;
20 from 19 is ¼", the same as 23 from 22 of back ;
Draw a line from 20 through 18 ;
21 is the forepart and step seam, and from it draw a parallel line with 18–20 ;
22 is the forepart neck-point ;
By the scye line 1–8 square up through 22 to 23 ;
23 from 22 is 1½" ;
Square across from 23 to 24 ;
24 from 23 is ⅜ths ;
Draw a line from 24 through 23 ;
25 is the forepart shoulder point.
By the scye line 1–8 square up through 25 to 26 ;
26 from 25 is 1" ;
Square across from 26 to 27 ;
27 from 24 of forepart is as much more

than 22 to 25, as 17 to 19 of back shoulder is wider than 6 to 7 ;
Draw a line from 27 through 25 ;
28 is the break ;
29 is the stand ;
Square across from 22 ;
30 is the break line continued from 22 ;
31 from 24 is the same as 30 from 22 ;
32 is squared across from 28 ;
33 from 24 is ¼" ;
Place the 36" forepart pattern with its neck-point 22 touching 33, and its crease line 29–28 on the crease line 32–31 ;
34 is where 29 touches the line 32–31 ;
Continue the neck.
Draw a line from 34 through 29 ;
35 is where this line touches the scye line ;
36 is the lapel step corner ;
37 is the corner of lapel ;
38 is found by drawing a line from 35 through 36 to the collar seam ;
39 from 38 is found by drawing a parallel line from 37 to 39 by 36–38.

POCKETS—BREAST POCKET

40 is the back of pocket, and remains stationary ;
41 is the front of pocket ;
42 is squared across and is ⅜" from 41 ;

HIP POCKET

43 is the back of pocket ;
44 is the front of pocket ;
45 is midway between 43 and 44 ;
46 from 45 is ⅜" ;
47 from 46 is ¼" more than 43 from 45.
Draw a line from 43 through 47 ;
48 from 46 is ¼" more than 44 from 45 ;
Draw a line from 44 through 47.

SECTION 6

Take the 36" forepart pattern and connect up front pitch to 27, the front scye ;
27 to 24, the shoulder ;
39 to 32, the lapel (the gorge section having already been marked in) ;
the remainder of the front by placing the bottom of the pattern on the line drawn from 17 and the front touching 7 ;
The side seam from 20 through 19, 9, 12, 14, to 17 ;

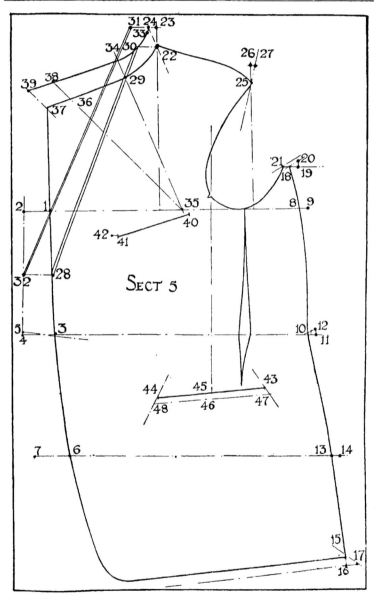

DIAGRAM 13.

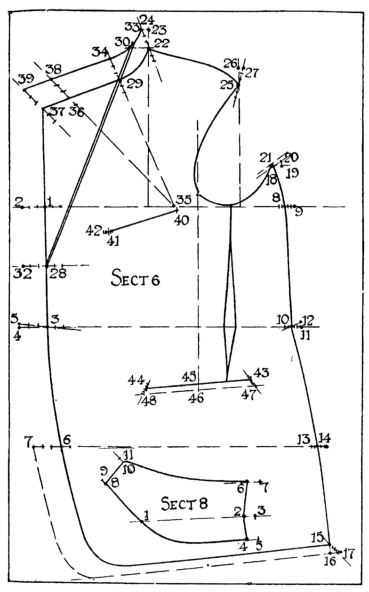

DIAGRAM 14.

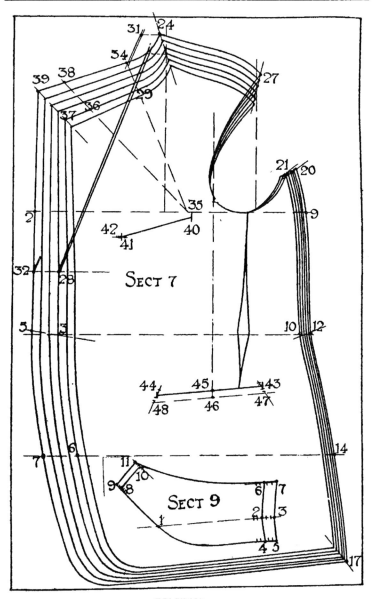

DIAGRAM 15.

The back section of scye at side seam to underarm cut.

SECTION 7

All spaces between all points may now be divided *as the back was,* viz., according to the patterns desired— 2″; 1½″ or 1″; in this case 2″ sizes

GRADING THE COLLAR
SECTION 8

1–2 is the crease;
3 from 2 is ⅜″;

5 from 4 is ⅜″;
7 from 6 is ¾″.

Measure from 29 to 36 of the 36″ chest and also the distance from 34 to 38, and note the increase.

Make 9 from 8 and 11 from 10 each this amount.

SECTION 9

This diagram shows the distance between all points divided according to the sizes desired, the 42″ chest being "filled in."

GRADING THE TOPSLEEVE

SECTION 10

It will be noticed that a " three-quarter " sleeve has been used, with 1″ seam displacement.

Draw the line o–o, the line 3–13 being parallel with o–o and 1″ away from it.

Place the front pitch point 1 on the line o–o ;

Point 2 at cuff is on the line 3–13 ;

Mark round the topsleeve ;

4 is on the line o–o, squared into 7 ;

5 is the hindarm, and is squared into from the line o–o.

6 from 5 is ⅓ of 4 to 5 ;

7 from 5 is ¾″, square up from 7 ;

8 from 7 is ½″, the same as 20 to 21, the coat back, Section 2.

Draw a line from 8 through 5 ;

9 is squared up from 6 ;

10 from 6 is ½″, 10 from 7 being ⅓ of 4 to 7 ;

11 from 10 is ⅔″ more than 6 to 9, ½″ being for the height from 7 to 8 and ¼″ being ⅓ of the back and forepart increase above the back pitch level.

Draw a line from 11 through 9 ;

12 is where the sleeve crosses the line 4–7.

13 from 2 is ¾″ ;

14 is the cuff hindarm ;

Square across through 14 from the line o–o ;

15 from 14 is ½″ ;

Square down from 15 ;

16 from 15 is ¾″ ;

Draw a line from 14 through 16.

SECTION 11

Divide the distance between all points according to the sizes desired and also " come in " from the 36″ for the sizes below 36″ chest.

Take the topsleeve pattern and connect up all points as in the diagram.

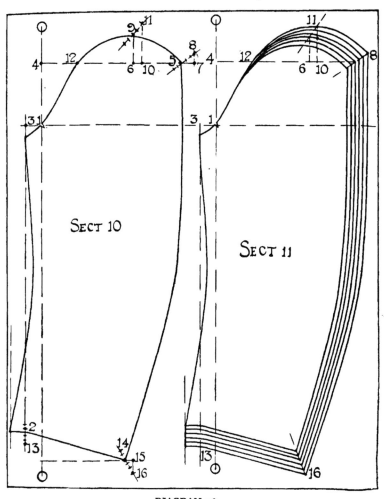

DIAGRAM 16.

GRADING THE UNDERSLEEVE

SECTION 12

Draw the line o–o, the line 2–12 being parallel with o–o and 1″ away from it ;

Place the cuff point 1 on the line o–o and the top at 2, which is on the line 2–12 ;

Mark round the undersleeve.

3 is on the line o–o squared into 5 ;

4 is the hindarm, and is squared into from the line o–o ;

5 from 4 is $\frac{3}{4}$″ ;

Square up from 5 ;

6 from 5 is $\frac{1}{4}$″, the same as 7 to 8 of topsleeve, section 10.

Draw a line from 6 through 4 ;

7 is the top of undersleeve ;

Draw a line from 7 parallel with the line 6–4 ;

8 from 1 is $\frac{3}{4}$″ ;

9 is the cuff hindarm ;

Square across through 9 by the line o–o ;

10 from 9 is $\frac{1}{2}$″ ;

Square down from 10 ;

11 from 10 is $\frac{3}{4}$″ ;

Draw a line from 9 through 11.

SECTION 13

Divide the distance between all points according to the sizes desired and also " come in " from the 36″ for the sizes below 36″ chest.

Take the undersleeve pattern and connect up all points as in the diagram.

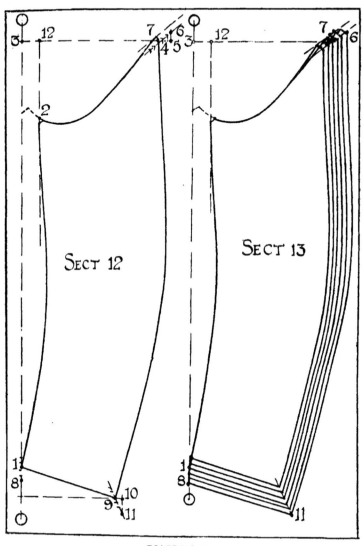

DIAGRAM 17.

GRADING THE VEST BACK

SECTION 14

It will be noticed that there is a line 16–17 which is below the actual breast line, this is due to the vest back balance being longer; the same will be noticed at the waist at 18–19.

Place the back pattern on a sheet of paper and mark it in; also mark the breast line, 4, or mark a line running through 16, the waist line 2, or mark a line running through 18.

From 2 at the waist go out to 3, the amount the centre of back waist has been suppressed, and draw the back construction line o–o.

By the back construction line:

Square across through 10 at the shoulder;

Square across through 13 which is about half the scye depth;

Square across through 16 at the scye line;

Square across through 18 at the waist-line;

Square across through 21 at the bottom of side seam.

6 from 1 is 1″;

By the scye line square up through 7 to 8;

8 from 7 is 1″, the same as 6 from 1;
Square across from 8 towards 9;
9 from 8 is ⅓″;
Draw a line from 9 through 7;
11 from 10 is 1″;
Square up from 11 to 12;
12 from 11 is ¾″;
Draw a line from 12 through 10;
14 from 13 is 1″;
Square up from 14 to 15;
15 from 14 is ½″;
Draw a line from 15 through 13;
17 from 16 is 1½″;
19 from 18 is 1¼″;
Square up from 19 to 20;
20 from 19 is ¼″;
Draw a line from 20 through 18;
22 from 21 is 1¾″;
23 from 2 is ¼″.

SECTION 15

Divide the distance between all points according to the sizes desired, and also " come in " from the 36″ for the sizes below 36″ chest.

SECTION 16

Take the back pattern and connect up all points as in the diagram.

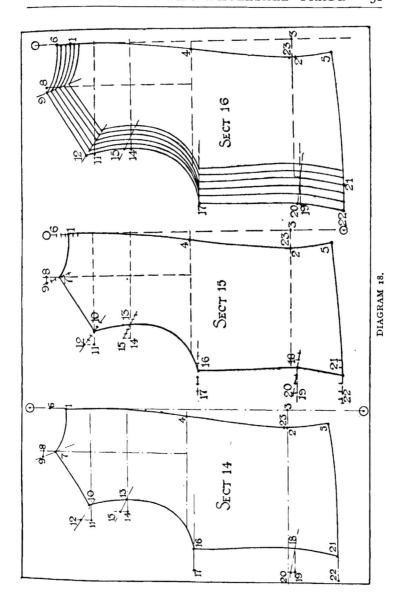

DIAGRAM 18.

GRADING THE VEST FOREPART

Section 17

Mark in the forepart pattern on a sheet of paper, marking the breast and waist lines.

1 is on the scye line;
2 from 1 is 1½";
3 is on the waist line;
4 from 3 is 1¾";
Square up from 4 to 5;
5 from 4 is ¼";
Draw a line from 5 through 3;
6 is the bottom of vest;
Square through 6 by the waist line towards 7;
7 from 6 is ¼";
Square across from 7 towards 8;
8 from 7 is 1¾";
Draw a line from 8 through 6;
9 is the bottom button or hole position;
Square across from 9 towards 10;
10 from 9 is 1¾";
Square down from 10 towards 11;
11 from 10 is ¼";
12 is the top of side seam;
13 is on the waist line;
14 is ¼" above 13 (the waist line);
15 is the bottom of the side seam;
16 is the front of scye;
17 is the forepart and neck point;
By the scye line 1–12 square up through 17 to 18;
18 from 17 is 1⅛";
Square across from 18 to 19;
19 from 18 is ⅜";
Draw a line from 19 through 17;
20 is the forepart shoulder point.

By the scye line 1–12 square up through 20 to 21;
21 from 20 is 1";
Square across from 21 to 22;
22 from 19 (the forepart shoulder) is as much more than 17 to 20, as 9 to 12 of the vest back shoulder is wider than 7 to 10;
Draw a line from 22 through 20.

WATCH POCKET

23 is the back of pocket;
24 from 23 is ¼";
25 is the front of pocket;
26 from 25 is ¾".

LOWER POCKET

27 is the back of pocket;
28 from 27 is ¾";
29 up from 28 is ¼";
Draw a line from 29 through 27;
30 is the front of pocket;
31 from 30 is 1";
32 up from 31 is ¼";
Draw a line from 32 through 30.

SECTION 18

Divide the distance between all points to the sizes desired and also " come in " from the 36" for the sizes below 36" chest.

SECTION 19

Take the forepart pattern and connect up all points as in the diagram.

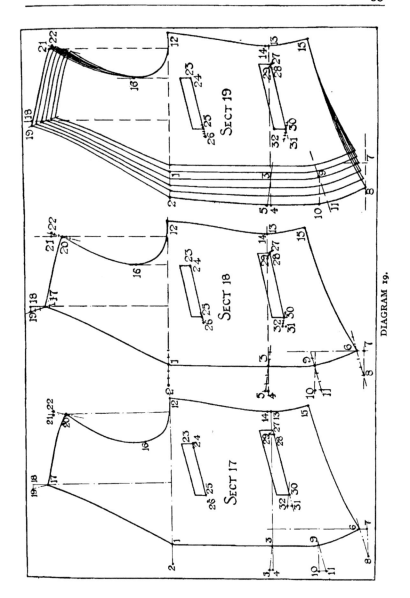

DIAGRAM 19.

LOOSE-FITTING OVERCOAT

GRADING THE BACK

SECTION 20

All points are found exactly as laid down in Section 2 (the jacket back), except that 28 from 5 and 30 from 29 are each 2″, which is equal to lengthening the coat 1″ per 2″ chest increase.

32 is midway between 5 and 13.

33 from 32 is the same as 28 from 5.

35 from 34 is ½″.

SECTION 21

This shows the distance between all points divided according to the sizes desired, the 42″ chest being "filled in."

36 is midway between 6 and 7.

37 is midway between 17 and 19.

Connect up and divide.

GRADING THE FOREPART

SECTION 22

All points are found exactly as laid down in Section 5 (the jacket forepart), except the length, 12 from 7 and 16 from 15, which are each 2″, as in Sections 20 and 21.

13 is midway between 15 and 6.

14 and 13 is the same as 7 to 12.

SECTION 23

This shows the distance between all points divided according to the sizes desired, the 42″ chest being "filled in."

40 is midway between 22 and 25.

41 is midway between 24 and 27.

Connect up and divide.

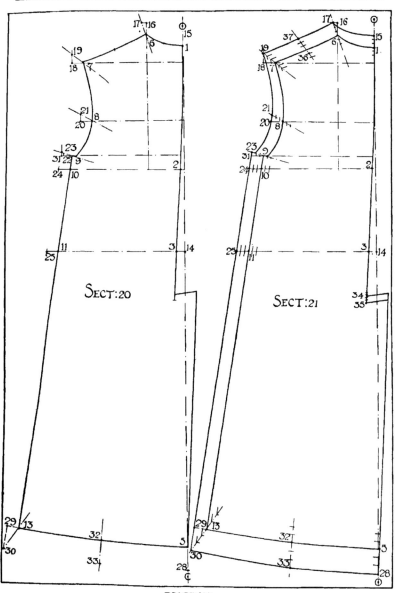

SECT:20

SECT:21

DIAGRAM 20.

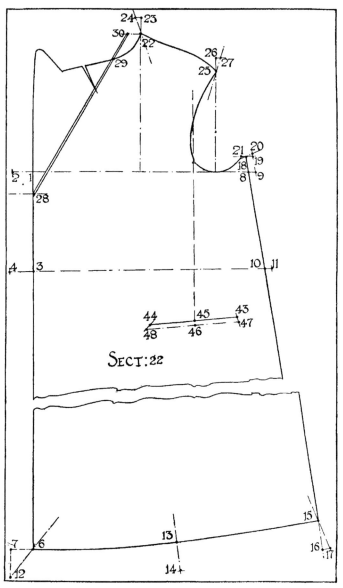

SECT: 22

DIAGRAM 21.

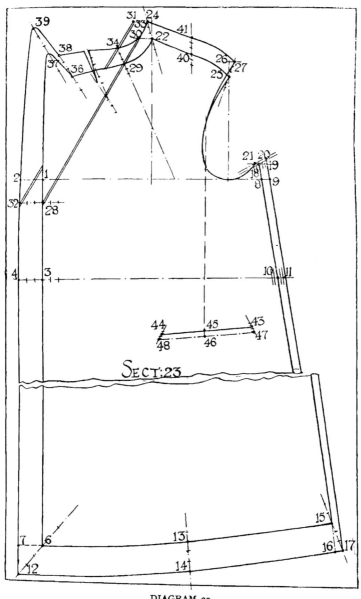

DIAGRAM 22.

THE SPLIT INSET SLEEVE

GRADING THE TOPSLEEVE

SECTION 24

Mark in the two halves of the top-sleeve, with the centre seams equally apart and parallel.

10 from 9 and 24 from 23 are each $\frac{3}{8}''$.

11 from 10 and 21 from 20 are each $\frac{3}{4}''$.

22 from 21 is $\frac{1}{2}''$.

15 from 14 is $\frac{1}{4}''$.

16 from 15 is $\frac{3}{4}''$.

7 from 6 is $\frac{3}{8}''$.

25 is continued from 19 and is $\frac{3}{4}''$.

27 is continued from 26 and is $\frac{3}{8}''$.

28 from 27 is $\frac{1}{4}''$.

SECTION 25

This shows the distance between all points divided according to the sizes desired, the 42″ chest being " filled in."

17 is found by connecting 7 and 16.

29 is found by connecting 22 and 28.

The undersleeve is graded as in Sections 12 and 13.

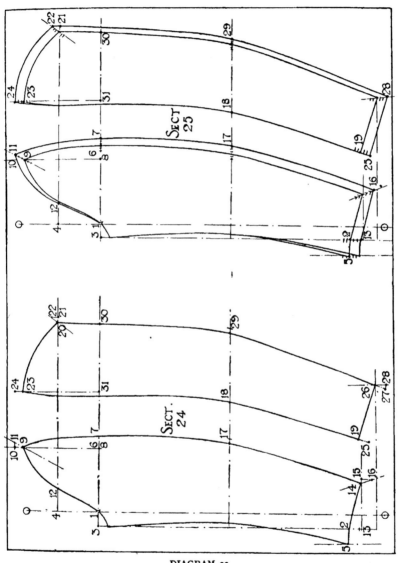

DIAGRAM 23.

RAGLAN OVERCOAT

GRADING THE BACK

SECTION 26

All points are found exactly as laid down in Section 20 (loose-fitting overcoat back).

SECTION 27

This shows the distance between all points divided according to the sizes desired, the 42" chest being "filled in."
37 is midway between 6 and 8.
38 is midway between 17 and 21.
Connect up and divide.

GRADING THE FOREPART

SECTION 28

All points are found as laid down in Section 22 (loose-fitting overcoat forepart).

The neck curve is found by going down from 26 to 27 ½", placing the 36" chest forepart with 25 on point 27, continuing the 36" neck curve to 28, and allowing ¼" beyond 28 to 30.

THE POCKET

33 from 31 is ⅜".
34 from 32 is ¾".
33 to 34 is the 42" chest.

SECTION 29

This shows the distance between all points divided according to the sizes desired, the 42" chest being "filled in."

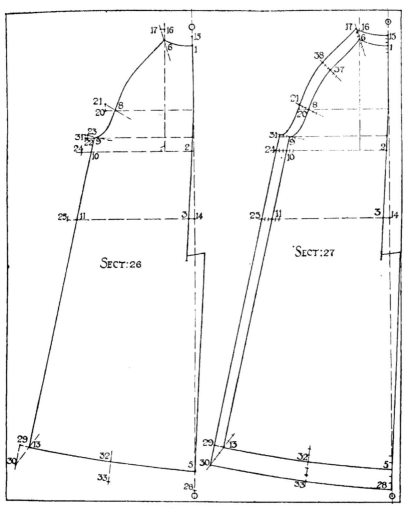

DIAGRAM 24.

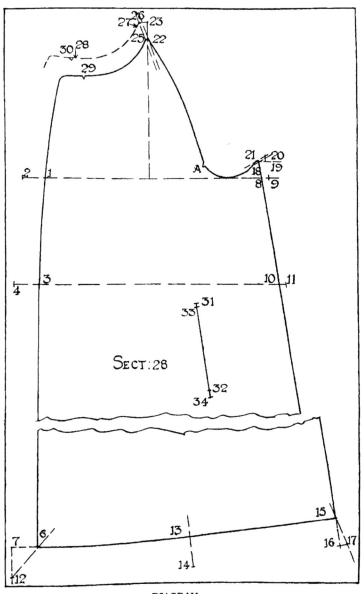

DIAGRAM 25.

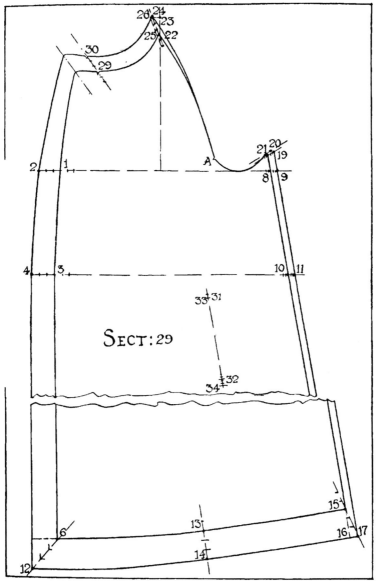

DIAGRAM 26.

RAGLAN TOPSLEEVE

SECTION 30

All points are found as in Section 24 and are also numbered in a similar manner, with the exception of the shoulder and neck-pieces, which are an addition to the split inset sleeve. Measure from the front pitch " A " to 22 of Section 28, then continue to 24 and note the increase of length from the 36″ chest to the 42″ chest, making 33 from 31 and 34 from 32 a similar amount.

Measure from the back pitch 8 to 6 of Section 26, then measure from 21 to 17 and note the increase of length from the 36″ chest to the 42″ chest, making 37 from 35 and 38 from 36 a similar amount.

SECTION 31

This shows the distance between all points divided according to the sizes desired, the 42″ chest being " filled in."

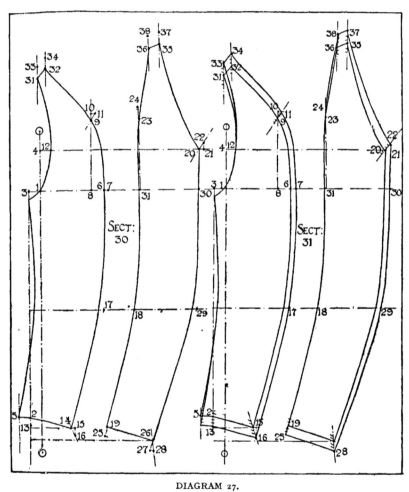

DIAGRAM 27.

CHAPTER IV

GRADING FOR THE WHOLESALE TRADE

By REUBEN SYTNER

LADIES' GARMENTS

LADIES' COAT.

GRADING THE BACK
SECTION L.1

Place the back pattern on a sheet of paper and mark it in.

Also mark:

The scye depth line: 2–10;

The waist line: 3–11;

The hip line: 4–12;

From 3 at the waist go out to 14, the amount the centre of back waist has been suppressed, and draw the back construction line o–o, in the same way that the pattern has been produced.

By the back construction line o–o:

Square across through 7, at the shoulder;

Square across through 8, at the back pitch;

Square across through 9, at the top of side seam;

Square across through 10, at the scye line;

Square across through 11, at the waist line;

Square across through 12, at the hip line;

Square across through 13, at the bottom.

15 from 1 is $\frac{1}{2}$".

By the scye line 2–10, square up through 6 to 16.

16 from 6 is $\frac{1}{4}$", the same as 15 from 1.

Square across from 16 towards 17.

17 from 16 is $\frac{1}{4}$": draw a line from 17 through 6.

18 from 7 is $\frac{1}{4}$": square up from 18 to 19.

PANEL FRONT

19 from 18 is $\frac{3}{8}$": draw a line from 19 through 7.

20 from 8 is $\frac{1}{2}$": square up from 20 to 21.

21 from 20 is $\frac{1}{4}$": draw a line from 21 through 8.

22 from 9 is $\frac{1}{2}$": square up from 22 to 23.

23 from 22 is $\frac{1}{8}$": draw a line from 23 through 9.

24 from 10 is $\frac{1}{2}$".

25 from 11 is $\frac{1}{2}$".

26 from 12 is $\frac{1}{2}$".

27 from 13 is $\frac{1}{2}$": square down from 27 to 28.

28 from 27 is 1": draw a line from 28 through 13.

29 from 5 is 1".

30 is $\frac{1}{4}$" (a seam width) beyond 22.

We now have the outline of the 40" chest back. Should one wish to grade up to 42" instead of 40", then in all cases increase the amount given by half as much again. For instance:

16 from 6 is $\frac{3}{4}$".

17 from 16 is $\frac{3}{8}$": and so on all through.

We are now ready to divide the space between all points according to the patterns desired. For instance, if the size grade is up to 40" chest (as in this case), all spaces are divided into equal parts.

When grading the sizes below 36", raise the waist line $\frac{1}{8}$" per size; in other words, shorten the waist length an extra $\frac{1}{8}$" per size below 36" chest.

66

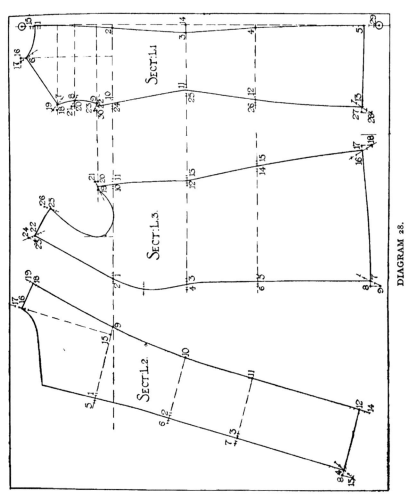

DIAGRAM 28.

LADIES' COAT.   PANEL FRONT (*continued*)

GRADING THE PANEL FOREPART

SECTION L.2

Follow the same procedure by marking both front sections of the forepart. It will be noticed that the chest, waist and hip lines are all squared by the centre of front and are parallel with the bottom.

5 from 1, at chest, is $\frac{1}{2}$".
6 from 2, at waist, is $\frac{1}{2}$".
7 from 3, at hip, is $\frac{1}{2}$".
8 from 4, at bottom, is $\frac{1}{2}$".
13 from 8 is 1" : draw a line from 13 through 4.
14 from 12 is 1".
15 is on the line 1–9 : square by it through 16 at the neck.
17 from 16 is $\frac{3}{8}$".
18 is the panel seam : continue the seam run.
19 from 18 is the same as 17 from 16.
The neck and lapel sections are found as laid down in the Gentlemen's section.

SECTION L.3

2 from 1 is $\frac{1}{4}$".
4 from 3 is $\frac{1}{2}$".
6 from 5 is $\frac{1}{2}$".
8 from 7 is $\frac{1}{2}$".
9 from 8 is 1" : draw a line from 9 through 7.
11 from 10 is $\frac{1}{2}$".

13 from 12 is $\frac{1}{2}$".
15 from 14 is $\frac{1}{2}$".
17 from 16 is $\frac{1}{2}$".
18 from 17 is 1" : draw a line from 18 through 16.
20 from 19 is $\frac{1}{2}$".
21 from 20 is $\frac{1}{4}$", the same as 23 from 22, Section L.1.
Draw a line from 21 through 19.
23 from 22 is $\frac{1}{4}$".
22–23 line is parallel with the chest line 1–10.
24–23 line is parallel with 22–1 line, the panel.
24 from 23 is the same as 18–19 of Section L.2.
26 from 25 is parallel with 23–24.
Check up the width of shoulder 17–19, Section L.2 and 24–26, Section L.3 with the increase of 17–19 of Section L.1.

SECTION L.4

This shows Section L.1 graded from 36" up to 40" and down to 32".

SECTION L.5

This shows Section L.2 graded from 36" up to 40" and down to 32".

SECTION L.6

This shows Section L.3 graded from 36" up to 40" and down to 32".

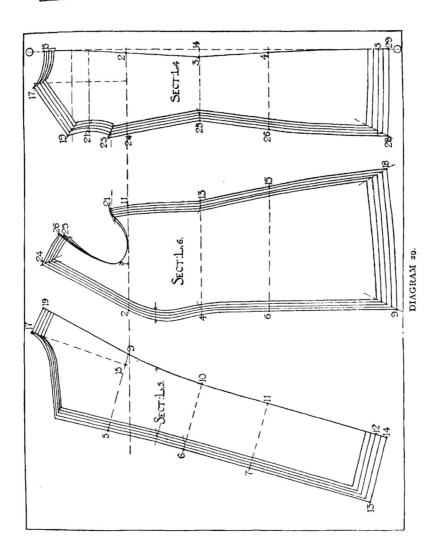

DIAGRAM 29.

LADIES' SIDEBODY COAT

GRADING THE BACK

Section L.7

All points are numbered and found exactly as in Section L.1.

GRADING THE FOREPART

Section L.8

5 from 1 is 1″.
6 from 2 is 1″.
7 from 3 is 1″.
8 from 4 is 1″.
13 from 8 is 1″ : square up from 15 through 16.
17 from 16 is ⅜″.
18 from 17 is ½″.
20 from 19 is ½″.
22 from 21 is ¼″.
23 from 22 is ⅜″ : draw a line from 23 through 21.
24 is squared through by 15–17 line.
25 from 24 is ½″.
26 from 25 is ⅜″ and is parallel with 24–19.
28 from 27 is parallel with 25–26.
Check up the width of shoulder 18–23 and 26–28 of Section L.8 with the increase of 17–19 of Section L.7.
30 from 29 is ¼″.
32 from 31 is ¼″.
34 from 33 is ¼″.
36 down from 35 is 1″.
37 from 36 is ¼″ : draw a line from 37 through 35.
The forepart is now ready for dividing the space between all points according to the patterns desired up to 40″ chest, as in this case.
When grading the sizes below 36″, raise the waist line ¼″ per size.

GRADING THE SIDEBODY

Section L.9

It will be noticed that I have made all allowances on the back seam. (This is optional.)
1 is the top of sidebody.
2 from 1 is ¼″ : square up from 2 to 3.
3 from 2 is the same as 22 to 23 of Section L.7.
Draw a line from 3 through 1.
4 is on the chest line.
5 from 4 is ¼″.
6 is on the waist line.
7 from 6 is ¼″.
8 is on the hip line.
9 from 8 is ¼″.
10 is at the bottom.
11 from 10 is 1″.
12 from 11 is ¼″ : draw a line from 12 through 10.
13 is at the bottom of underarm seam.
14 from 13 is 1″.
The sidebody may be divided in a similar manner to the forepart and back.

GRADING THE SIDEBODY

Section L.10

In this case all the width variation is made at the underarm seam.
1 is on the chest line.
2 from 1 is ¼″.
3 is on the waist line.
4 from 3 is ¼″.
5 is on the hip line
6 from 5 is ¼″.
7 is at the bottom.
8 from 7 is 1″.
9 from 8 is ¼″.
10 is at the bottom.
11 from 10 is 1″.
12 is the top of sidebody back seam.
13 from 12 is the same as 22 to 23 of Section L.7.

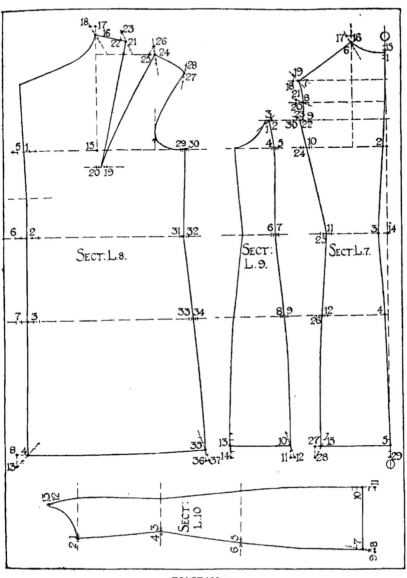

DIAGRAM 30.

LADIES' SIDEBODY COAT (*continued*)

GRADING THE SIDEBODY (*continued*)

SECTION L.11

This shows Section L.7, the back, with all the grades filled in up to 40″ and down to 32″ chest, 2″ sizes.

SECTION L.13

This shows Section L.9, the sidebody, with all the grades filled in up to 40″ and down to 32″ chest.

SECTION L.12

This shows Section L.8, the forepart, with all the grades filled in up to 40″ and down to 32″ chest.

SECTION L.14

This shows Section L.10, the sidebody, with all the grades filled in up to 40″ and down to 32″ chest.

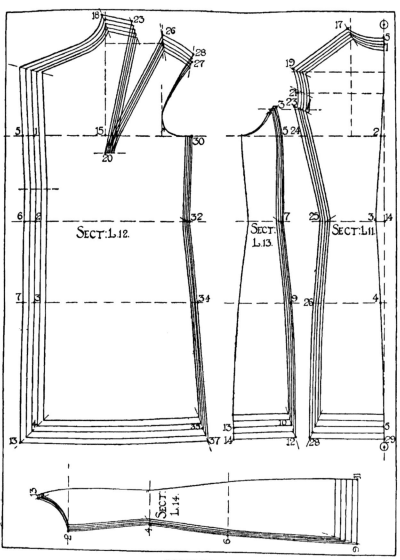

DIAGRAM 31.

THE SLEEVE

GRADING THE TOPSLEEVE

SECTION L.15

It will be noticed that a three-quarter sleeve has been used, with 1″ seam displacement.

Draw the line o–o, the line 3–13 being parallel with o–o and 1″ away from it.

Place the front pitch, point 1, on the line o–o.

Point 2 at the cuff is on the line 3–13.

Mark round the top sleeve.

4 is on the line o–o, squared into 7.

5 is the hindarm, and is squared into by the line o–o.

6 from 5 is half of 4 to 5.

7 from 5 is ½″ : square up from 7.

8 from 7 is the same as 20 to 21, the coat back, Section L.1.

Draw a line from 8 through 5.

9 is squared up from 6.

10 from 6 is ¼″ : 10 from 7 being one half of 4 to 7.

11 from 10 is ½″ more than 6 to 9.

Draw a line from 11 through 9.

12 is where the sleeve crosses the line 4–7.

13 from 2 is ½″.

14 is the cuff hindarm : square across through 14 by the line o–o.

15 from 14 is ¼″ : square down from 15.

16 from 15 is ½″ : draw a line from 16 through 14.

GRADING THE UNDERSLEEVE

SECTION L.16

Draw the line o–o, the line 2–12 being parallel with o–o and 1″ away from it.

Place the cuff point 1 on the line o–o and the top at 2, which is on the line 2–12.

Mark round the undersleeve.

3 is on the line o–o squared into 5.

5 from 4 is ¼″ : square up from 5.

6 from 5 is the same as 7 to 8 of Section L.15.

Draw a line from 6 through 4.

7 is the top of undersleeve.

Draw a line from 7 parallel with the line 6–4.

8 from 1 is ½″.

9 is the cuff hindarm.

Square across through 9 by the line o–o.

10 from 9 is ¼″ : square down from 10.

11 from 10 is ½″.

Draw a line from 9 through 11.

SECTION L.17

This shows Section L.15, the topsleeve, with all the grades filled in up to 40″ and down to 32″ chest.

SECTION L.18

This shows Section L.16, the undersleeve, with all the grades filled in up to 40″ and down to 32″ chest.

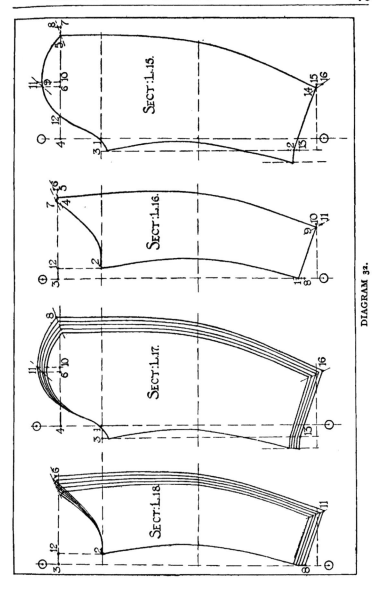

DIAGRAM 32.

CHAPTER V

LAYS OR ECONOMY IN CUTTING

By REUBEN SYTNER

IT is surprising to anyone who has had experience in the wholesale, to see the amount of waste in the custom trade when cutting. As an instance, the usual procedure is to cut off a 1¼ yard length for the trousers and pass this over to the trousers cutter. The suit lay takes 2 yards and 32″ in one case ; assuming that we deduct the trousers length, this leaves 1 yard and 23″ : what kind of jacket and vest can one cut from this length ? The " cheap lay " takes 1 yard and 25″, without any inlays and a pieced facing, so that this in itself ought to convince anyone of the avoidable waste. True, the trousers are cut out by a junior, and the wage cost is therefore lower ; but do the wages saved fully compensate for the material wasted ? I doubt it. In the wholesale trade men are fully occupied day after day doing nothing else but planning lays and making perforated lays in which all avoidable waste is eliminated.

In order to test lays and prove that garments have been planned from the smallest possible amount, it is usual to examine them for " daylight," i.e. waste. Each size is usually contrived in three widths—54″ ; 56″ ; 58″ ; and sometimes 60″.

The average is tested as follows : Multiply the length by the width, e.g. 104″ by 56″ = 5,824 square inches ; divide by 54 and 58 respectively, and if the length taken by the lays does not agree with the test, there is something faulty, one or more of the lays taking too much material. It may be necessary to divert a seam in the three-quarter sleeve, or give the trousers seat-pieces or waistbands. In doing this the comparative cost of labour and material must be studied. For instance, if the material saved is worth 3d. and the extra labour entailed would cost 3½d., it is obviously cheaper to waste the material. When costs are equal, the following points must be taken into consideration :

1. The appearance of the garment.
2. Whether labour or material is most easily procurable.
3. The time taken in production, whether it affects delivery.

If a saving of 9*d.* in material would entail an additional 9*d.* in *making* costs, all other things being equal, and the garments being wanted, it would be preferable to waste the material and save the making cost. As the latter must of necessity mean time taken in making, this would also keep up production. If the makers are wanting work and the garments are *not* urgently needed, then save the material and pass the saving on to the operatives in extra work, i.e. wages. Keep the staff occupied and help to cut down overhead costs.

The whole business of wholesale production is not quite so haphazard as those outside are given to believe. Economic laws can no more be ignored in wholesale tailoring than in any other business, and production and system are important factors.

Production costs always reflect themselves in selling prices, and the former are constantly in the limelight, the saving being passed over to the purchaser, " the man in the street."

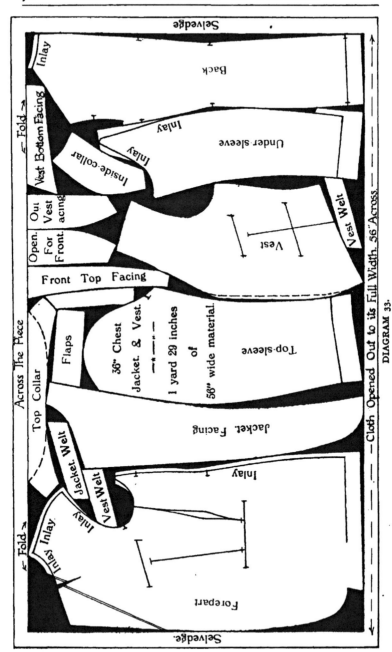

DIAGRAM 33.

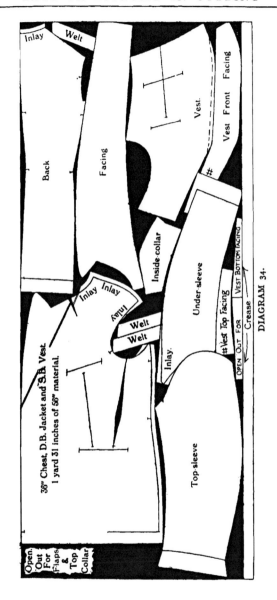

DIAGRAM 34.

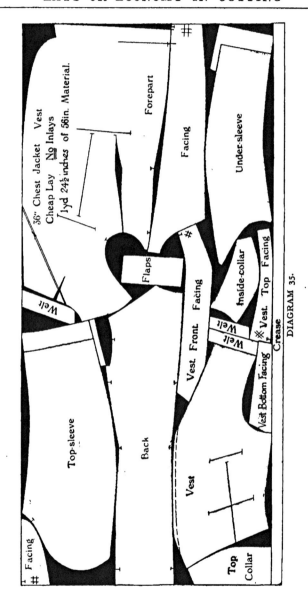

DIAGRAM 35.

PLATE VII

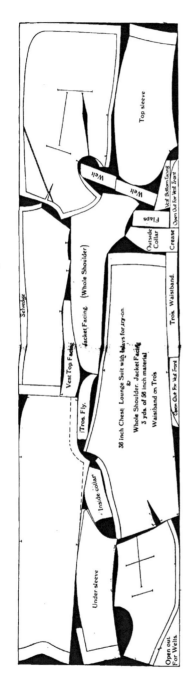

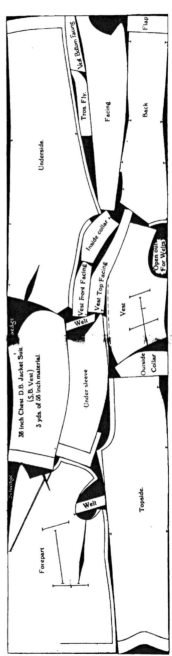

ECONOMY LAYS.

PLATE VIII

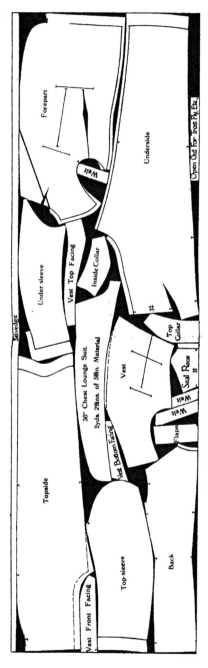

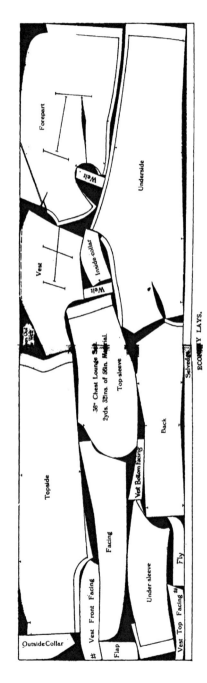

ECONOMY LAYS.

PLATE IX

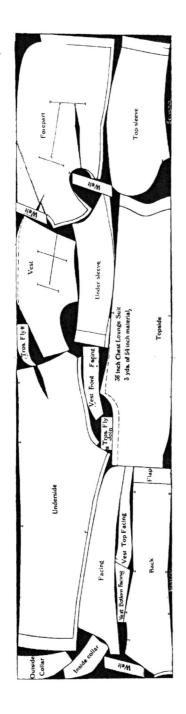

36 Inch Chest Lounge Suit
3 yds. of 54 inch material

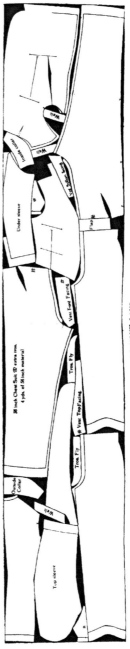

36 Inch Chest Suit 30 extra rm.
4 yds. of 56 inch material

ECONOMY LAYS.

CHAPTER VI

CUTTING LADIES' GARMENTS (NETT) BY SHOULDER MEASURE SYSTEM

By F. G. STOREY

(Designer, Messrs. John Barran & Sons, Ltd., Leeds)

LADIES' LONG COAT

Diagram 36

MEASURES :—*Natural waist* $15\frac{1}{4}''$; *full length* $44''$; *half back* $6\frac{3}{4}''$; *elbow* $18''$; *full length sleeve* $28\frac{1}{2}''$; *bust* $36''$; *hips* $40''$; *shoulder measure* $24''$; *forearm* $17''$. *Two-thirds shoulder measure* $= 16''$; *add* $1''$ *for ease, making* $17''$, *which is the working scale.*

THE draft is produced nett—that is, all seam allowances and turnings must be added.

DRAFT

Draw line O to E the full length, $44''$;
A from O is $1\frac{3}{4}''$.
B from A, one-third scale.
C from O, natural waist length.
D from C, $7''$ for hip line.
Square out from these points.
F from O, one-sixth scale ; square up $\frac{1}{4}''$ and shape back neck.
G from A, one-third scale plus $\frac{1}{4}''$.
Square down to H.
Connect $\frac{1}{4}$ to G and shape back shoulder seam.
U from G one-eighth scale ; apply width of back $6\frac{3}{4}''$ at this point.
J from H one-quarter scale plus $\frac{1}{2}''$.
K from B one-half bust plus $1''$.
Square up to L from J ; also down to Q and up to P from K.
L from J one-half scale plus $\frac{1}{2}''$.
Square from L to P by L J.
P is the point of intersection of lines LP and KP.

M from L one-sixth scale less $\frac{1}{2}''$.
N is midway between L and P.
Connect M to G and make MM from M back shoulder width less $\frac{1}{4}''$.
Come up from J $1\frac{1}{2}''$ and forward $\frac{1}{4}''$.
Draw scye MM to $\frac{1}{2}$, round through back scye to GG, which is $\frac{1}{2}''$ outside G.
R from Q $\frac{1}{2}''$; draw centre line from P through R.
Square down from M to 7 one-sixth scale.
Square out from 7 to 8.
Draw gorge line as diagram, dropping slightly below 8.
Measure M to N and take this amount out in front vee of gorge.
CC from C, one-third scale plus $\frac{1}{4}''$.
DD from D as CC from C plus $\frac{1}{2}''$.
9 from B one-third scale plus $1''$.
Shape back from 9 through CC and DD to point 5.
3 from CC $\frac{1}{4}''$.

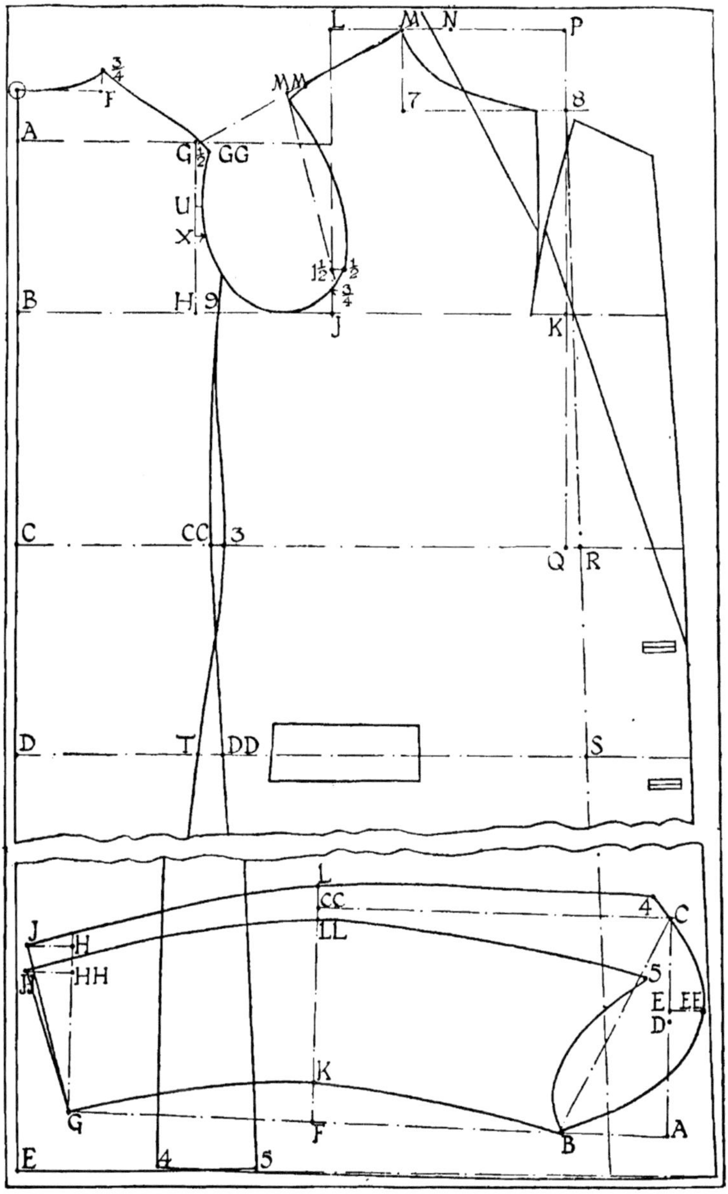

DIAGRAM 36.

Measure D to DD; place this amount at S and measure out to T the hip measure plus 1".

Shape side seam from 9 through 3 and T to point 4.

Add 3½" beyond centre line for front overlap.

SLEEVE

Draw line A to G.

B from A same as U from H on coat draft.

Square out from A to C.

C from B same as U to GG and MM to point ¾ measured straight.

D is midway between C and A.

E ½" from D nearer C.

Square up from E to EE 1¼".

Shape sleeve head from B through EE to C.

Square down from C to CC by CA.

Measure back width; place this amount at C and measure to CC the elbow length, continuing to J the sleeve length.

Point F is squared from CC by CC to C.

K from F, 1¼".

L from CC, ¾".

G from B the forearm measure.

Square out to H and make H ¼ scale plus 1"; square down to J.

Connect G to J for run of cuff.

4 from C same as X from U on coat draft; in this case 1".

Draw hindarm seam from 4 through L to J.

LL from L, 1¼".

JJ from J, ¾".

Sweep point 5 from 4 by CC.

Measure from front pitch to X on coat draft and make 5 from B this quantity plus ½".

Draw underside of sleeve from B to 5 as diagram and hindarm of underside from 5 through LL to JJ.

Draw forearm seam from B through K to G.

LADIES' COSTUME COAT

Diagram 37

MEASURES :—*Natural waist* 15¼" ; *full length* 27" ; *half back* 6½" ; *elbow* 18" ; *full length sleeve* 28½" ; *bust* 36" ; *hips* 40" ; *shoulder measure* 24" ; *forearm* 17". *Two-thirds shoulder measure* = 16" ; *add* 1" *for ease, making* 17", *which is the working scale.*

THE draft is produced nett—that is, all seam allowances and turnings must be added.

DRAFT

Draw line O to E, the full length, 27".
A from O, 1¾".
B from A, one-third scale.
C from O, natural waist length.
D from C, 7" for hip line.
Square out from these points.
F from O, one-sixth scale ; square up ¾" and shape back neck.
G from A, one-third scale plus ½".
Draw back shoulder seam from ¾ through G to GG, making GG ¾" from G.
Square down from G to H.
U from G one-eighth scale ; apply back width at this point.
X from U, 1".
J from H, quarter scale plus ½" ; square up to L.
L from J, half scale plus ½" ; square out to P by LJ.
K from B, one-half bust plus 1".
Square down to Q and up to P from K.
Point P is intersection of lines from K and L.
N is midway between L and P.
Connect N and G for front shoulder.
MM from G, 3½".
Come up 1½" from J and forward ½" for front of scye.
HH is midway between J and H.
Lower shoulder point at MM, ½".
Draw scye from ½ below MM through front of scye point HH and back width to GG.
R from Q, ½".

Draw centre line from P through R to bottom of coat.
Draw front shoulder from N to ½" below MM.
NN to Z is the amount of difference between N to MM and back shoulder width.
Square down to 7 from N one-sixth scale.
Square out to 8.
Draw gorge as diagram.
Square down to W from HH.
Suppress side seam ¼" each side of W.
Add 1" each side of V and shape side seam of back and forepart as diagram.
Panel seams may be added to taste : the following will be a guide :
2 from A, 5".
3 from B, 4½".
4 from C, 4½".
5 from D, 4½".
6 from E, 4¾".
Connect these points up for back panel.
Suppress ¾" as at 9 ; shape sidebody seam through 6–5–9–3–2, nipping out ¼" above 2.
RR from R, 5½".
SS from S same as RR to R.
Rule front panel through SS to RR up to point 12, which is 2" below bust line.
Suppress ¾" as at 10 and square down to T.
Connect 12 to NN and 10–12 to Z.
NN is 2½" from N.
Add 1½" button stand ; shape lapel as diagram.

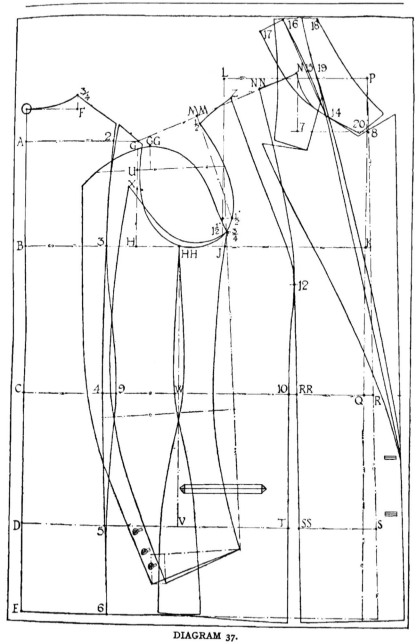

DIAGRAM 37.

SLEEVE

The sleeve is constructed the same as for long coat, making elbow width and cuff width ½″ narrower.

COLLAR

Come forward from N 1″ to 19 and rule crease row of lapel through this point.

Point 14 is where the crease row crosses gorge line.

15 is midway N 19.

Rule 14–15 to 16.

15 to 16, back neck width.

17 from 16, the stand.

18 from 16, the fall.

Draw sewing-on edge of collar from 17 through 14 to 20, nipping out ½″ as at 20.

Shape collar end to taste.

CHAPTER VII

LADIES' LEATHER GARMENTS

By W. H. HULME

(Head Teacher—Clothing Trades Department, Leeds Technical College)

SUEDE leather, so useful for sports purposes, can be obtained in a wide range of colours. Many of the newer art shades are very becoming when worn with a suitable skirt of sporty cut.

In designing and cutting garments of this material it must be borne in mind that the typical sports jacket will take five skins, the average working out about 32 square feet altogether. Grade I skins cost about 1s. 4d. per square foot ; Grade II 1½d. less. Few suitable skins are more than 29″ long with a maximum width of 20″. The design must be so ordered that the various parts come out of the skin without piecing.

The pelts are not uniform in thickness, and the thin, weak places must be so arranged in the lay that they come in those parts of the garment least subjected to strain. The normal type of jacket will not be more than 28″ long. If greater length is needed a yoke seam may be placed about the breast line. Pleats, back and front, may be arranged as required. For a golfing jacket pleats are, of course, desirable. A seam at low-hip may be inserted and covered by a half belt. Pleats will therefore run between yoke and hip.

Any outside pocket will be of the patch variety, with or without flap. If an inset pocket is demanded, it should be finished with a welt, which gives the best result in this material. The lining should be of a sound silk fabric, which has been shrunk with a " dry iron " before cutting.

Suede will press quite well, if a not-too-hot iron and dry rag are used. The surface can always be restored after pressing. Secure the edges by sewing in, when " running-on," an inch-wide strip of rubber fabric such as " Q-N," or similar

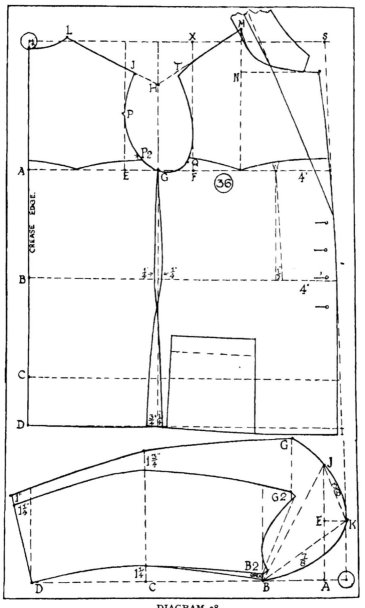

DIAGRAM 38.

preparation. The bottom and sleeve-hands may be secured in the same way.

Do a bare minimum of basting, and do not make up as an open coat, but bag the job, even at the bottom. The button-holes will be of the same material. See that a " leather " needle is placed in the machine. Above all, do not handle the job more than is necessary.

If, in the course of making, the suede becomes marked, do not apply benzine or any other liquid stain remover. Any marks may be removed by lightly rubbing with clean, fine sand-paper.

Diagram 38

SYSTEM FOR SUEDE SPORTS JACKET
Scale = half breast measure.
($\frac{3}{8}''$ seams allowed.)

Square O–S, O–D.
O–A = $\frac{1}{3}$ sc.
O–B = natural waist.
O–D = full length 27".
B–C = 7".
Drop $\frac{1}{2}''$ from O.
O–L = $\frac{1}{4}$ sc.–$\frac{1}{4}''$.
L, $\frac{1}{4}''$ above line.
A–E = $\frac{1}{3}$ sc. + 1".
A–F = $\frac{2}{3}$ sc.
A–W = $\frac{1}{2}$ breast.
G centre E–F.
E–P = $\frac{1}{4}$ sc. + $\frac{1}{2}''$.
G–H = $\frac{1}{3}$ sc.

From X, $\frac{1}{6}$ sc. + $\frac{1}{2}''$ forward, rising $\frac{3}{4}''$ to M.
Connect L–H, M–H.
J = $\frac{1}{4}''$ out.
M–T = L–J.
F–Q = $\frac{3}{4}''$.
M–N = $\frac{1}{6}$ sc.

SLEEVE

O–A = $\frac{1}{12}$ sc.
O–B = $\frac{1}{3}$ sc.
B–D = 17".
C = half B–D.
B–J = P–J–T–Q on jacket draft.
Displace seam from J, 3" to G.
E = half A–J.
B²–G² = Q–P².

CHAPTER VIII

COLLAR CUTTING AND MAKING FOR LADIES' GARMENTS

By PHILIP DELLAFERA

APART from the styles which are used for men's garments, collar cutting and making for ladies' garments is quite a different matter, although the general principle is the same. In order to cover as much ground as possible, I have selected a few styles which are always popular, and am omitting the masculine styles which, of course, would be treated in the same way as if they were for men's garments.

Diagram 39. Section A

THIS depicts the cutting of a fairly deep collar extending to the end of lapel and which is made from cloth.

The crease edge of lapel is marked from 2 through 3 to bottom, point 2 being fixed at $1''$ from neck-point.

Continue this line from 2 to 4, making this quantity equal to back neck plus $\frac{1}{2}''$.

Sweep 5 from 4, making this distance $1\frac{3}{4}''$.

Draw straight line from 5 to 3, then square from this line to 6 and 7.

6 from 5 = $1\frac{1}{2}''$.

7 from 5 = $3\frac{3}{4}''$.
8 from 7 = $\frac{3}{4}''$.
9 is $\frac{1}{4}''$ below top of lapel.
10 is fixed at $9\frac{1}{2}''$ from 8, and $3\frac{1}{2}''$ from 9.

Draw centre back seam from 6 through 5 to 8; fall edge from 8 to 10; collar end from 9 to 10 and sewing-on edge from 6 to 9, the run of seam being $\frac{1}{4}''$ below the neck of coat.

SECTION B illustrates a portion of forepart which is used for the double collar.

SECTION C shows the cutting of the double collar, which is intended to be made from cloth ; it is almost a straight piece of material.

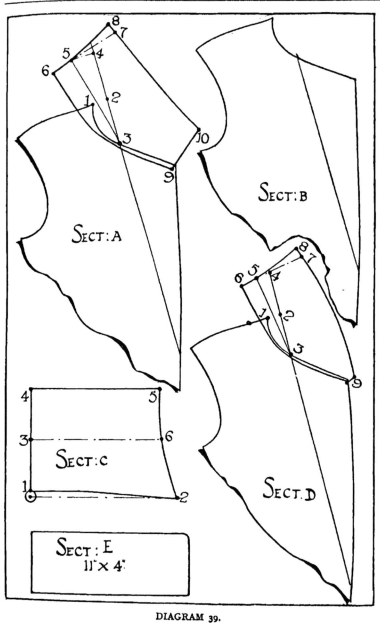

DIAGRAM 39.

To draft same, square construction
   lines 0, 2, 4.
1 from 0 = $\frac{1}{4}''$.
2 from 0 = $10\frac{1}{2}''$.
3 from 1 = $3\frac{1}{2}''$.
4 from 1 = $7''$.
Square across from 3 and 4.

5 from 4 = $9\frac{1}{4}''$.
6 from 3 = $9\frac{1}{2}''$.
Draw sewing-on edge from 1 to 2 ;
   collar end from 2 through 6 to 5 ;
   top edge from 4 to 5 and centre
   back from 1 to 4.

SECTION D shows the cutting of a deep roll collar, which may be covered with fur.

Points 1, 2, and 3 are the usual quantities in order to get the crease edge
   of lapel.
Continue the crease edge from 2 to 4,
   making the distance equal to the
   back neck plus $\frac{1}{2}''$.
Sweep $1''$ from 4 to 5 and draw straight
   line from 5 to 3, this being the crease
   edge of collar.

Square 6 and 7 by line 3–5.
6 from 5 = $1\frac{1}{2}''$.
7 from 5 = $3\frac{3}{4}''$.
8 from 7 = $\frac{3}{4}''$.
9 is made $\frac{1}{2}''$ beyond the end of lapel.
Draw centre back seam from 6 through
   5 to 8 ; fall edge from 8 to 9, and
   sewing-on edge from 6 to 9, making
   the run of seam $\frac{1}{4}''$ below the gorge.

SECTION E illustrates the ordinary straight collar, which is usually covered with fur of some description ; it is merely a straight piece of material, $11''$ in length (this, of course, being half the actual size) and $4''$ wide.

Diagram 40. Section A

THIS diagram represents the cutting of a " stole " collar and is arranged so that the lapel rolls right to the bottom of forepart. In order to get this effect, a large dart is required in forepart, the size of this being obtained by turning back the lapel to the point at which it is required and then cutting off the amount which shows itself beyond the fold of front, the line being indicated from 3 downwards and usually taking the position of the ordinary crease edge, which is found by going out 1″ from 1 to 2 and drawing it straight through 2 and 3.

To draft the collar, continue crease line from 2 to 4, making the distance equal back neck quantity plus ½″.
Sweep ½″ from 4 to 5 and square 6–7 by line 3–4.
6 from 5 = 1½″.
7 from 5 = 2¼″.

8 from 7 = ½″.
9 is the end of lapel.
Draw centre back from 6 to 8 ; sewing-on edge from 6 through 3 to 9, and fall edge from 8 to 9, making this run in line with edge of lapel.

SECTION B shows the upper portion of forepart suitable for a double stand collar ; the neck must be cut higher than usual, so that the collar fits well up in front.

SECTION C illustrates the outline of collar and is drafted as follows :

Square construction lines 0, 2, 5.
1 from 0 = ½″.
2 from 0 = 8½″.
3 from 1 = 3½″.
4 from 3 = 4″.
5 from 4 = ½″.
Square across from 3 and 5.

6 from 5 = 9¼″.
7 from 3 = 8¼″.
Draw sewing-on edge from 1 to 2 ; centre back from 1 to 4 ; top edge from 4 to 6, and collar end from 2 through 7 to 6.

SECTION D shows the cutting of a small collar suitable for coat frocks ; it is similar to the ordinary step, but extends to the end of lapel.

Point 1 indicates the neck-point of forepart ; 2 is located at 1″ out from neck-point, then the crease edge is drawn from 2 through 3 to bottom of lapel.
Continue crease edge from 2 to 4, making this equal back neck quantity plus ¼″.
Sweep 5 from 4 making it ¼″ ; then square 6 and 7 by line 3–5, which indicates the crease edge of collar.

6 from 5 = 1¼″.
7 from 5 = 2″.
8 from 7 = ½″.
9 from ¼″ below end of lapel ; and 10 is fixed at 6″ from 8 and 2″ from 9.
Draw sewing-on edge from 6 to 9 ; centre back seam from 6 to 8 ; fall edge from 8 to 10, and collar end from 9 to 10.

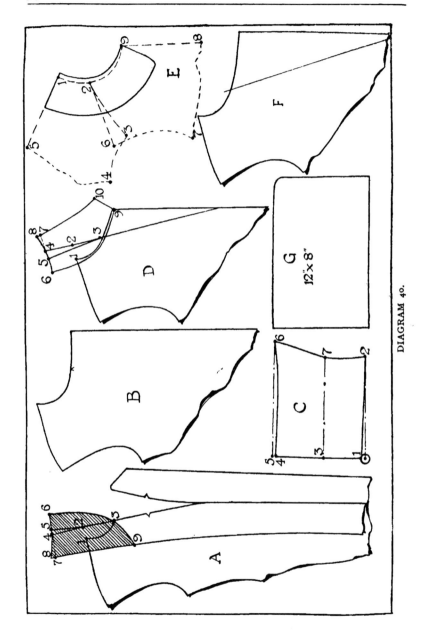

DIAGRAM 40.

SECTION E illustrates the method of the laid-on collar which is also used for coat frocks.

This collar is obtained by placing the back and forepart together in such a position that the neck-points are level and the shoulder ends overlap about 1″.

The outline of back is indicated by points 1, 2, 3, 4, and 5 ; whilst the forepart is marked by points 2, 6, 7, 8, and 9.

The solid line clearly illustrates the shape of collar ; it is cut $\frac{1}{2}$″ smaller at the neck to allow for the seam and is about 3″ wide all round, the front being cut away slightly and rounded.

SECTION F represents the shoulder portion of forepart which is to be finished with a deep fur collar. The gorge must be cut fairly high, so that when the collar is turned up it will fit nicely round the front of neck.

SECTION G shows the outline of collar, the actual size being 24″ × 8″, the diagram showing half this length.

Fur collars are usually cut perfectly straight, consequently the under collar must be cut in the same way, the length being regulated according to size of garment.

Diagram 41. Sections A, B, C, and D

THIS diagram illustrates the making of the collar which is shown in the cutting diagram, Section A.

First of all, cut out the canvas which must be on the bias ; then sew up the centre back seams of both under collar and canvas, and finally baste the two together in readiness for padding.

SECTION A illustrates the under collar with the back seam pressed open, whilst

SECTION B shows the collar nicely padded ; the stand is stitched out and the drawing-in thread is also marked along the crease edge.

The under collar may now be joined to the neck of coat, or, if desired, the collar may be made up completely before it is put on to the coat.

SECTION C portrays a portion of the collar joined to the neck ; it is seamed right to the end of lapel and slopes in an outward direction, this being shaped according to individual requirements.

Sometimes the facing and outside collar are cut in one piece, the seam being made at centre back ; in this case the under collar must be joined to the coat before the facings and outer collar are put on.

The finish of this style of collar is purely a matter of taste ; the edges may be left quite plain, or they may be stitched about $\frac{3}{8}''$ off as indicated by SECTION D, which shows the lapel turned over with the collar.

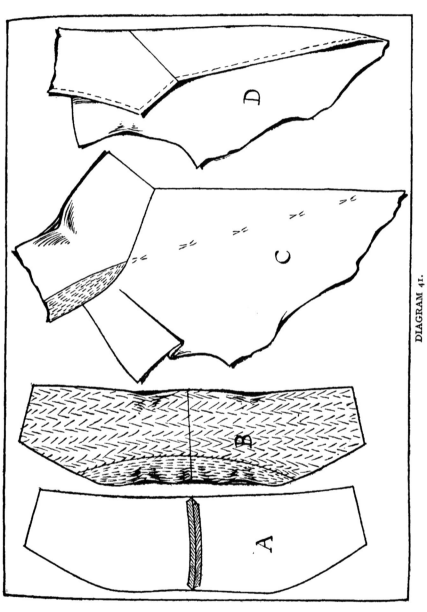

DIAGRAM 41.

Diagram 42. Sections A, B, and C

HERE is shown the making up of a cloth double collar, which is cut as SECTIONS B and C of diagram 42.

The collar is practically a straight piece of material; it may be interlined with a soft canvas, but there is no need for any padding, because this style is intended to be worn in almost any position.

SECTION A illustrates the actual length of under collar; it must be stretched slightly at the centre of sewing-on edge and the fold is indicated by stitch marks, this being fixed about half the width of collar.

SECTION B shows a portion of collar sewn into the neck; it reaches right to the end of lapel, and the edge is continued perfectly straight for a few inches and then it springs out slightly.

This shape is not absolutely necessary, but it gives a very smart effect when turned over.

A few rows of stitching may be made at the collar end as indicated on SECTION C, which shows the finished collar and lapel turned over in its correct position.

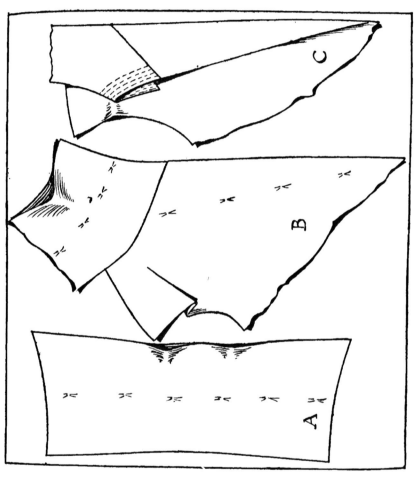

DIAGRAM 42.

Diagram 43. Sections A, B, C, D, E, and F

THIS diagram illustrates the making up of two styles which are very popular, especially for overgarments.

The neck in each case is the same, the only difference being the shape of collar and the method of trimming ; one is a roll collar, whilst the other is simply a straight collar extending right to the end of lapel.

SECTION A illustrates the roll collar padded and stitched out ; the drawing-in thread is also marked, and both edges have been stretched.

SECTION B shows a portion of the collar seamed into neck of forepart ; the line of crease edge is plainly indicated and the run of outer edge is also shown ; this should be one continuous line with front edge.

Presuming this collar is going to be covered with fur, it will be necessary to turn the edge in, basting it down to the canvas ; and then the fur collar, which has been specially prepared to the desired size, is felled on, taking special care not to get it too tight across the lapel.

SECTION C plainly shows this method of finish ; the lapel rolls fairly low and the collar has been well shaped.

Fur collars may be cut out and made up by the tailor, but it is far better to get a furrier to make them up, as they specialise in this work. It is only necessary to supply a pattern of the shape required, and the collar will be made up ready to be felled on to the cloth under collar.

SECTION D illustrates the straight collar ; it is just a straight piece of material about 4″ wide and of sufficient length to go round the neck of coat.

It is sewn in quite plain ; it may be interlined with a soft canvas if desired, and the shape of end is indicated by SECTION E, where a portion is joined to the forepart. Here again the finish is a matter of taste ; it may be trimmed with fur, similar to the roll collar, or it may be covered with astrakhan or similar material, as shown by SECTION F, which illustrates the finished collar and lapels, the latter being cloth, whilst the former is made from astrakhan.

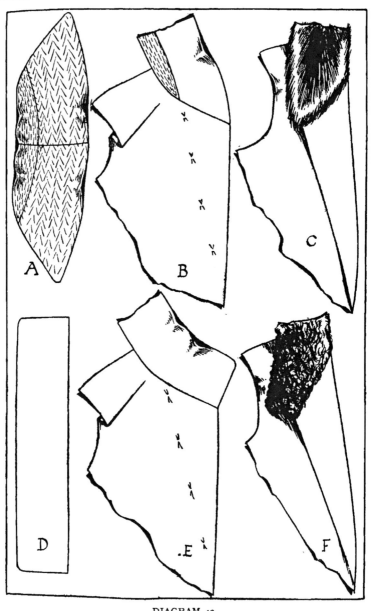

DIAGRAM 43.

Diagram 44. Sections A, B, and C

I NOW come to the stand and fall collar, which is a great
favourite with many ladies ; it consists of a straight piece
of material cut in such a way that it will stand up round
the neck for a few inches, then turn over nicely, falling over
the shoulder ; the fronts are pointed and cut away.

It is most effective when plain material is used for the
garment and a border of check or plaid material put on the
collar and cuffs, the border being cut on the bias to give the
best effect.

SECTION A illustrates the full size of collar laid out flat ;
the sewing-on edge is slightly stretched at the centre of back ;
the border has been put on, and the stitch marks indicate the
fold which is made when the collar is turned over.

When the collar is sewn into the neck of coat, it does not
go right to the end of the lapel, but extends to a point about
3" back from front edge in the case of a double-breasted coat
and about 2" back in a single-breasted garment.

The collar ends are only intended to meet ; therefore the
end of collar must be so arranged that it reaches a point as
near as possible the centre of front on forepart, this being
located by a notch and adjusted when fitting the coat.

SECTION B clearly illustrates the collar sewn into the neck
and finishing well back from the front edge.

SECTION C shows the effect of the collar turned over ; the
under collar, which is cut the same shape as SECTION A, is seen
joining the forepart, whilst the outer collar with the plaid
border is also plainly illustrated.

This type of collar may be worn turned down flat in the
ordinary way if desired.

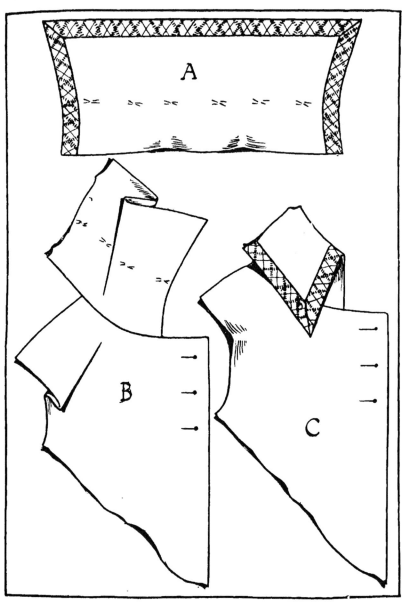

DIAGRAM 44.

Diagram 45.   Sections A, B, and C

THIS diagram shows the ordinary collar which is usually put on coat frocks; it is made up in the same way as an ordinary step collar, except that it is made to reach the end of lapel.

SECTION A shows the under collar; the stand and fall edges have been stretched; the stand is stitched out, and the fall is nicely padded, so that a good shape will be obtained.

It is sewn into the neck in the usual way, the outline of same being indicated by SECTION B, which shows a portion of collar fastened to the forepart.

The facing is made from the same material, but sometimes silk is used for the outer collar, in which case this may be put on over a cloth collar or direct on to the under collar, with an interlining of domette or similar material.

The edges of collar may be finished with a row of silk braid, as shown by SECTION C. In this case the collar is made up in the usual way and simply bound with the braid.

Sometimes the edges are just placed together and seamed up with the braid; this makes a very thin edge and is certainly a good method.

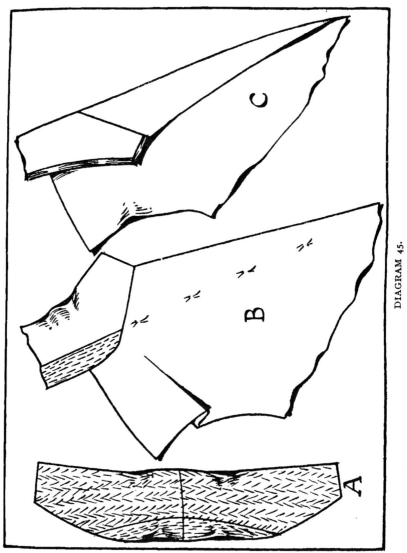

DIAGRAM 45.

Diagram 46. Sections A, B, C, and D

THE laid-on collar is not used very much, but is certainly a very useful style for frocks or dresses.

There are two ways of putting on this collar; one is just seamed on and turned over, the seam being neatened or hidden by making a row of stitching under the collar near the seam ; whilst the other method is by laying the collar on the neck, leaving sufficient material to be turned inside ; the neck is then neatened either with the lining or a strip of binding.

First of all, the collar must be lined, and this is done by basting it on to a piece of lining as shown by SECTION A, and the outer edge seamed right round from end to end.

It must then be pressed into shape, so that it resembles SECTION B, which shows the collar ends brought together at the front and a small portion turned in at the top, this being eventually turned in the inside of neck when the collar is put on.

SECTION C illustrates the collar laid on back and forepart, the dot and dash line round neck indicating the actual neck of garment, whilst the solid line at neck shows the amount that the collar is overlapped for turning in.

SECTION D shows the collar turned up and indicating the actual line of neck ; the dot and dash line being the collar, whilst the solid line is the neck of back and forepart.

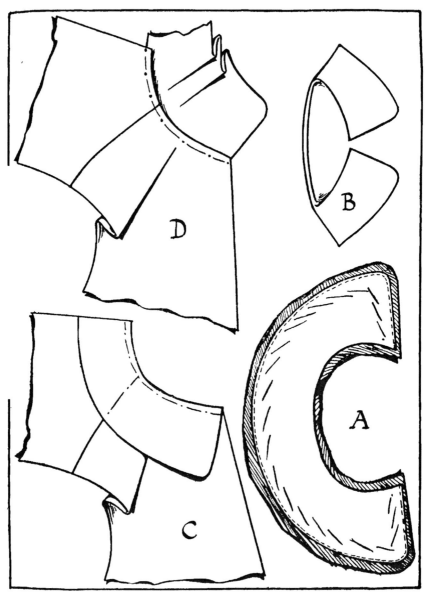

DIAGRAM 46.

Diagram 47. Sections A, B, and C

THIS shows the making up of the " stole " collar. First of all, sew up the breast dart and proceed to make up the under collar (SECTION A), which is done in the usual way. The under collar is then sewn into the neck and pressed round, so that it takes the shape required. Here it should be mentioned that the collar must be kept as short as possible, so that it pulls the lapel well back from the front edge ; in fact, the lapel is turned back the whole length of forepart, and for this reason the collar must be regulated so that it is nice and clean.

It will be found that the front edge will require a fair amount of drawing in to get it to fit well. The position of this is indicated at bottom of breast dart on SECTION B, which illustrates the dart seamed up and pressed open, in addition to a portion of the collar.

The completed shape of front is illustrated by SECTION C. It will be seen that the lapel is turned back all the way down, and the position of under collar seam is indicated by dot and dash line.

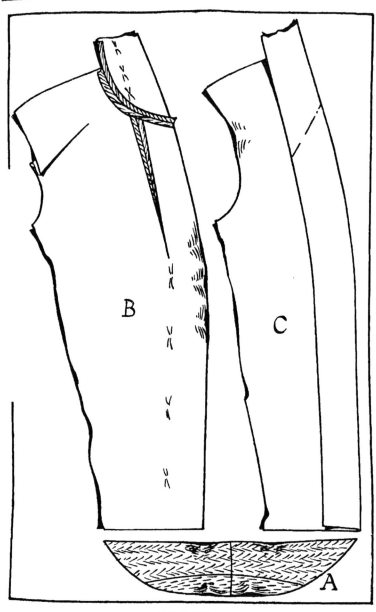

DIAGRAM 47.

Diagram 48. Sections A, B, C, and D

THIS diagram illustrates the making of the ordinary square fur collar, which is worn in almost any position.

The under collar is simply a straight piece of material about 8" wide and of sufficient length to fit the neck, usually about 24" in length.

SECTION A illustrates the fur collar, which must be specially prepared. It is lined with a thin layer of wadding and covered with a piece of domette; the edges turned in and a piece of tape sewn round, this being used to sew on the cloth collar.

SECTION B shows the cloth collar sewn into the neck, and press studs are indicated, these being used for fastening the collar up in the position indicated by SECTION D.

SECTION C illustrates the collar doubled over and the lapel rolling down to the waist line.

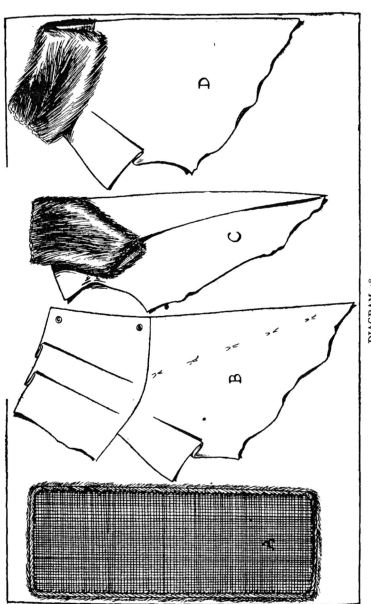

DIAGRAM 48.

CHAPTER IX

THE TAILORS' SHOP

By H. R. SKIPPER

The Exterior—The Shop Front—Signs—Window Fittings—Interior Fittings and Fixtures—Importance of Proper Lighting and Heating.

THE EXTERIOR

THERE is a saying that the appearance of a home portrays the mind of the housewife. It can also be said that the appearance of a shop portrays the mind of its proprietor. A retailer whose display front looks drab and untidy gives the impression that his goods, too, are drab and untidy.

Retailers do not always realise that their efforts to increase sales are often marred to a great extent by dingy and unattractive shop exteriors. The first impression potential customers have of a business is conveyed by the shop front, which will either induce them to enter the premises or pass on to a more attractive establishment. Why is it the " big " stores attract so many people ? It is not always because they give better value for money, for the average retailer is able to supply most, if not all, of the same class of merchandise that is sold by the multiple shops. No, the reason for the " big " stores " pull " is because of their attractiveness.

A bright, attractive shop front in a dingy or uninteresting street is bound to attract attention, and, what is more, custom.

Speaking broadly, an establishment for men should possess a certain severity both inside and out, just as a man's club or the smoke-room of an hotel is designed on severe lines. Men's shops should be strictly businesslike. By that is meant a shop should be fitted so as to give the maximum amount of service with the minimum of delay.

The modern tendency among shopfitting specialists is to concentrate more and more on the use of lighter and less costly

PLATE X

GLASS FRONTED SHOW-CASES WHICH ALSO ACT AS WARDROBES.

The new shop-fitting idea is to stock and display at the same time.

PLATE XI

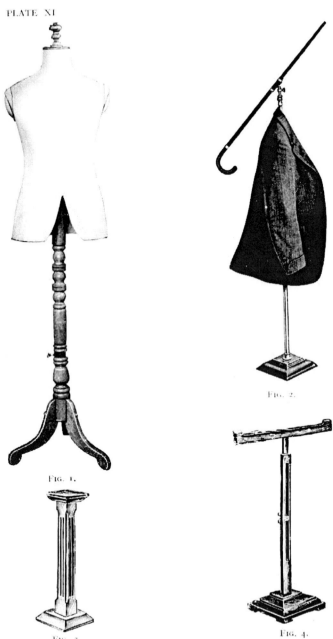

FIG. 1.

FIG. 2.

FIG. 3.

FIG. 4.

A GROUP OF INDISPENSABLE FITTINGS.

PLATE XII

FIG. 1A (Dressed).

FIG. 2.

FIG. 1B (Undressed).

FIG. 3.

DISPLAY ACCESSORIES FOR THE TAILOR.

PLATE XIII

FIG. 1.

FIG. 2.

FIG. 5.

FIG. 4.

FIG. 3.

MODERN IDEAS FOR DISPLAY STANDS.

PLATE XIV

A TAILOR'S OAK DISPLAY STAND.

(Pollard's.)

PLATE XV

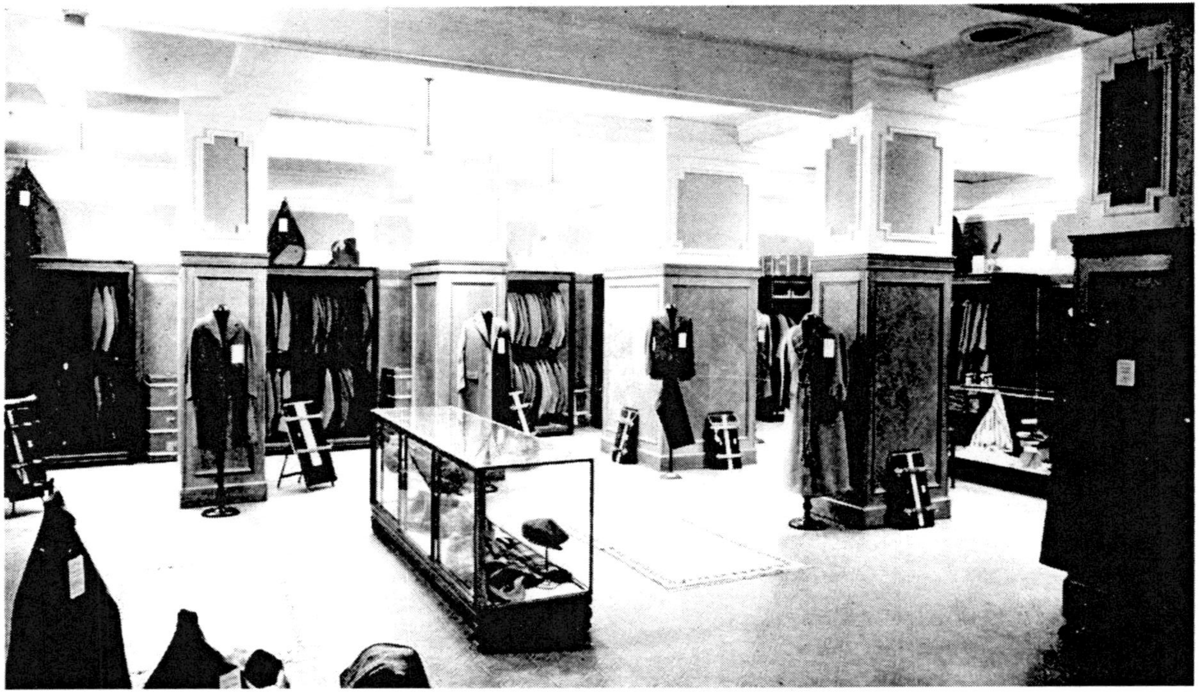

By courtesy of] [E. Pollard & Co., Ltd.

A MEN'S WEAR READY-MADE DEPARTMENT.

Showing the dignified effect obtained by the use of modern show-cases and display fittings.

PLATE X

MODERN SHOP-FITTING.

materials than those of former days. Whatever the retailer may have in mind as to what he considers would suit his requirements, it would be better for him to lay his plans before one of the many shopfitting specialists before coming to a decision. The specialist has a collection of records and a wide experience that enable him to lay a selection of possible schemes before his client with the least waste of time.

THE SHOP FRONT

Nowadays the most popular material used in the construction of a shop front is bronze metal. This is generally used on a backing of wood, weighs less than plain bronze metal and is cheaper. An important advantage of this material is that it needs little cleaning. Wood is still used for shop fronts to a large extent, oak and mahogany being the more popular. A front that is well painted, grained and varnished either in mahogany or oak colour looks exceedingly well and possesses an advantage over the polished front favoured a few years ago.

Stone and metal, when they are used for frontages, lend themselves to particularly artistic fascias and signs. White marble with bold bronze Roman letters gives an air of distinction to any window and entrance. One of the great advantages of metal is that it can be moulded into so many designs that appear light and attractive to the eye and yet are not fragile like plaster or wood.

The material used for the lower part of the shop front, known as the stall-riser, looks well if it corresponds with that used for the remainder of the shop front.

THE SIGN

The shop sign, or fascia, is one of the most important parts of the shop front. This should be dignified, discernible at a distance, pleasing in appearance, and in harmony with the general design of the shop. As regards the usual fascia, a wooden frame with the letters under glass is probably the kind in most general use. Variations of this simple form of sign are the coloured glass panel with gold-embossed letters, and the polished wooden frame with metal lettering. Incised gold letters on glass is an effective style. This can be varied in colour. Perhaps the best fascia for a tailoring establishment is one made of white marble with bronze metal letters. Such a fascia has a striking and handsome appearance.

It is advisable for the retailer to have his name below the window as well as above it. Many shoppers will look at a window and not take the trouble to notice the retailer's name over the premises. For this reason it is a good plan to place the name on a stall plate just below the window. On account of their exposure to wear and tear stall plates are more often than not made of metal. They may be cast bronze with polished letters, or repoussé copper plate, in which case cast letters are also used. The class of letter is capable of almost infinite variation to suit the taste of the owner of the business. The first object of any lettering is obviously to communicate information and to do so in a dignified manner. Before deciding on the style of fascia, stall plates, etc., it is the wisest plan to allow the shopfitter to submit drawings that have been prepared in connection with the whole design. Signs that might look well by themselves, or on one building, can easily look quite out of place on another.

Outside projecting signs and hanging signs are the traditional method of advertising in some districts. Although there are certain drawbacks to projecting signposts when they are placed over the ordinary sidewalk, in the case of vestibule entrances, and particularly arcades, such indicators have a distinctly decorative as well as a publicity value. A somewhat similar idea is the hanging lit-up sign that so many shops exhibit inside the window. Metal signs with pierced letters are the most suitable for electric light.

THE WINDOW

The window may be described as the retailer's chief advertisement. Small retail shops usually possess but two windows, and these not of the largest. The retailer must, therefore, concentrate his attention on securing from them the maximum display value. The entrance to the windows should be wide and tall enough to allow of easy access, and should never be completely blocked by the goods.

It is always well to have the windows constructed on generous lines as regards dimensions of depth and breadth, as it is easy by means of partitions and screens to divide them up if necessary for dressing. Light panelled oak with glass over is one of the most practical backgrounds for enclosed windows. It lends itself to almost any purpose, and does not shut out light. Side partitions are usually light in colour, cream being a popular favourite.

For the floor of his window, the tailor can choose between a finished material in the shape of parquetry or similar highly polished surface treatment, and plain boarding which requires a covering of some sort.

Parquetry is the most durable material, but, if desired, a cheaper form of flooring may be obtained. This is a composition mounted on prepared canvas and supplied in squares of about 2 ft. ready for laying.

SHUTTERS AND SUN-BLINDS

Sun-blinds and shutters are the tradesman's two principal defences against theft and the weather. In the case of a shop that happens to be on the sunny side of the street, adequate protection against the full force of the rays is essential in almost every business.

The class of sun-blind usually fitted in front of a shop is of the self-acting spring-roller variety, the fabric being either sail-cloth or coloured linen-tick.

These blinds are fitted into special container boxes of seasoned wood, fronted with a loose moulding that is in keeping with the front itself. If side blinds are used they should be of the same material and colour as the main blind.

The old flat wooden shutters are hardly ever used now. The most popular type is the roller-shutter of either wood or metal. However, there is a tendency in the tailoring trade to leave the windows exposed even over the week-end.

THE ENTRANCE

The window having done its part in attracting custom, the potential customer must naturally proceed to the entrance to make his purchases. This should be on the same level as the street in which the shop is situated. It is far better to have a sloping entrance rather than a step, which is often the cause of accidents.

The door should admit of easy opening and closing. Doorways should be wide enough to permit easy entrance by two or more people both coming in and going out. The doorway should not be obstructed by show-cases.

FITTINGS

There is still plenty of room for individual effort in constructing tailoring displays, and the enterprising retailer is in the fortunate position nowadays of having a host of fittings from which he can select to assist him to make an effective window display.

Display fixtures are the basis of well-dressed tailoring windows, and a supply of the following types will be found most useful :

Draping Blocks.
Display Forms.
Stands (wood and metal).
Attachments for Stands.
Trouser Rails.
Pedestals.
Shelves.

The foregoing are used in window displays as well as the showroom. For the showroom the following articles are indispensable :

Counters.
Chairs.
Wardrobes (glass fronts).
Trouser and Mantel Rails.

A good deal of care is necessary in selecting display appliances. It is wise, in the first place, to purchase a few good appliances rather than a quantity of cheap articles. Cheap fittings are rarely durable.

There are various styles and types of individual fixtures used in the average tailoring establishment and the fixtures here described and illustrated are regarded as specially suitable for giving maximum effect in displays in tailoring.

Forms for displaying men's jackets, jackets and vests, overcoats, women's coats and costumes, are made in a variety of shapes and styles. The forms in general use for displaying the garments mentioned are those known as Bust Forms. Such forms consist of a papier-mâché bust, mounted on an adjustable pillar or standard. The bases and knobs are made of metal in various finishes ; others have fitments of metal and wood combined. For all-round utility, the wood-fitted combination forms and stands are most desirable. An excellent example is that shown in Plate XI (Fig. 1) by Harris & Sheldon, Ltd. This is telescopic and can be used either for a jacket and vest or overcoat.

The stands best adapted for use in tailoring displays are

those known as T-stands. Such stands may be of wood or metal, and consist of a base standard, extending rod and a cross-arm.

Metal stands are made in a great variety of design of round or square tubing, plain or fancy, with round or square bases of porcelain or of metal. A very effective T-stand is shown in Plate XI (Fig. 4) by Dudley & Co., Ltd. This is made of solid oak, polished with extra heavy moulded base with four feet to prevent vibration. It is useful for displaying trousers. That illustrated measures 30 in. high when closed and extends to 48 in.

Pedestals are suitable for tailoring displays, and the solid kind like that shown in Plate XI (Fig. 3) by Dudley & Co., Ltd., are available in various heights.

DRAPING BLOCKS

A number of draping blocks are indispensable in a tailoring establishment. These consist of a wooden top and bottom connected by strips of wood, and covered with straw board and brown paper. In Plate XII, Figs. 2 and 3, and Plate XIII, Fig. 5, are shown the kind in general use. Fig. 3, Plate XII, is suitable for displaying trouserings, whilst Fig. 3, Plate XII, and Fig. 5, Plate XIII, are used for displaying suit, overcoat, and costume lengths.

A useful stand for displaying suitings and trouserings is shown in Plate XII, Figs. 1A and 1B (Dudley & Co., Ltd.). This is made in heavy oak and measures: Height 24 in., distance back to front 29 in.

Papier-mâché vases, an example of which is shown in Plate XIII, Fig. 4 (Dudley & Co., Ltd.), are a welcome change from the usual drape block for use in displaying suitings. Display vases lend an air of dignity and charm to window displays and greatly enhance their appearance and attractiveness.

The stand illustrating the walking stick and coat (Plate XI, Fig. 2) (Harris & Sheldon, Ltd.) can be extended up and down to suit individual dressings. It is supplied with a steel bronzed upright on a square oak base having a hook at the top to suspend the garment.

The easel stand (Plate XIII, Fig. 2) by Harris & Sheldon, Ltd., is adjustable to any angle and can be extended up and down. This was specially designed for displaying cloth lengths for one of the big London stores. It has met with exceptional demand by tailors all over the country. It is mounted on a heavy metal base and is supplied in Florentine bronze finish.

A unique all-metal suit stand is illustrated by Plate XIII, Fig. 1 (Harris & Sheldon, Ltd.). This is suitable for displaying a pair of trousers with a coat, one sleeve folded inside the other and hanging from the hook which appears at the top of the stand. The garment has then the appearance of being on a complete bust and makes an attractive display. Another suit display stand is shown in Plate XIII, Fig. 3 (Pollards). This is of solid oak, has a hook for hanging jacket to shelf and a cut-out for trousering.

For ready-to-wear departments there is nothing to beat the centre wardrobes. These are adapted for men's and boys' suits and overcoats, and an average size has a capacity of 90 or 100 pieces. These wardrobes have plate-glass tops and sides, the glass used in the backs, ends, and doors being of double strength. The cabinets being of glass, do not obstruct the view of the floor, and have the additional advantage that they provide facilities for display as well as storage. They can be moved to any position desired, and the frames are available in a variety of materials. Dimensions vary according to requirements.

Wall cabinets are also available on similar lines and they can be built upon the unit principle by the use of detachable cornices and pilasters. One up-to-date type has a recess in the centre, lined with mirrors, which is well adapted for the purpose of a fitting-room.

The tailors' oak display stand shown in Plate XIV (Pollards) is specially suitable in the show-room. The example shown measures 4 ft. high and has a 23-in. top. It is mounted on castors and is used to carry samples of cloth. This useful time-saver can be made to any other sizes or in any kind of wood to match the other furniture in the shop.

As regards the decorations of a clothing establishment, these should be as unobtrusive as possible so as not to detract the attention from the goods themselves. All decorations and furnishings should be a background to the wares for sale, and not be allowed to compete in any way with them in arousing interest on the part of a visitor to the shop.

Floors can be advantageously covered with composition if the boards are in a bad condition. This composition saves the wear of the matting or carpets. If a new floor is being put down polished parquet with carpet runners gives an impression of luxury and comfort. Linoleum or rubber tiles are more popular, however, for the furnishings of men's shops.

The illustrations on Plates I, X, XV, and XVI show how

a pleasing result can be obtained by the use in the most restrained manner of the simplest materials. These pictures are interior views of well-known men's wear shops and show the fine effect of a happy combination of a plain and business-like design and a strictly " mannish " atmosphere.

Taken together, these illustrations are fairly typical of the several kinds of arrangement most suitable for the interior construction of a clothing store. It will be noticed that white ceilings in panels and shaded lights are an effective method of decoration. Mirrors, when used, should not be overdone.

The Fitting Room

It is essential that the tailor have a fitting room, and where it is desired to add to or enlarge the fitting rooms already in use the retailer has an extensive range of choice of different types of panelling at his disposal. With regard to the equipment and furniture of a fitting room, this must naturally be in proportion to its size. There is no doubt that a wall fitting with panelled sides and mirrored front is the most efficient method of storing partly finished garments awaiting trying-on. It takes up less space than the old type of fitting consisting of rows of fixed racks. The new sliding racks make it possible to pack the garments closely together, but without confusion or over-crowding ; while, by merely pulling out the rack, any individual customer's order can be picked out instantly. The mirrored doors can be used in addition to or instead of the usual fitting-room mirrors.

Lighting the Premises

To have well-lighted windows is to realise the importance of carrying the same effect inside the shop by efficient interior illumination. If the shop lighting is neglected the window conveys a false impression, for a customer coming into a badly lighted shop after inspecting a well-lighted window display experiences a feeling of disappointment.

As far as window lighting is concerned it is no exaggeration to say that it costs no more to light a window well than to light it badly. The whole secret of window lighting lies in proper reflection. The retailer has to remember that effective lighting does not merely mean a sufficient light or a bright light or a good light, but a light which is sufficient and good for his particular purpose, which is to make his establishment look attractive and enable him to display the articles he wishes to sell to the greatest possible advantage. Light, as far as the shopkeeper is concerned, has to attract attention and illuminate effectively.

The trader who is anxious that his shop shall be well lighted and at the same time be totally devoid of any element of glare, cannot do better than examine the catalogues of firms producing the various types of translucent fittings and reflectors.

Traders whose shops are lighted by gas have an almost equal range of fittings from which to make their choice. Gas is claimed to be more economical in use. The incandescent gas light possesses the advantages of steadiness and brilliancy and is well diffused. It approximates very nearly in quality to daylight, which is an important consideration where colours are concerned.

HEATING THE SHOP

The purpose of heat, which should be distributed as far as possible evenly, is to give warmth and cheerfulness. The position of a fire or radiator should, therefore, be carefully selected, and in this respect expert assistance will be useful.

There are a multiplicity of heating devices from which the trader can make his choice. He must, however, make up his mind whether he intends to use electricity, gas, oil, or water as mediums of heating.

A very popular method of heating stores is by means of locally heated radiators deriving their heat from gas burners underneath or from radiators giving heat from hot water circulating from a boiler. In the latter case, the hot water is circulated through radiators of a suitable size placed in position selected for the purpose.

Gas stoves are favoured in many shops. They give a pleasing and warm effect. They offer many advantages over other systems both from the point of view of convenience and appearance. Gas radiators can be used as independent units and are thus not dependent upon central heating supply.

An alternative method of heating the shop is by means of anthracite stoves. These appliances can be placed in front of an existing grate, or may be connected to any existing brick chimney by means of metal piping. Once an anthracite stove is lighted it can be left alight for the remainder of the winter season.

The use of electricity for heating is not so universal as gas, but it has some possibilities especially for supplementary purposes. In a fitting room, for instance, it may be necessary to provide heat during the presence of a customer and obviously a radiator which can be switched on and off in a moment may then be highly convenient.

For quite small shops, electric fires of the reflector type are to be obtained in a form of pedestal heaters.

Unless rebuilding operations or extensive structural alterations are in hand, the problem of heating will merely resolve itself into adopting the best and most economical devices which are available and suitable for the system already employed.

CHAPTER X

WINDOW-DRESSING FOR TAILORS

By LUNGLEY POWE

(Director of Hector Powe, Ltd., London)

THE subject of window-dressing is so much in evidence to-day that any work dealing with the Tailoring Trade would be incomplete without at least one chapter devoted to it. I am, however, in this position : knowing something of the history of the trade, I realise fully that to many members of the craft both advertising and window-dressing seem a downward step. Let me explain. Tailoring, in its earliest days, was an honourable profession ; it brought men into intimate contact with the King and his great nobles, as well as dependents. It was as much a necessity as food ; in some cases, more so. It needed no flourish of trumpets ; no shop-window front. It was just there. Every stitch in every garment was put in by hand, and good, solid businesses descended from father to son ; it being the pride of the former to initiate the younger generation into the mysteries of cutting and sewing. It was a craft wherein comfortable, if not brilliant, fortunes could be made, for its intimate nature suggested ways of augmenting income ; as, for instance, when the Lord of the Manor was temporarily pushed for ready money.

Progress, that juggernaut which crushes so much in its triumphal march, has wrought many changes. It is not in my province in this article to trace the results of the introduction of the sewing-machine ; electric power ; the first ready-to-wear factory, etc. We all know that these things exist. What is so often forgotten, however, by those who essay to bring the tailoring trade " up-to-date " is this : Up and down the country, as well as in Savile Row, Jermyn Street, Bond Street, etc., there are men engaged in the trade whose ancestors were the trusted friends of the great ones of their day ; to these men blatant self-advertisement and the glaring lights of a shop-window are as repellent as factory-made clothes. One has only to visualise for a moment historic firms such as Poole & Co., Hill Bros., Hawkes & Co., Huntsman, and Scholte displaying dummies ticketed " As worn by H.R.H. the Prince of Wales," etc. etc., to understand that there are certain well-defined limits in this complex trade of ours.

Because of these things, I am writing as an ordinary middle-class tailor to my middle-class confrères. We are engaged in business to-day to make a living ; we are bound to make ourselves felt or perish. We cater for the great majority, but, because the market is a large one (far greater than at either extreme), competition is fierce, hence our belief in the adventitious aids of advertising and window-dressing.

THE MIDDLE-CLASS POINT OF VIEW

I should like, at the outset, to make the position perfectly clear by defining what I mean by " middle-class." We never touch the level of the " Fifty-shilling " man ; but neither do we charge our customers twelve or fourteen guineas for a suit. Our prices range from 4½ to 10 guineas, which means an average of about 6 guineas a suit.

We are constantly changing our displays during the season, but we always make a point of appealing to the middle-class young man. We are all young in the firm ; the directors are young, and, like our customers, " just ordinary middle-class men." This is the class we want to attract, for the young man has a future with possibilities. The older generation offers far less scope, and, what is more important, the discrimination and " dress-consciousness " of the young man of to-day is a wider medium for the spread of his tailor's name. We therefore dress our windows to attract him. As we ourselves grow older, it may be that our views and policy will change accordingly, and our appeal be made to older men.

TWO DISTINCT APPEALS

There are two distinct ways of appeal from a shop-window. The first is to cram it with coats and suitings, and when a prospective customer passes, if he needs a particular colour he may perhaps buy should he see just the one shade he wants. The second way is to dress a window to create desire ; and, as a firm, we have decided very strongly in favour of the window that creates desire, not the type that fills a want. There is all the difference in the world between a window dressed to show a little bit of everything and the window dressed to create desire—tastefully arranged *without too much in it.*

THREE TYPES OF SHOP FRONTS

There are three entirely different types of shop fronts. Take, for instance, the barber with his pole. He makes no display ; he simply says, " I'm here." The tobacconist, on the other hand, with his window full of cigarettes, says, " I've got them " ; but we try to make each one of our windows say : " You need me." To make this point clearer, for its importance cannot be too strongly stressed, look at any jeweller's window in the provinces. It is absolutely full, and one has great difficulty in choosing anything from it : it is a window dressed to fill a want. In London to-day jewellers are beginning to realise the value of open dressing, especially those who stock imitation jewels. Pearls are laid out on velvet cushions—just a few sets in a window—and they are put there to tempt the heart of the passer-by, to create desire. No one can fail to understand the subtlety of the appeal, nor the difference in the two types of window.

We, as a firm, are specialists in every sense of the word. We never show two different commodities in the same window. For example, if our appeal is on dress wear, nothing else is shown ; if on lounge suits, only *one* colour is on view ; if it is a question of price, our appeal is directed to the pocket of the man in the street, *one* price only ; if it is sports wear, then nothing but sports wear is shown, and so on. Of course, there is a possibility of missing business sometimes, but one must have a definite policy, and we are confident that it is the *specialised* window which makes the greatest appeal.

AVOIDING THE " TRAM-LINE " PRINCIPLE

In window-dressing, as in business, one has to study the psychology of the crowd, that is, of course, if it is the crowd one is out to attract. It is recognised that most people live on " tram-lines." That is to say, when a man leaves his office he goes along the same street and lunches at the same restaurant, day after day. He never sees some streets at all ; and others only by chance when some particular object takes him that way. That is why windows dressed on the " tram-line " principle, the same thing day after day, never arouse any interest. If, however, a continual change of idea and appeal is made each week, imagination and curiosity are both stimulated, and people begin

PLATE XVII

A "SALE" WINDOW WITHOUT THE WORD "SALE."

A good "reason why" the public should buy is given on the show card. The poster attracts the public; the show card tells the story, backed by a Chartered Accountant's Certificate to prove the selling at cost—truth in advertising. The window is purposely a little overcrowded, a necessity when pushing in dull times.

to look out to see what such and such a firm is showing. In this way interest is created—and business follows.

A very important plank in our policy is " Truth to the Public." We hear a great deal about " Truth in Advertising," and the same thing applies in display. " A price in the window is worth two in the shop," and, acting on this maxim, everything in our windows is priced plainly, but not too blatantly. It is possible to ruin an otherwise perfect window by a gaudy card or over-coloured price ticket. All cards should be in perfect keeping with the background, fixtures, and the rest of the display.

I think that in London, at any rate, windows are steadily growing more honest. The man who tries to stimulate trade by showing " bankrupt stock " does not accomplish his object. The public knows that it is nothing of the sort, and has no use for the goods.

TESTING RESULTS

We have followed this particular window-dressing policy for many years, and have faith in it ; but this faith is backed up by practical tests. We make it a rule to take the results of all our windows in this way. When a man orders a suit, he is asked if he has been in before just as a preliminary to checking his measurements. If the reply is in the negative, we ask if he has been recommended, and if this is not the case, then he must have been attracted by the window. These questions, of course, are asked in a tactful manner : under no circumstances is the customer cross-examined. The results thus obtained teach us remarkable things. Windows on which we pride ourselves have failed to attract ; others have turned out winners when we have least expected it. It is never safe to prophesy what will happen, but we live to learn, and if the results from a certain display are not good, we cut it out of our programme. Of course, in working out results every factor is taken into consideration, such as the weather, general conditions, etc., and daily reports are sent in to headquarters from the branches.

From the point of view of sales a casual observer might remark that the results of all the care and trouble expended on window-dressing are very disappointing. Our turnover shows 75 per cent. of business done is due to old customers repeating their orders ; 15 per cent. the fruit of personal recommendations, and only 10 per cent. traceable to window display. This percentage does not really give the window sufficient credit, as it must be borne in mind that if the standard of appeal dropped the 75 per cent. would not keep coming back, while the recommended customer would not deal with us if the windows did not display the quality he expected.

THE POLICY BEHIND THE WINDOW

I cannot stress too strongly the importance of the policy *behind* the window. We do not look upon our windows *merely* as a medium for selling our goods ; we make them render us greater service. We make them sell our publicity. We synchronise our window display with our press advertising, and by putting in copy (display or otherwise) of what we are showing, our windows help our newspaper advertising.

Another tremendous factor in window display is light, and it is our policy to present a totally different picture from our competitor next door. For instance, when the daylight method was first introduced, we had nothing else in our windows, and the effect was remarkable. A man passing on the opposite side of the road could see our competitors' line of yellow light ; then appeared the clear blue light which made our shop stand out vividly and impress its personality on all and sundry. When imitation, that sincere, but most trying, form of flattery, made many other shopkeepers take up daylight lamps, we resorted to coloured ones. For example, if we were showing a special line of wine-brown suitings, then the lighting was slightly contrasted in order to emphasise the particular shade of brown. And this illustration brings me to another potent factor in successful window-dressing—the mobile mind. Public opinion and public fancy are two of the most fickle things in the world, and a brain which cannot anticipate change; which dare not face risks, must be content with two or three stands of cloth.

Having tried, as far as possible, to describe our own particular policy, I will, in conclusion, formulate a few definite principles.

A FEW DEFINITE PRINCIPLES

The first point in figure-dressing is to study the garment to be displayed and then make the appeal as life-like as possible, with the most striking features to the fore. Shirts, collars, and ties are important, and should be chosen with proper regard to the suit. A real knowledge of how a suit should fit is essential for the would-be window-dresser. The coat, if on a dummy, must be as if worn. No display man can make a badly cut coat appear good, however hard he tries to alter it with padding ; in fact, padding is strictly forbidden. In order to make this feasible, our dummies are made to our own specification and are an exact reproduction of a normal 36″ chest youth of to-day. This method is valuable in that a prospective customer may have the model out of the window to try on, which often results in an immediate sale. And, most important of all, nothing is faked and the window models are made *in exactly the same way* as our ready-to-wear stock. Thus two birds are killed with one stone : all the ready-mades can be used in the windows and all new window shows can be put into ready-made stock. In my opinion, the average tailor's window model looks an impossible creation—impossible to wear and often impossible to buy ! There is no royal road to success, but infinite care, patience and, above all, an observant eye and brain, will eventually achieve it.

CLOTH DRAPING

Volumes have been written on this subject. No one, I think, can lay down laws on the matter, but, as a principle, there is no doubt that cloth draped in simple form and *loosely* will always look better and attract sooner than the hard, closely-creased effects of a few years back. My own endeavour is always to make an attempt at the natural, for when the cloth is made up into the suit, who finds hard, straight lines ? The prospective customer, looking in your window, will most certainly be attracted by a natural effect, and that is why pins and creases are forbidden with us, and folds and draping take their place.

THE BACKGROUND

Just as we, in our firm, are advocates of simplicity of display, so do we believe in the background that enhances the value of the goods, but does not detract attention from the commodity to be sold. Oak is often used to show up brighter or lighter shades of suiting, and certainly always creates the effect of solidity and strength. But with the more sombre blues and browns, it is apt to make a window too dark. Various experiments have been tried with more neutral woods, such as cedar, (a grained medium grey), and on the whole I prefer this colour for a permanent background. The careful use of simple additions such as trellis-work, stone vases, or the new textophoto picture, often add an effective setting to display. But it is imperative to guard against overloading with decorations an otherwise good window, so producing an effeminate result. Fussiness and futility will send a prospective customer straight into a rival establishment, even though the windows of your competitor are carefully veiled with a wire blind !

Reflecting Personality

May I add just this one word of advice ? The tailor who is to make the most use of his window will make sure that it reflects the *personality* of his shop. The man in the street, the passer-by, has only the window to guide him before making a purchase ; it is often only a very small item which will influence a purchase *here* or *there*. The shop-keeper who is out to get maximum results from his labours will, if he be wise, never rest satisfied with the window of *to-day* ; to-morrow he will try to do better, and, if he tries hard enough, he will !

PLATE XVIII

DISPLAYING DRESS WEAR.

The accessories, the top hat and stick, the lamp-shade and chair (always of best quality) create an interior effect. The Japanese screen as a background lends the colour so essential to an otherwise sombre effect.

(Price tickets had not been added when the photo was taken.)

PLATE XIX

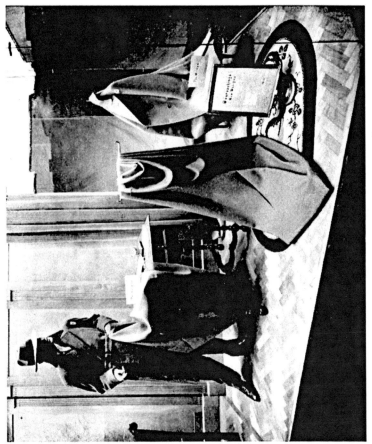

AN OVERCOAT DISPLAY FOR WINTER.

The material, the material made up, and the coat in wear. The natural stance of the wax figure and the "homely" effect of the cigarette and gloves demonstrate "the ease of buying in an H.P. shop" which is one of the advertised features.

PLATE XX

SELLING A DESIGN THROUGH THE WINDOW.

The Ripple Weave, a new design, was pushed through the effectiveness of the textophoto as a background. Electric lighting with a ripple effect was used behind the picture of the river. Both the enlarged reproduction of an H.P. advertisement and the show cards are worthy of note.

PLATE XXI

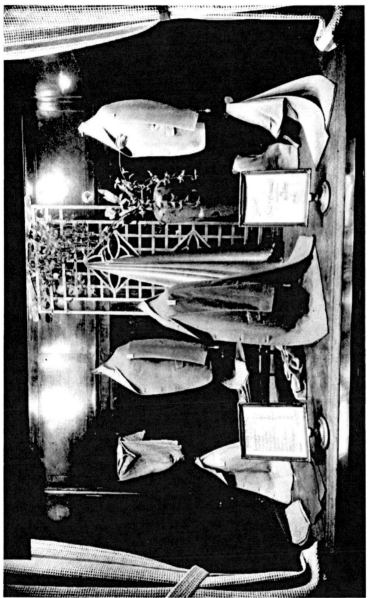

SELLING READY-TO-WEAR.

The natural draping of the garments is demonstrated in this window. Balance of the window, it will be noted, is gained rather by colour and depth than equality on both sides.

CHAPTER XI

LIGHT AS A SELLING FORCE FOR THE TAILOR

By VICTOR HYDE, M.C., M.J.I.

The Concealed-light Source—Ineffective Window Lighting—A Specimen Tailor's Window Equipped—The Cost—Public Interest Aroused—Over 1,000 Lighting Hours—Value of After-hour Lighting—Automatic Time Switch—Spotlights and Floodlights—Movement as a Means of Attraction—How to Employ Colour—The Decoration Lamp for the Window—Exterior Electric Signs—Lighting the Showroom—How Many Fittings ?—Fitting-room Illumination—Light and Working Efficiency—Custom follows the Light.

METHODS of business development are many and varied. We advertise, we employ good salesmen, we build up goodwill, and so obtain fresh custom by recommendation. We instal an imposing shop front, and employ other appropriate means for sales promotion, but what of artificial illumination ?

Light is one of the most potent of all advertising aids· for the tailor. It has changed public shopping habits ; it has made trade brisk where before it was slack ; it has doubled profits attributable to the influence of the window, and it has enabled shops situate in side streets to compete successfully with the more populous and popular main thoroughfare. More and better light has all this to its credit.

The methods of illumination which I propose to review in these notes were those employed in every one of the above-quoted examples, and before I enter upon a detailed discussion of them it will be not a little suggestive and instructive to note exactly what happened to bring about these trading results.

In Grey Street, Newcastle-on-Tyne, a peculiar trading problem arose. Almost the whole of the foot traffic, containing, we may say, a tolerably large proportion of custom for the tailor, kept to the east side pavement ; the west was comparatively neglected, to the trading detriment of the shops hereabouts. Then the latter were persuaded to double the intensity of their window illumination. The effect was instant, and greater than ever anticipated : as many as had previously used the east side of the street crossed over to the more spectacularly lighted west side, to the obvious financial gain of the latter. Light, and light alone, was responsible. That is where light changed a public shopping habit.

A ladies' tailor in the West End of London was once asked why, in broad daylight, he kept his window lights burning. His reply was significant. " Whenever business is slack," he said, " I have the lights switched on, and in fifteen to twenty minutes the shop is as busy as it conveniently can be." That is where light turned slack into brisk trade.

My third example of where modern lighting arrangements sold the goods is the case of another London shop. With six lamps lighting the window, this trader estimated that his per hour profits directly attributable to the window were 20 per cent. higher than when there were only two lamps ; after he had increased six to fourteen lamps he reckoned that the same profits had taken a further rise of 16 per cent., or 36 per cent. in all as a result of installing twelve additional lamps. Once again was light the salesman.

Finally in proof of the selling power of adequate light, well disposed, let us turn our attention to a side street in a West of England town. An interesting experiment was made. The intensity of the window illumination was very considerably increased, with the result that for every single person using it hitherto eight now passed down it, attracted by the brighter light centre : in other words, the trade prospects of the shopkeepers were raised 800 per cent. This particular example of the power of light proves that tailors so situate geographically —off the main thoroughfares, that is—can always overcome any comparative disadvantage arising out of such a trading position.

THE CONCEALED-LIGHT SOURCE

We can now, with infinite profit to the tailor and his business, examine critically into the constituents of the illumination which effected these, and other, cash gains.

The ideal principle in window lighting is to conceal the source of the light ; after all, it is only the display to which it is desired to draw attention, and any disturbing factor coming in the way, as lamps and fittings, is poor showmanship, and a hindrance to the main objective. It was to hide the source of the illuminant that top-lighting was introduced, and such is the basis of all the most successful window-lighting installations to-day.

The ideal application of this basic principle is by way of the silvered-glass shop-window lighting reflector and clear gas-filled lamp. These are installed in the front and sides of the window ceiling—hence " top-lighting." The forte of the reflector is to collect and control the light rays and make a maximum effective use of them, while the clear gas-filled electric lamp is light source for the tailor's window in its highest form. The reflector directs the whole of the light from each lamp employed downwards on to the display, and the result is a display of men's and women's suitings, habits, costumes, and the rest, that is bathed in a brilliant yet soft white light, in which those twin enemies of fine illumination, glare and shadow, are conspicuously absent.

The reflector system is quick and easy to install, without dislocation of business, and can be adapted to any structural arrangements or type of window fitment, and to any area. Spread over the years of service a good installation will provide, as a business overhead charge the cost can be expressed in terms of halfpence a month.

INEFFECTIVE WINDOW LIGHTING

Compare for a moment less effective methods of lighting the front of the shop. Some tailors employ the totally-enclosing or semi-open glassware diffusing fitting depended by chain from the window ceiling. Now, these make for good enough lighting in their way—in fact, in their proper sphere, it is impossible to improve upon them—but the window is hardly the place for them. The resultant light is neither so powerful nor concentrated as that from the reflector in the ceiling.

This practice, however, is infinitely preferable to inferior lamps, sometimes naked, and equally inferior fittings employed in the same way—hung over the display. Relatively few tailors favour this arrangement, and it needs but a brief marshalling of its disadvantages to put it out of the reckoning all together. What happens ? In the case of naked lamps the eye can be temporarily " blinded " by coming into direct contact with them, and full attention is diverted from the display, where it is wanted, to that which illuminates it. Under such conditions also, valuable light, because it is not under proper control, is wasted in sideways and upwards directions, and glare and shadow will generally exist. Lastly, lamps and fittings so disposed harbour dirt and dust, which reduce their primary efficiency. With top-lighting it is a different story entirely.

A Specimen Tailor's Window Equipped

How many reflectors and lamps will the tailor need? It depends on the window area. Suppose we take a frontage of 9' to 10', by a height of 7' and a depth of 5'. While this is not typical of the trade, it is sufficient to serve as a working example. The adequate illumination of such an area will call for not less than six reflectors and six 100-watt clear gas-filled lamps, less powerful lamps, as 60-watt, not meeting the case. For the purpose of concealing the reflectors—handsome and not unsightly in themselves—from exterior vision, a valance or pelmet, in a choice of materials supplied by the shopfitter, should be hung across the entire frontage to a depth of about 1' to 2' from the top of the window. In addition to tending to concentrate more attention on the tailoring display by thus covering the light source, this device provides a pleasing and artistic finish to any window.

The foregoing specification is for one window only; a second one of the same size would, of course, take identical equipment.

The Cost

What will be the initial cost? The reflector varies from 15s. up to 30s. and more, with a sound enough type either at the lower of these figures or not exceeding £1. The 100-watt lamp costs 5s., so the equipment specified can be obtained for an outlay of £7 10s. (£6 for reflectors and 30s. for lamps). A 9' long pelmet is purchasable around £2 for a good quality, and a few shillings more if the tailor decides to incorporate his initials, trade-mark, or other device on it. Then there will rank wiring and contractor's installation charges.

What will be the maintenance cost? This is easily determined. Six 100-watt lamps are the equivalent of three-fifths of a unit of electricity, which they will burn in the hour. The cost of electricity per unit varies with different supply areas, but suppose we put it at 5d. the unit. On this figure the tailor may burn his window lights for no more than 3d. an hour. Later I shall show how this cost may be even lower.

Public Interest Aroused

What public interest may be looked for ? Here we reach an intensely instructive, not to say provocative, stage in the study of light and its selling potentialities. Some two or three years ago a series of highly valuable tests were conducted over several hundred shops in various parts, including those of several tailors. The purpose of the tests was to draw a line between intensity of illumination and drawing power. It was conclusively proved that while two 100-watt lamps were the means of attracting an hourly window audience of 200 passers-by, six such lamps gained the attention of close upon 250 in the same period, with from fourteen lamps persuading very nearly 300 of the public to pause and inspect the display. In other words, you can definitely control public interest in the tailoring window by the intensity of the light there employed. The tailor, indeed, who exceeds the minimum number of lamps (and reflectors) necessary for adequate illumination is fully justified of his action and greater expenditure by virtue of the bigger public he is drawing. He might even double the necessary number of lamps and still, for this reason, be acting wisely.

While I have anticipated most, if not all queries likely to be put, I regret that, to the nearest pound or ten pounds, I cannot determine the accretion of profits accruing to the tailor from these " more and better " window-lighting arrangements. There is this that can be said, however, that every passing crowd drawn to the tailor's window contains, in the aggregate, its percentage of customers, if not to-day then on some future occasion, for light is like newspaper advertising—repetition soon makes for impression, and from impression we pass to those other steps in " the sale," which are desire, conviction, and order.

Over 1,000 Lighting Hours

If the necessity for, and value of, a modern system of illumination in and about the tailor's premises were not already clearly apparent, a moment's consideration of the total number of hours when light can be advertising the shop and its location will certainly emphasise the case for putting light in proper order. First there are the hours, autumn and winter, between dusk and the closing of the shop, or 200 hours ; secondly ranks the time in the same seasons from the closing of the shop to the public's bedtime (say, 11 p.m.), or 600 hours; thirdly is the period, in the months of longer days, between the dusk which falls (allowing for the Daylight Saving Act) after the shop is closed and 11 p.m., or 250 hours, or 1,050 hours in all, or 44 days, which is almost one-eighth part of the whole year. If we include the hours of darkness on Sundays, which I have omitted from these calculations, we must add another 170 hours. From the " time " angle alone, then, it is worth while putting light on the best possible basis, is it not ?

VALUE OF AFTER-HOUR LIGHTING

A practice which has developed considerably of recent years is after-hour or " late " lighting. Indeed, if shop salesmanship is to be fully progressive, the days when the windows are put in darkness with the closing of the shop must pass. It is true that at these times the public cannot enter and order, neither can they buy the goods advertised on the midnight electric sign or in the newspaper they read when the shops are closed, but, as in these cases, if they are sufficiently impressed they will make a mental or other note and buy on some future occasion.

The public which, on any fine night, is about the streets till a late hour, indulging the shop-gazing habit, is a large one, and the shop which is in darkness, however arresting the display, misses a score of opportunities for impression and suggestion.

Special rates are often available for shop-window lighting during these hours. Certain electricity supply authorities offer the tailor a reduced " after-hour " tariff whereby the 4d., 5d., or 6d. a unit up to 6 p.m. may be reduced to as low as 2d. after that hour. Thus the six lamps which cost 3d. an hour at other times may be burnt for a fraction over 1d. an hour after six o'clock, or continuously till 11 p.m. for as little as 6d. (These figures allow for six 100-watt lamps consuming three-fifths of a unit in the hour.) In return, the tailor can reasonably anticipate that during this period, approximately 1,250 passers-by (or five times the 250 which six lamps will attract in one hour) will not only see but inspect his display. According to the size of the district, this figure may be greater or less.

AUTOMATIC TIME SWITCH

More particularly where no one remains on the premises after business hours, attention to the lights at these late hours is inconvenient, if not sometimes altogether impossible. A time switch, however, can be installed whereby the lamps are ex-

PLATE XXII

FIG. 2.—THE SAME REFLECTOR EQUIPPED WITH A COLOUR SCREEN. THE LATTER IS CLEARLY VISIBLE ACROSS THE FACE OF THE FITTING.

FIG. 1.—A SCIENTIFICALLY DESIGNED REFLECTOR FOR CONTROLLING THE LIGHT IN A TAILOR'S WINDOW.

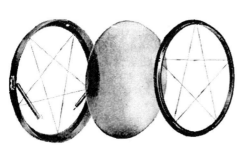

FIG. 4.—AN EXAMPLE OF THE TOTALLY ENCLOSING GLASSWARE DIFFUSING FITTING FOR INTERIOR ILLUMINATION.

FIG. 3.—A COLOUR LIGHTING ATTACHMENT FOR THE WINDOW REFLECTOR.

The lighting fittings illustrated here are examples of manufactures by the General Electric Co., Ltd., Magnet House, Kingsway, London, W.C.2.

tinguished at any predetermined hour, with personal control obviated. The same device will also switch on the lights in summer when darkness does not fall till one, two, or more hours, according to the individual time of closing, after the end of the day's business.

SPOTLIGHTS AND FLOODLIGHTS

Auxiliary window-lighting equipment are the spotlight and the floodlight, valuable, yet not essential supports to the reflectors. The tailor may desire, periodically, to impart added emphasis to his display or some section of it. At such times these appliances will function to good purpose. The spotlight will throw a concentrated beam of light on any one part of the window, with the floodlight increasing the intensity over the whole dressing. In price they are two to three times the cost of the reflector, and employ special types of the gas-filled electric lamp. The method of installation is the same as in the case of the reflector—i.e. in the window ceiling. In a large window a sound spotlight arrangement is to fit one at each corner and one central in the front of the window.

MOVEMENT AS A MEANS OF ATTRACTION

If, now, the tailor could add movement to these excellent lighting arrangements he would be adding very materially to the drawing power of the front of his premises. The public is always sufficiently intrigued by movement to the extent of stopping to look, and while one has noted such devices as the whirling kaleidoscope in some tailors' windows, it is not such that I have in mind, but coloured light. The changes that can be rung from ordinary white light to colour, and as between colour and colour, are tantamount to movement, and the cheapest form of window movement the tailor can devise. With colour at his command he will have the satisfaction of knowing that his windows will be an approximately 40 per cent. greater draw than with standard lighting effects, for whereas up to 250 an hour will note the display in the ordinary way, the figure may well rise to 350, and more, under the subtle urge and influence of colour.

HOW TO EMPLOY COLOUR

The foundation for the most spectacular exposition of colour is the reflector system. The only additional equipment required is a colour-screen outfit, the colour films—red, green, blue, yellow, and so forth—fixing across the open face of the reflector, and turning the light from the lamps into almost any desired colour. They are as easily removed again for white lighting as they are fitted in the first place. The cost of a colour outfit is around 20s.

By way of helpful example, we will equip three of our six reflectors for colour effects, and leave the others free for white lighting. Taking alternate reflectors, we can utilise, say, red, blue, and green. Now, if we instal a flasher, and have the reflectors wired on separate circuits, each working independently of the rest, a variety of changes is at our command. At fifteen seconds, half-minute, or other intervals, we can have a sequence as : white-green-red-white-blue-white, which, because of the movement afforded in each successive change in the colour of the light, is infinitely preferable to colour effects which are stationary only. A " chain " group of men's tailors in London features a delicate blue light in its windows by night, but in this case colour is not given its greatest opportunity, by reason of the fact that there are no automatic changes.

Just as tailoring displays change with the seasons, so can the appropriate and seasonal colour note in the lighting be found. In this regard, the attributes of the chief colours should be noted. Red, orange, and yellow are warm and exciting, with green producing cheerful effects. In combination with yellow, green is tranquil, cool, and soothing in effect. Blue sesults in coldness, gravity and serenity, while a blue-green is sober and sedate in tone. Purple light will provide the impressive atmosphere desired for an evening dress window—and so on.

Certain obvious colour schemes are suggested by this list. A red or yellow light, for example, would harmonise with and support a winter-wear window ; green would be in keeping with the spring suitings display, and a yellow-green, or even a blue, with the summer dressing.

The alternative—and it is not a good one—to colour films attached to the reflectors is the artificially colour-sprayed lamp, used, perforce, lower down in the window. The spraying, however, means the loss of the greater part of the effective light of the lamp, with the result that the only virtue in this type of illuminant is the admittedly high decorative value, which, in window lighting, takes second place to intensity. Further, the cost would be greater.

THE DECORATION LAMP FOR THE WINDOW

Sundry tailors, feeling the need for some decorative seasonal lighting, have favoured the decoration lamp, a small olive-shaped bulb made in outfits of nine and eighteen lamps ready wired for festooning round the window or for use in other display directions. In a variety of colours, they provide a most charming and alluring effect, and are particularly appropriate to the Christmas season and winter months. Like the colour-sprayed lamp, the whole of their value lies in their decorative qualities, and not in the power of light they give, for which, of course, they should not primarily be used.

EXTERIOR ELECTRIC SIGNS

Before we entirely leave the front of the shop, why not an electric sign to advertise the location of the business? The publicity value is a high one and the cost reasonable. The most advantageous position is horizontal to the entrance, with the sign readable on both sides, so that the public approaching from either direction, and on both sides of the street, can see the wording. A flashing sign is preferable to any other sort, the reason being the same as in the case of coloured light in the window—resultant movement. All in, including lamps, wiring, and installation charges, a suitable and high-class sign can be erected for £10, and less for the less pretentious designs.

LIGHTING THE SHOWROOM

The main requirements of interior illumination are adequate diffusion without glare or shadow and light which is at least the equal of ordinary daylight.

A fitting that can be thoroughly recommended is the totally-enclosing glassware diffusing unit, as decorative as it is efficient in its primary purpose. It is supplied in a variety of patterns and sizes, in plain or decorated glassware, from 20s. up to four and five guineas in the more elaborate models. It has the merit of being dustproof, so saving labour in cleaning and tending to prolong the life of the lamp. Employing the same lamp as in the window, the 100-watt clear gas-filled, it provides a perfect light, brilliant yet devoid of all glare, subdued and mellow, and such that one can " look into " the glass of the fitting and experience no inconvenient or " blinding " effects. An important point is the penetrative quality of the illumination : there are no dark corners when this form of lighting is used, and no risk of the customer standing in his own shadow to inspect materials.

How Many Fittings ?

The totally-enclosing fitting can be installed, either on the chain suspension principle or, in the case of a low ceiling, fitted flush with the latter. To assist in determining the number which the tailor will require, we will suppose a showroom interior 24' wide by 50' deep. The proper spacing of the units described is 12' apart, therefore adequately to light this size interior two rows of four in depth would be required. The cost, in lamps and fittings, need not exceed £10. The needs of both larger and smaller areas can be gauged from this example. Wherever there is more than one floor to equip it is advisable to standardise one type of fitting throughout.

The tailoring floor of one of the largest London stores employs not far short of one hundred totally-enclosing fittings, and their high artistic value is strongly brought out in this extensive installation. There is no doubt whatever that in appearance alone they make an appreciable contribution to the " furnishing " of a shop.

Fitting-room Illumination

An ideal arrangement in the fitting room is the small opal globe fitted flush with the ceiling and employing a 40- or 60-watt clear gas-filled lamp. This is far more effective practice than the naked lamp on the usual cord suspension, where valuable light is wasted, with glare both for the cutter and the customer if the unprotected lamp is not of the sprayed variety (the invariable rule, by the way, being : clear filaments where there is a fitting, sprayed or coated lamps if there is no fitting).

Light and Working Efficiency

Illumination such that customers can see cloths and styles under conditions approximating to daylight, and without standing in their own light, is not, however, the only ideal at which to aim in the interior : well-disposed light in the work-rooms will increase the happiness and efficiency of the staff and assist production in general. On the negative side, the extent of the damage to eyesight through defective workroom lighting is far larger than it need be, and eye-strain inevitably means a lower standard of work.

And so one reaches the end of a brief and critical review of light in its proved capacity as a potent selling agent for the tailor. That there is room for an improved standard of

PLATE XXIII

FIG. 5.—A SPOTLIGHT.

FIG. 6.—THE BESPOKE WINDOW OF THE
WOOLWICH CO-OPERATIVE SOCIETY.

The lighting is on the reflector principle, with the lamps
and reflectors manufactured by the General Electric
Co., Ltd., Magnet House, Kingsway, W.C.2.

illumination in the trade is indicated by a recent survey of conditions. In this only 19 per cent. of tailors' shop lighting was passed as " excellent " (meaning that the methods described in these notes were followed), while a corresponding proportion classified under " fair " and " good " claimed respectively 21·4 per cent. and 40·6 per cent.

Custom follows the Light

To-day, with competition in the business at a fine point, it is the scientifically lighted shop that has a pronounced start in the race for the public's custom ; indeed, fine, " clean "-looking lighting is an absolute necessity if the tailor is going to establish that atmosphere of well-being and efficiency which is so necessary. Much hangs upon first impressions, and because it is the first part of the tailor's premises to be seen, the lighting in the window cannot receive too much consideration and care ; then pleasing first impressions must be perpetuated within. A bright light centre is an unfailing public draw, and where the public is drawn there does trade go. There is, indeed, such a thing as persuading a person into a want. Good salesmen are doing it every day ; another type of salesmen which does it is—light.

CHAPTER XII

BUYING A BUSINESS

By ELLIOTT STONE, M.J.I.

(Late Acting Editor, " Men's Wear Organiser ")

IN buying a business the first necessity is capital. How much have you and how much must you allow out of that amount for the purchase of the business ?

It will readily be understood that in considering the purchase of a business it is essential that provision be made for carrying it on afterwards.

Usually this question of the financing of the business after it has been bought is not taken sufficiently into consideration, and, in consequence, many businesses fail through want of enough capital.

Consider, first, the amount of capital available, and then we can decide how much to allow for the actual purchase money.

You will probably have saved some money and be willing to use this in the business. Or you may have been fortunate and have had money left to you. Possibly friends will be willing to help you. Your insurance policy will be valuable ; it represents a certain sum of money which can be used if necessary. There will be other possessions of some value. Whatever you have that is either ready money or something that can be conveniently turned into money, add it all together (*under*-estimating anything of doubtful value), and call this your available capital.

In passing, let me say definitely that in any instance where money is lent to you for the business by a friend or relative, it must be clearly understood and agreed in writing that this loan does not give the lender any right or authority to interfere in any way with the conduct of the business. If it is one friend or person who is lending a substantial sum, make him a partner. This need not give the friend any authority so far as the business is concerned. It will mean that you will have to give him a generous interest on the money he lends. You must also, in any case where money is lent, have a definite and written agreement as to the repayment. Let it be clearly stated that you are at liberty to repay the loan by giving notice to that effect.

Having come to a fairly accurate total as regards the amount of money you can call upon if required, it is necessary to try to decide how much of this amount you can safely put into the purchase of a business.

Bear in mind that to be short of ready money in a retail business is a very serious matter. It leads to all kinds of inconveniences ; you lose discounts and you lose the opportunity of buying to the best advantage.

The chief items to be considered in trying to find out how much money you will need for the business itself, after the purchase money has been paid, are : the rent, rates and taxes, the staff salaries, the workmen's wages, lighting, heating, water, telephones, and a fair amount for redecorating the shop. This last must not be done in a niggardly fashion. Ample must be set aside for it. Another large sum will be allotted to the item of stock ; this will be taken as the average amount of stock to be carried.

It is clear that, until a business is in mind, this calculation can only be made very approximately, but anyone having in mind the buying of a business will naturally have an idea of the class of trade and the volume of it that can be managed.

It will be found, in practice, that about half the amount of available capital should be used for the purchase of the business and the other half for carrying it on.

Trading as a Limited Company

Another point, in passing, should be mentioned. It is very much better to carry on your business as a Limited Company. Small retailers are inclined to object to this method, but it is a much more satisfactory way. One great advantage is that, trading as a Limited Company, it prevents your creditors (should you come to grief) from taking more than the actual business assets. As a private individual your creditors can take all your personal effects as well. There are many other advantages, and the man who is buying a business should, at the same time, arrange to have it turned into a Private Limited Company. Then, if you have any need for extra capital, or any friends who would like to come in with you, the matter is a simple one. Nor will it be found that your creditors will be so objectionable in times of stress. There is, too, a goodwill value in the fact of trading as a Company; the public invariably assume that the Limited Company is a much more important concern.

It is not a very expensive process; the whole thing can be done for less than twenty pounds, unless you are very ambitious.

GOODWILL AND STOCK

The value of a business usually depends upon the goodwill, the stock, the lease, and the position and locality of the premises, and the profit that has been made.

Taking goodwill, we want to know how many years the business has been established, whether the business has steadily increased, if there is credit given and, if so, whether the accounts are paid reasonably well.

Obviously, if a business has been established for some years and has been doing an increasing turn-over, then there is an evidence that the business is a good one and has been conducted on the right lines. Such a business will be likely to continue to give good results unless, just previously to the business being put on the market, there have been bad management and neglect.

The value of the goodwill can be gauged fairly accurately by taking the net profits for the last three years and totalling them. This is only a good guide when it is clear that the business has been properly conducted and also, when it is not likely that the proprietor is able to take a number of the customers away with him.

(In this connection, see to it, at the very commencement, that you get a very clear agreement that the person who sells you the business will not open again in your district for several years. When selling, a man will give such an undertaking in the most generous terms, and that is the time to make him do so. There will be a foreman or other important member of the staff whom it will be as well to come to terms with for at least a year. This will make sure that he does not open against you in the hope of taking with him some of the customers.)

The stock is a matter of mutual arrangement between the buyer and the seller. When, as it not unusually happens, the price asked is considered too high, it is as well to call in a professional valuer. This saves bother and it satisfies the buyer that he has got fair value.

LEASES AND THEIR CLAUSES

The lease needs careful attention, and a solicitor should always be consulted before any definite arrangement is made. The lease may be only for a few more years, the greater part of the period covered having gone. If at all possible the owner of the premises should be seen and asked to grant a new lease, or, if he will not do that, try and persuade him to give you an "option of a renewal" at a reasonable rent. In any case, you want to have an idea what you will have to pay when the end of the present lease arrives, else you may find that the rent is prohibitive.

The lease must also be studied carefully in order to know exactly what it contains. There may be clauses which make it impossible for you to carry on any other trade but that of a tailor. This is not an advantage to you, because there may be an opportunity to develop the business in some other class of trade.

The worst of all is the dilapidations clause. This is almost invariably inserted in the case of a shop lease. The tenant has to keep the premises in good repair and, if any alteration is done to the building (even if the landlord gives his consent), the tenant will be liable for the cost of replacing what has been altered.

➤ These clauses cannot be helped, but they should be noted, and it must be recollected that they take from the value of the lease.

To get some idea of the value of a lease, inquiries should be made to the manager of a local bank or to the estate agent. These gentlemen are well able to state the fair rental value of any premises in their district. So that, suppose the shop you have in mind has a present rental value of one hundred pounds a year and the lease has seven years to run at seventy pounds, this would give a sum of just over two hundred pounds as the value of the lease. *But*, from this figure must be taken a substantial sum for dilapidations. Be careful about this and allow plenty. When you get to close quarters with the man who is selling the business, have a surveyor to go over the premises and estimate the cost of putting them into the condition set out in the lease. This would enable you to deduct from the value of the lease the sum given in the estimate.

What usually happens is that the whole matter is made into one of bargaining ; you will have to pay more than the actual value of the lease, but, if you know the exact value (or thereabouts), it will prevent you paying too much. Recollect that you get an extra value in the lease, if it is for any length of time, by the fact that the value of business premises invariably goes up.

THE POSITION OF THE PREMISES

The position of the premises has a distinct bearing on the value of the business. Some positions are obviously first-class ; there is always a flow of the very people you want for customers. Other positions will never help the business very much. Your difficulty will be to make up your mind to take the better position, if there is a choice.

Here let the writer urge any business buyer not to get into a dull, stale street, no matter how favourable an offer seems. Businesses in such positions can be had at very low prices, and they are dear at any price, because there is little chance of a really big business being developed. In such thoroughfares the tailor will usually get a bare living. Whenever possible the business in the good shopping position should be bought. This will cost more money, but (if you know your job) it will be much the better investment. Besides, you can always get a good price for a business in a shopping spot.

But, after all, the best indication of the value of the business is the amount of profit it has made. There may be the question of the ability of the proprietor, but, as the buyer, that is to your advantage.

SEEING THE BALANCE SHEETS

Most businesses are now conducted in such a way that there is some kind of balance sheet to be seen which shows what the proprietor has made in the way of *net* profit.

The first thing to consider is the length of time shown by the balance sheets. If these go back for, say, six years and they show a steady profit and an increasing one, this is satisfactory. But these profits should be compared with the amount of trade done in the same periods. If this profit is in the region of ten per cent. of the turn-over, then you may be assured that the business has been well done. Look at the figures for the last year of the trading. If this shows an unusual increase both in the trade done and the profit made, beware. The

vendor has been using special means to do more trade ; he may
have been giving worse value, and this will reflect on the business
in the future.

Pass Books and Income-tax Receipts

It is not enough to take the balance sheet for granted, even
if got out by an accountant.   Get also the pass book of the trader
and also his income-tax receipts.   For the last year the income
tax paid may show a very good sum, but this should be taken
carefully.   In selling businesses it is not unknown for the
proprietors to pay more income tax than they have actually
made themselves liable for in the business.   A buyer, not
knowing this, may take it for granted that the business has
been successful to the extent indicated.   That is why the
income-tax receipts for several years should be examined.

In some trades credit is given and, in the change-over, some
of the debts will have to go with the business.   This is not an
easy matter to arrange.

Directly any serious negotiations are commenced the proprietor of the business should be particularly requested not to
take any drastic measures in his efforts to get in as much money
as possible before he sells.   In nearly every instance where a
business is going to be sold, the first thing is to press the customers who owe money.   This has the result of causing many
of them to become offended, and they will probably go elsewhere in the future.   This is the thing which the new proprietor should try to avoid.   Make an arrangement whereby
you will undertake to collect the outstanding debts and pay
them over at stated periods.   If you do this there will be less
chance of the customers getting threatening letters and other
annoyances, and you will retain many whom you would otherwise have lost.   This matter of the book debts is an irritating
one because, unless there is a mutual agreement not to worry
the people who happen to owe money, a serious loss of reputation and business will result.

The Question of Book Debts

If some fair figure can be agreed upon it is better to buy the
debts, though this means another call on the capital.   But on
no account pay for them until you have had an opportunity
of sending to every one of the debtors.   A fair price to pay,
assuming that reasonable credit has been given, is half of their
face value.   This of course only applies to what may be called

good debts, those that have been incurred within a reasonable time or are owing by standard customers.

In your search for the business which seems good to you, be careful not to be too much influenced by friends who pose as being clever men. There are so many people who think themselves competent to give advice. But only very few are really competent. It is better to pay a good lawyer and an accountant rather than to be led to make a mistake by someone who wants to look clever but is not.

A final word. Be patient, and do not buy unless you are quite satisfied that the business is sound and the price fair.

CHAPTER XIII

INSURANCE FOR TAILORS

By ELLIOTT STONE, M.J.I.

(Late Acting Editor, " Men's Wear Organiser ")

IT is, perhaps, somewhat trite to say that the tailor cannot be too careful about his insurances. Yet this warning is not always acted upon.

A tailor, lacking for the moment the assistance of his porter, went out to pull down the sunblind. He was not aware that the hook was loose, and in the result a lad, walking under the blind, received a blow on his head and was seriously ill for some time. This cost the tailor a good deal and, in addition, he has always the recollection of the damage done.

A porter, cleaning the windows of his employer's shop, danced about on the top of the steps in a mood of frivolity. He fell and injured both knees, with the result that he was incapacitated for a long time and the tailor had to pay. Fortunately, in this instance, he was insured.

While one does not want to behave in an extravagant manner when becoming the owner of a tailoring business, it is common sense to make quite sure that every possible risk is fully and properly covered.

VALUE OF A REPUTABLE AGENT

It is as well to consult some agent of established reputation. If such a person cannot be discovered, an inquiry to the editor of a trade journal will usually bring anyone into touch with a reliable and capable person or firm. On no account do business with some friend of a friend of yours who professes to be able to see you through at a much lower fee than anyone else. Choose your insurance agent as carefully as you would choose your doctor and your solicitor. It will mean a very great deal to you should any emergency arise.

The great advantage in doing your insurance through a

reputable agent is that, in the event of any claim, he will see to it that you get the full compensation to which you are entitled, and he will also see to it that you are insured completely and against all possible risks.

It will, at first, seem that the costs of the insurances are excessive. This is because there is a general idea that if one is insured against fire to the extent of five hundred pounds and there is a fire that causes damage to that amount, the insurance company will pay that sum as compensation. This does not follow because, if the stock (or whatever it is that is insured) happens to be of the total value of a thousand pounds, the insurance paid will only be half the actual amount of damage. A moment's consideration will show that this is but fair to the insurance company, though, at the moment of loss, it will seem the reverse.

Obviously, then, the first need in connection with insurance is to know the value of the goods or premises upon which the premium has to be paid. If a competent valuer is called in, he will get out a list covering every item concerned and the value of it. This list will be useful in the case of fire, and it can be used as the basis of the amount to be insured.

Various Forms of Insurance

There are a number of insurances which the tailor should take out as soon as he is in possession of a business.

The obvious one is that of fire. But, over and beyond the loss of the goods by fire, there is the fact that if the premises are damaged it may seriously hinder your business until the necessary rebuilding has been done. The usual method is to insure against loss of rental value and also against the loss of profits. If this sounds like going to the extreme it must also be remembered that there is always the risk present, and that the amount of the premiums is very small indeed in proportion to the value of the insurance effected. Besides, the retailer who is fully insured sleeps much more soundly, especially if he lives away from the business.

Then there is, for the tailor particularly, the insurance against workmen's compensation. This, again, is a risk which cannot be ignored, and it should be covered liberally. The death of a man is no slight risk and, if a complete insurance is not arranged, it may well mean the ruin of the trader who employed him.

A necessary insurance is that which covers the business

man in such matters as damage by water and other similar risks which do not come under the heading of fire or of burglary. It has not been unknown for both the fire and burglary insurance companies to decline to compensate for a water damage done because a burglar caused a fire. One gets the basement flooded and the contents spoilt : a costly business for the tailor who stocks his suits there and may have several valuable fur coats in the room at the time.

The risk of burglary is another necessary matter which should not, on any account, be neglected. You may find that the insurance company will insist upon several protective bars and other items, but safety is a valuable asset in a business such as tailoring.

Your plate-glass windows and mirrors should be insured. These have a habit of getting broken on occasions and, though the premiums are high, they are well worth it. One smash, and the premiums of many years are saved several times over.

There is, again, what are known as third-party risks. Here is the need of providing against any damage which may be done to any person outside the staff. As in the instance given at the beginning of this article, there are occasions when accidents happen through your fault or the fault of your staff. These can easily be very costly indeed, and it is folly not to be quite covered against any claim in connection with them.

Not the least of the advantages of this form of insurance is the fact that the company concerned will take over all the business in connection with the claim. They are well able to deal with the demands made and, from long experience of such matters, will be able to do it to the best advantage.

The tailor has not usually a very large staff, but even so, there is always the risk of dishonesty. The messenger lad gets into bad company and, on an occasion, is tempted to omit to pay in some money that has been paid to him. It is satisfactory, in one sense, to be assured that whatever money is lost in this way will be repaid by the company to whom you have been paying premiums.

In the shop, too, there will be members of the staff who have opportunities to handle money, and it will make for more peace of mind if the precaution to guard against loss from this source is taken before the accident happens. Even in a small business it is not possible to keep an immediate track of moneys paid in or which come by post. The insurance acts as a means of avoiding losing any serious amount of money from this cause.

Care in Filling up Forms

To make out the necessary proposal forms a good deal of care is required. If you are acting through an agent he will help you and will see that you do not omit any vital facts. What you need to be most careful to do is to get the statements accurate. The insurance companies are very keenly organised concerns, and they exist for the purpose of making money ; they are, in fact, retailers of insurance. So that, if there is any flaw in the proposal form it may mean that the insurance is not sound and you will not get any compensation in the case of accident.

Also, it may be possible to get a lower premium if certain facts are stated and if there are conditions which are in favour of the retailer. On the other hand, if, for instance, one's premises are next door to an oil shop, the premium will be higher. The thing is that the whole transaction must be fair and square. You may feel inclined to withhold facts which will increase the premiums, but this is not advisable. What is essential is that your policies should be quite in order. They should fully cover every phase of the risk concerned, and the company must be a first-class one, so that you can rely upon reasonable treatment if and when the time comes.

Be very careful to read the policy through before it is finally passed to the insurance company. A document of this kind is not always easy to understand, but it is the business of the person who is seeking insurance to know exactly what the whole matter contains. Your agent should see that your interests are carefully studied, but it is not advisable to trust blindly even to him. In any case, it is the barest business precaution to understand precisely what you are giving and getting. Once the document is signed and in the hands of the company it is usually too late to make any amendments unless extra payment is made. In this instance you are buying insurance, and in this type of buying, as in most others, it is the buyer who must beware.

Something of this necessary caution will be appreciated when it is mentioned that, in the majority of policies, there is a provision in favour of the company which makes it impossible to bring an action in the Courts against them, no matter what your claim.

If you mention this to your agent he will tell you that it is customary. At any rate such a fact will put you on your guard and urge you to study the policy with the utmost care and attention. Do not be afraid, as many people are, to show that you do not know all about your insurances. There is no reason why you should be expected to be fully familiar with this phase of business, and there is, therefore, nothing to be ashamed of in being ignorant about it. If there is anything you want to be enlightened upon, consult your agent and, if his reply does not seem quite satisfactory, take advice from someone whom you know to have experience and honesty. But be quite sure that you know exactly what arrangements you are making with the insurance company.

PROMPTNESS IN NOTIFICATION

If, unfortunately, you should have a fire, or any other accident of the kind that is covered by insurance, get into touch with the company as soon as possible. If you can telephone, do so, but it is always as well to send a written notice in addition. It will readily be understood that it is generally a very great advantage for the company to have immediate notification. They have a very keen system of dealing with any matters of claims, and the sooner they are able to make a start, the better for all concerned. You will get much better treatment if the best help is given on your part. For small claims it will be found that the companies act very promptly and generously, provided that the occurrence is obviously a straightforward one. Naturally, if the claim is a large one, a good deal of investigation may have to be made, and it is only fair that every chance should be given to get the matter settled at the earliest moment to the satisfaction of both parties.

If you have employed an agent to attend to your insurances, advise him immediately any accident happens. If he is available he will know how to set about getting the damage assessed, and his knowledge and experience of these matters will enable you to avoid a good deal of unnecessary trouble and waste of time.

When it is a burglary that has occurred the police should be sent for instantly. In this way some of the stolen property may be recovered, and there will be less doubt about your eventual claim.

NATIONAL HEALTH INSURANCE ACT

There are two other forms of special insurance with which the employer of labour must become familiar. The first of these is in connection with the National Health Insurance Act.

It is as well for the tailor to get a copy of this act and study it carefully. Also, a consultation with the local authority will help to get a clear definition of your duties.

This act provides for the possible sickness of the members of the staff, and it affects almost all employees who are between the ages of sixteen and seventy and whose salaries do not total more than two hundred and fifty pounds a year. The cost of this insurance is paid jointly by the employer and the employee. The whole of the amount is first paid by the employer, who purchases the necessary stamp and has it put on to the appropriate card. The employer is then entitled to deduct from the employee his part of the cost. The stamping should be done by the employer at the time the wages are paid, and it is necessary to have this card stamped even though only a part of the week has been worked and paid for. One occasionally hears of tailors who fail to attend to this part of their business, but such neglect is stupid ; this insurance is now a part of the everyday routine of trading and commerce generally, and it should be included in the regular duties. Note that it is the business of the employer to see that the card is produced by the employee, and, if there is any difficulty about this, a duplicate card can be obtained. But the onus is on the employer, and it will not excuse him to say that the card was not handed to him or that he could not get it.

Still another special insurance in which the employer is vitally and financially interested is in connection with the Unemployment Insurance Acts. It is a complicated business, and needs very great patience to understand. The main issue is that there is a payment by the employer and also by the employee, which results in a fund from which unemployment payments are made. The best way to deal with it is to go to the local authority and get them to explain what you want to know in connection with your own business. This will usually be found to be quite satisfactory.

INSURANCE POLICIES AS FINANCIAL ASSETS

There is just one other suggestion in connection with insurances. Every man should be insured, but, for the business man, there is an added advantage in the fact that he can use his policies to raise money.

By taking out what is called an endowment policy, money can be put aside each year (or quarterly if this suits better), so that at the end of twenty years, or any other arranged period, the whole of the money saved is returned, and with it a considerable sum in the form of a bonus. All the time this policy has been in force there has been the fact that, had the insured person died, the full amount of the policy would have been paid over as well as the proportion of the bonus due.

This is an excellent means of saving money. It also provides a sum of money available for emergencies. Another advantage : up to a certain amount the money paid for this insurance is not taxable, so that there is a saving of several pounds each year on this premium. There are few ways whereby one can get such a good return for money invested.

CHAPTER XIV

SALES LETTERS

By ELLIOTT STONE, M.J.I.

(Late Acting Editor, " Men's Wear Organiser ")

FOR the tailoring trade the sales letter is one of the best means of getting more business. It is inexpensive ; the amount spent can be regulated to whatever sum is required ; there is very little waste ; you can get right into the home or the office of the person whom you want to get for a customer.

It is true that there are still a number of people who jeer at the circular letter, but that is, primarily, because the letter is not well done. It is certain that if the letter is properly planned it will be the means of bringing to the business concerned much more profit than the letters have cost.

On the other hand, it is not fair to expect the sales letter to work miracles ; it will not, though it is surprising how much it can be made to do. There is also the follow-up letter which is, in effect, a part of the art of selling by letter. The point is that, unless the advertiser is unreasonable, it will usually be found that the properly got out sales letter will be a very good investment. That is what all advertising should be.

A sales letter can be said to be successful if it has the effect of making the reader do what the letter suggests or urges that he should do. Even if it makes the reader inclined to do so it will not have been a failure, nor can it be counted an actual loss if it just manages to give the reader a good impression of your firm.

WHAT THE SALES LETTER MUST DO

It will be readily remembered that the easiest way (and almost the only way, where the tailoring trade is concerned) to make a man do something is to convince him that it is worth his while to do it. The majority of men need clothes and eventually must have them. But this is not to say that they will come to your shop ; they may do so, but you want to make sure of their custom. There are a considerable number of possible customers who pass your premises and may be attracted into it by a well-dressed window. There are many times more possible customers within the radius of your district, but they will not know about your shop and your business unless you take measures to tell them. Even then, they will not be inclined to go out of their usual way unless you are able to convince them that it is worth their while to do so. That is what your sales letter has to do.

The actual sales letter is the most important of the items which make for success, but it is not the only thing. There are several other factors to be considered and which have a direct bearing on the result.

Take the sales letter first. The actual sheet of letter paper is the beginning of the process of making the whole communication attractive to the reader.

I am a great believer in colour for the letter paper. What happens is, that when you send a man a letter on a coloured paper, he is at once attracted by it—if it is unusual and not objectionable. So the reader is inclined to read what you have put on the coloured paper. For ordinary correspondence this coloured paper idea is good, because it makes your letter easy to identify, and each time it is seen it recalls your name and business to the person who has received it.

There is an abundance of beautifully tinted letter papers to be had, and the fact of the colour does not add to the cost.

NECESSITY OF GOOD STATIONERY

The paper must be of a good quality. Think, to yourself, if a young man came into your shop and asked for a position as salesman. If he is well-dressed he gets a good hearing ; if he is shabby and his clothes of the very cheap variety, you scarcely trouble to listen to him ; you have immediately made up your mind that he is not any good. Something like this happens when a man receives a letter done on flimsy and cheap paper ; he instinctively feels that the goods cannot be satisfactory.

There is so little difference in cost between a poor paper and a good one that there should never be any question as to which to have. The paper should be fairly substantial in weight and solid to the feel.

The printed matter on the letter paper should be in some dark colour to tone with the tint of the paper. Think carefully about how you lay it out on the sheet. Try to arrange it so that it looks neat and, at the same time, a little out of the ordinary. Your printer will usually set up the matter in the same way that he has done many others, until he has got into the habit of doing it in that one way. You want to avoid this. Even if the printer charges you extra for a proof, never mind, it is very important to get a good-looking letter heading.

I suggest that, at the top of the sheet and taking about two inches right across, you should have your name and address, with the telephone number. Do not make the mistake of having your name in very big letters. It is a little humiliating, perhaps, to know that your customers are much less interested in your goods than in your name, but this is so, and it is as well to bear this in mind. Even on your letter heading it is as well to refrain from distracting the attention of the reader from the trade you do to your own name.

At the left-hand side of your letter heading have what is called a panel in a box rule going from just below the top matter to near the bottom. This rule should be a very light one and in a very fine dotted pattern. The idea of it is merely to give the information inside it a tidy appearance.

Inside this long panel have brief details of any feature of your business which will interest the customer and help to increase his confidence in your ability to tailor well.

If you have been established a considerable time, this is an item in your favour. If you have had any very complimentary letters from some leading public man or similar important person who will be known to the people to whom you are likely to send, put one or two of the best phrases in the panel and add the name of the writer. You may be an agent for some special goods ; this can go in. Also insert one or two prices of your leading lines. At the bottom of the panel, put a short statement about your ability to tailor well and your guarantee that in the event of orders being given, you will see that they are quite all right in every way.

The matter in the panel should be in sections and in very neat and light-faced type. You do not want to get a heavy effect.

Take care about this letter heading. Try to imagine what effect it will have on the man who receives it. If necessary, reconstruct it ; it is so important in the result of getting your new customers, that the extra trouble and expense will be more than made up.

Now for the letter itself. It has been proved fairly conclusively that the limit of keen attention which a man will give to an ordinary letter is about two hundred words. One of the most successful tailors in London has made much of his success because of his ability to write sales letters. He seldom uses as many as two hundred words. Nor, I think, is there any need to do so.

A Snappy First Paragraph

The first thing the letter has to do is to attract the attention of the reader. Some part of this will have been done by the letter itself, and the first paragraph must add to this attention and to the interest also. Something must be put into that first paragraph which will cause the reader to read further. I usually allot about twenty words to this.

Let me give you an example of what is meant. It is assumed that you are writing about clothes and tailoring. The first paragraph of the letter might be something like this : " There are times in the affairs of men when it is of the utmost importance for them to be well-dressed." Here we call attention to clothes and pave a way for the next paragraph which goes on to give details of what you have to offer.

A sales letter should never be in the nature of a general statement. You must always have some special purpose in writing to your prospect. You have rebuilt your premises, or bought some exceptionally good cloth, or the season's cloths are to be cleared ; better still, you are offering a special group of suitings to a limited number of customers (or prospects) in order to induce them to try your tailoring. It can be stated definitely that special offers are one of the very best means by which the tailor of a medium-class trade can get new business. But the offer must be a really good one ; it is fatal to do the thing badly.

In your second paragraph you can give the details of what it is you have to interest the reader. Keep always in mind the fact that the customer (or reader) is only interested in what will be an advantage to him. He is not a bit interested in your need for clearing the goods, unless, in consequence, he can get a suit at a cheaper rate. Bear this always in mind, so that whatever you say will be to give the reader the idea that he will benefit. You ought to be able to say all you need in fifty words.

The third paragraph is the most difficult. In it you have to try to convince the reader that he must on no account miss such an opportunity. Every selling argument must be put in and each will have to be condensed to the least possible. For this paragraph sixty words are allowed. Imagine that you are trying to convince a very obstinate person to give you an order. Think of all the objections he would make and use the answers as selling facts.

In the fourth paragraph there should be a guarantee ; this is one of the things that ought never to be omitted from a sales letter. One of the greatest difficulties to overcome in the mind of the possible buyer is the suspicion which is in his mind. Almost every man has been swindled during his lifetime, and he is therefore inclined to think that this might happen again. That is the reason why a clear guarantee should be included in the sales letter.

The fourth paragraph is the most suitable one because, by the time the reader has got to it, he will be inclined to give you an order, and the guarantee will increase his confidence in your offer.

Add also in this section of the letter any details that will make it easier for the reader to do business with you. Tell him the simplest way to get to your shop and the hours you are open. It is usual for a retailer to think that the locality of his shop is known to everybody in the district. This is not so, and it is advisable to make sure that there is no doubt about this in the mind of the man reading your letter. If you can offer to send a man to the private address, this is a feature in tailoring which is productive of good results. The promise of patterns is also worth while, though this ought to carry with it the reply postcard (stamped) ; or it may happen that, in the case of a special offer of one kind of cloth, a pattern is sent with the letter.

At any rate, this fourth paragraph should make it as easy as possible for the reader to get to your shop and to give you the order. You can allow about fifty words for this.

The last paragraph must be in the nature of a final urge. It must be made to say " Do it now," but without using that much over-worked phrase. There is an inclination to tell the reader that, unless he takes immediate advantage of your offer he will lose a good bargain. This is a little dangerous. Anything which seems to suggest a threat must be avoided. You are very anxious to get a new customer or to encourage an old one, and you are making a special offer for that purpose ; but you can only do this for a certain time. This is the tone of the last strong urge, and a definite date or period of time must be given.

How to Use the Postscript

It will be found that the postscript can be used as a means of some special emphasis. You can use the argument of the short time during which the offer is to last and say something like : " Just ten days to take this excellent opportunity—we urge you to take it now." Or you can repeat one of the strong selling arguments. It should have been mentioned earlier that, in planning a sales letter for a medium-class tailoring trade, price should not be the standard of your appeal. It is value which is the best incentive at the present time.

Having decided upon the reading matter of the letter, it now has to be done out in duplicate typewriter type. Have this done by a first-class firm, in a dark-coloured ink other than black, and then sign all the letters yourself (or by someone whom you employ), using Indian ink. This means a little trouble, because the signing must be done carefully and neatly, but it is well worth while. The jet black signature at the bottom of the letter will give it a very good effect.

There remain the envelope and the additional contents of the letter. It is strongly advised that a good quality stiff cartridge foolscap envelope be used. (Consideration must be given to the needs of the typewriter.) This has the advantage of being a very much better-looking envelope than the small size generally used. It also means that the letter itself, and the other contents, will not need to be folded very much ; they will therefore be in better reading condition when actually in the hands of the reader.

The letters should be addressed by typewriter, and the list of addresses should be carefully selected by someone who is very familiar with the district. This is a part of the process which pays for care and attention. If no recent directory is available there are addressing agencies where the envelopes can be addressed.

In the envelope with the sales letter it is as well to put some other advertising matter. A very effective enclosure is a facsimile testimonial letter done out exactly as it is received and with the best parts underlined. Another idea which has been proved to be excellent is the blotter. This, in spite of its age, is still an effective means of bringing business. There are many wholesale firms and manufacturers connected with the tailoring trade who issue advertising matter. Where possible, good specimens of these advertisements should be obtained and used in the letter. There may not be any direct results, but eventually inquiries will come for the goods advertised. Where a special offer is being made, it is very advisable to insert a pattern of the cloth. Do this really well if at all.

Keeping the whole letter under two ounces, it can be sent by the halfpenny rate, and if the envelope is a good one, it will be delivered in good condition.

It is as well to try to get the letters delivered at the time most suitable for the class of person addressed. For a medium-class district and trade, Tuesday, Wednesday, or Thursday, by the last post, are the best times for the letter to arrive.

CHAPTER XV

BOOKKEEPING FOR TAILORS

By SYDNEY C. JONES, F.C.P.A.

(Secretary, London Area, National Federation of Merchant Tailors (Incorporated))

A NUMBER of my readers will no doubt have heard the expression or proverb, " Tailors make bad business men." I do not think that tailors are in any way unique in this deficiency—the same observation would no doubt apply with equal force and truth to traders in other spheres, but, be that as it may, there is no denying the fact that bad business men are bad bookkeepers, or, to put it another way, they fail to realise the necessity for efficient bookkeeping. There is very little difference between bookkeeping for tailors than for any other branch of commercial life. In saying this I refer to actual bookkeeping in so far as " Personal " and " Impersonal " accounts are concerned, but there are differences in every trade, which lead to, and need, different methods of recording in order that business may be facilitated. Bookkeeping may be simple or elaborate, according to the size of the business, and may be determined to a certain extent by the labour available—that is to say, on how much can be set aside for bookkeeping assistance. In the country districts where the business is necessarily restricted, a tailor would only require the services of a bookkeeper for a few hours monthly. In somewhat larger centres he may have such services once a week, and again, firms situated in busy centres, enjoying a larger trade, may employ a whole-time bookkeeper. The purpose of this article is to assist perhaps the former trader more than the latter—that is, to suggest an efficient method of bookkeeping according to needs and the assistance available for the provision thereof.

It must, however, be borne in mind that there are certain underlying principles in bookkeeping which must be adopted, no matter what assistance is employed.

Let us here for a moment consider for what purposes book-keeping is necessary.

Firstly, it is to enable a trader to see by the Sales Ledger at a glance by whom money is owing for goods sent out, and also quite readily the total sum owing.

Secondly, and this is of equal importance, to ascertain just as easily by the Bought Ledger to whom money is owing for goods received and the total liability.

Thirdly, to enable him at a given period, which should certainly not be for longer intervals than one year, to ascertain the result of his trading for the period, i.e. profit or loss, and by means of a Balance Sheet or Statement of Affairs to see what his Assets and Liabilities are, and his resultant capital or deficiency.

There are two definite systems of bookkeeping—Single Entry and Double Entry—both possess their respective advantages and disadvantages, but owing to the exacting needs of present-day commerce and the advanced commercial education now available, the former is gradually becoming obsolete, but it may as well be dealt with, for, after all, this article would not be complete without outlining both systems. The " Single Entry " system, if it may be termed a " system," since it requires very little time for its operations, will necessarily interest traders in a small business. Whichever method, however, is adopted, there is one book which must be used, it is the very basis of a tailor's system, and that is the numbered Order Book, which sets out the customer's name and address, measurements, cloth number, etc., and is perforated to allow one portion to be torn out and attached to the garment when cut and ready to be sent to the working tailor.

On page 163 is a facsimile of one page of this very important book which can be obtained from or through most booksellers.

SINGLE ENTRY

This method, which only recognises the "personal" aspect of a transaction, leaves entirely unrecorded those of an " impersonal " character, and therefore the only books kept are personal ledgers, i.e. Sales and Bought Ledgers. In practice, however, a Cash Book is now usually kept, which really means that the Double Entry system is partly incorporated into the Single Entry method.

Next to the Order Book above described, the Cash Book is of great importance. The number of columns must depend to

Customer's Name.

130505. Coat.

Try on	Time	Send	Call

130505. Vest.

Try on	Time	Send	Call

130505. Trousers.

Try on	Time	Send	Call

130506.

Try on	Time	Send	Call

a large extent on the bookkeeping knowledge of the tailor himself, or of the bookkeeper employed, as must also the fact whether bank and cash transactions are recorded in the one book, or whether separate cash books are used, one called the Cash Book and the other Petty Cash, illustrations of different styles will be found following.

The *capital* of a business is the term used to signify the balance of the total assets after deducting the total liabilities at a given date. In Single Entry this can be ascertained by preparing a Statement of Affairs, which is really a schedule of assets, comprising book debts, stock, fixtures, furniture, cash in hand and at bankers, etc., etc., and of the liabilities, representing creditors, loans, and expenses accrued due on a given date, such as rent, electric light, gas, rates, etc. The increased balance of the former over the latter (after making adjustments for extra capital put in the business during the period and for moneys drawn out) will indicate, after comparing with the similar statement, previously taken out, the profit or loss on trading during the period. Separate schedules of debtors and creditors must be extracted from the Sales and Bought Ledgers respectively, and only given in total in the statement. Opportunity should be taken when compiling the Sales Ledger balances to place in separate columns :

1. Accounts likely to be beyond recovery.
2. Overdue accounts, and
3. Current accounts

as the lists will be found useful when dealing with the two former categories.

The first should be urgently dealt with, and written off if bad, while prompt steps should also be taken with the overdue accounts to try and avoid their becoming like the former—that is, bad debts.

The assets should be set out on the credit, or right-hand, side of the paper, and the liabilities on the left-hand, the difference being capital (or deficiency), and which should be inserted to enable the two sides to balance.

A Statement of Affairs is very similar to a Balance Sheet, but the latter is the term used to describe the position at a given date when a Double Entry system of bookkeeping has been employed. One may say this is delightfully simple, and that it is unnecessary to do more, but this thought is elementary, as on a closer examination it will be appreciated that there is no check to prove whether the schedules of debtors and creditors have been taken out correctly or whether any assets which have been increased by cash expenditure during the period have been properly dealt with. In Double Entry bookkeeping such mistakes would be revealed, as the books must balance if arithmetically correct, of which more will be said later. A further disadvantage is that as there are no " impersonal " accounts, such as goods bought, sales, wages, salaries, rent, lighting, etc., trading and profit and loss accounts cannot be prepared. These are very useful, as they help one to ascertain that the costs of operating the business each year are in favourable comparison with the previous years, and that the percentages of gross profit and net profit to turnover are up to a working standard. It is very important that the value of stock on hand at the end of a trading period should be recorded in a systematic manner, and a value placed on each item at cost, or market price, whichever is lower. The stock sheets or stock book should be extended and checked. The total, of course, represents the figure which should appear in the Statement of Affairs (or Balance Sheet).

The Double Entry system affords the following advantages over Single Entry.

1. At the end of a financial period, when all transactions have been posted (entered up), a schedule of the balances on each account can be compiled. This schedule is called a Trial Balance, and if both columns agree it will show that the books are arithmetically correct. (Sales and Bought Ledger totals should be recorded in separate schedules and the total of each brought into the Trial Balance.)

2. The " impersonal " transactions are recorded which allow of their being collated in a classified form. The excess of total credits over total debits (as shown in the Trading and Profit and Loss Account) representing profit for the period, or loss if the position is the reverse. This enables a trader to compare year by year his trading result, and to keep down wasteful expenditure.

3. The arithmetical correctness of the Trading and Profit and Loss Accounts will also be proved, apart from compensating errors, by the drawing up of a Balance Sheet.

The entries in a balance sheet are a classified summary of the remaining open balances after Trading and Profit and Loss Accounts have been debited and/or credited. The assets are set out on the right-hand side and the liabilities on the left.

For a small tailoring business where the bookkeeping is to be on a Single Entry basis, the following books are indispensable:

> Customers' Order Book, numbered and as described.
> Sales Ledger.
> Cash Book.
> Bought Ledger (optional).

Let us see how these are applied.

Assume that Mr. Sharp orders a bespoke suit; the first thing to be done is for his name to be entered in the Order Book, using three slips, one each respectively for the coat, vest, and trousers. When the material is cut, attach one portion of each slip to each garment to send to the work-hand. This will subsequently be returned with the garment, and will in effect contain a history of the detailed operations carried out. The portion retained in the book should bear the date, customer's name (and address when not otherwise known), material pattern number, woollen merchant's initials and his stock number, measurements, and price. If the latter is entered at the time, disputes as to price are often avoided.

The next entry is for an account to be opened in the Sales Ledger, and debit the amount of the suit, quoting in the folio column the Order Book number. This constitutes an easy cross-reference for future orders. The Sales Ledger folio should also be entered in the Order Book. These entries are shown below. Other orders will, of course, be treated in the same way.

On the assumption that the cloth was selected from a pattern bunch, the material will have to be ordered. This will be delivered, together with an invoice. The clearest method of recording this invoice is to open an account in a bought ledger in the name of the merchant, and credit such account therewith. The name of V. Good & Co. has been chosen, and the account and entry are shown below.

The Cash Book, which, it is suggested, should be of the columnar type, should record on the left-hand side all moneys coming into the business, including amounts drawn from the bank, and on the right-hand side all payments made by cheque and by cash. When the book is totalled (it is suggested once a month) the difference between the receipts and expenditure should agree with the bank balance and cash in hand, and in this way both Cash Book and Bank Pass Book are " proved." The balance at the end of the month should be recorded separately as bank and cash in hand, and cash in hand only brought forward at the beginning of a new month. This will be a help when reconciling the Bank Pass Book.

The entries on page 167 should be continued for similar transactions during the financial year, and at the end of such period a Statement of Affairs should be prepared to ascertain the financial aspect of the trading period, that is, the amount of profit made or the extent of the loss suffered. The method of compiling such a statement is shown below as well as a summary to indicate the profit for the year.

The Schedule of Sundry Debtors should have three columns for purposes already mentioned.

For a tailor able to employ clerical assistance the Double Entry system of bookkeeping is strongly urged, and the following books are usually employed :

Order Book (as previously described).

Sales Day Book (or Journal as it is sometimes called) and Sales Ledger.

Bought Journal and Bought Ledger.

Cash Book and Petty Cash Book.

Impersonal and Private Ledger (combined). (Where it is

ORDER BOOK

		130505	130505
Date January 1, 19—			Customer's Name—B. Sharp
Price (S.L. 1) . . . £7 7 0		1.	Coat
Material No.		2.	Vest
Woollen Merchant's Initials		3.	Trousers
		4.	
		etc.	

SALES LEDGER (A/c)

Dr. B. SHARP **Cr.**

19—		O/No.	£ s. d.	19—		C.B.	£ s. d.
Jan. 1.	To D.B. Reefer Suit	130505	7 7 0	Jan. 10	By Cash	1	7 7 0

CASH ACCOUNT

	Receipts.	£ s. d.		Expenditure.	Draw-ing Wages A/c. £ s d	B.L. A/c. £ s d	Cash Pur-chases. £ s d	General Ex-penses. £ s d	Rent. £ s d	Sun-dries. £ s d	Dis-counts. £ s d	Amounts paid into Bank. £ s d
19—			19—									
Jan. 1.	Balance b/f Cash in hand	5 8 0	Jan. 3.	Wages	2 18 6							
			4.	Self.	5 0 0							
1.	Drawn from Bank	5 0 0		Cash Purchase (B. & Co.)			7 6					
5.	,, ,, ,,	10 3 3	5.	Paid to Bank								3 10 0
6.	,, ,, ,,	25 0 0		Packing Boxes				10 6				
10.	B. Sharp (S.L. 1)	7 7 0		V. Good & Co. (B.L. 1)		1 7 9					9	
			6.	Rent, Dec. Qtr.					25 0 0			

Further columns could be used for other items of expenditure of a recurring nature if desired, but head one "Sundries" for non-classified entries. Cheque payments to assist in verifying Pass Book could conveniently be entered in red ink.

BOUGHT LEDGER (A/c)

V. GOOD & CO.

19—		C.B.	£ s. d.	19—		£ s. d.
Jan. 5.	To Cash and Dist. 9d.	1	1 8 6	Jan. 1.	By Invoice*	1 8 6

* This being a "single" entry, there is no cross-reference.

desired to keep certain accounts, such as capital account, loans, etc., separate, two ledgers can be used instead of one.) This does not alter the system. Let us again assume the customer's name is Sharp. The first entry to be made on his placing an order is in the Order Book, where the procedure is just the same. Following this instead of putting the amount of his order direct to the Sales Ledger, it should be entered in the Sales Day Book (as shown). From here it is posted (entered) into the Sales Ledger to the debit (left-hand side) of the account opened therein in the customer's name. By this means the Double Entry is completed, viz. by crediting sales and debiting the customer. The monthly total in the Sales Day Book being credited (right-hand side) to a " Sales Account " in the Impersonal or Private Ledger. When the invoice is received from

STATEMENT OF AFFAIRS

(As at December 31, 19—)

To Sundry Creditors . . .	£592	By Fixtures and Fittings . .		£50
Capital %, being excess of assets		Stock		150
over liabilities at this date .	588	Sundry Debtors . . .		876
		Cash		104
	£1,180			£1,180

CAPITAL SUMMARY

	Capital at December 31, 19— .	£588
	Add Drawings for year . .	260
		848
	Less opening Capital, December 31, 19— . . .	492
	Net Profit for the year . .	£356

As mentioned in reading matter, as these books are kept on a Single Entry basis no Purchase, Sales, or other Impersonal Accounts have been kept, and therefore profit can only be ascertained by preparing a Statement of Affairs and Capital Summary.

LIST OF DEBTORS

(December 31, 19—)

Ledger Folio.		Doubtful.			Overdue.			Good.		
		£	s.	d.	£	s.	d.	£	s.	d.
3	A. Black .	3	13	6						
4	L. Brown .				5	5	0			
5	C. White? .							7	7	0
6	B. Jones .							6	6	0
8	A. Marshall				4	14	6			
10	G. Simpson	2	12	6						
	etc.									

V. Good & Co. for the material bought, it is entered into the Bought Journal and an account opened in the Bought Ledger. The firm is thus credited with the amount of the goods supplied, and purchases account at the end of the month (when the monthly total of purchases is posted) is debited to an account opened in the Impersonal Ledger headed " purchases " (or " goods bought "), whichever is preferred.

The Cash Book should have at least two columns on each side, one for cash receipts and discounts allowed to the customer (left side) and one for bank payments on the right-hand side and discounts allowed by the supplier. On the principle that all moneys coming in should be banked (and this is a vital principle in all businesses), such a Cash Book is really a record of bank transactions, and should be balanced each month after verification with the Bank Pass Book. Cash payments should be dealt with separately in a Petty Cash Book. Money drawn from the bank for cash payments should, after being recorded in the Bank (Cash) Book, be debited in the Petty Cash Book (left-hand side), and all cash used of the money so debited should be entered in the right side of the Petty Cash Book in columnar fashion. Once a month this book should also be totalled and balanced with the cash actually in hand. The balance (to assist in balancing next month) should be brought forward on the debit side as the first entry of a succeeding month, etc. The monthly totals of expenditure in the Petty Cash Book should be debited to accounts concerned opened in the Impersonal Ledger.

By a short study it will be seen that every transaction in the business by the Double Entry method (of an accountancy nature) will have been dealt with in two aspects, viz. debit and credit. The Sales Account will have been credited with the total sales during the month (per the Sales Day Book) and various Sales Ledger Accounts (customer's) debited with the daily entries therein.

The Purchases Account will have been debited with the total goods bought during the month, and the merchants from whom the said goods were purchased individually credited in the Bought Ledger, through the Journal, with the respective amounts of their invoices.

Discounts.—The monthly total of discounts on the debit (left-hand) side of the Cash Book must be debited to a Discounts Account (left-hand side) in the Impersonal Ledger, and the total on the credit side of the Cash Book credited to such account.

DOUBLE ENTRY BOOKKEEPING

ORDER BOOK   (As for Single Entry)

1.   SALES DAY BOOK

19—. Jan. 1.	B. Sharp, D.B. Reefer Suit				Order No. 130505	L.Fo. 1	£ 7	s. 7	d. 0
	Monthly total, say .						£156	8	0

SALES LEDGER

1.   *Dr.*   B. Sharp   *Cr.*

19—. Jan. 1.	To D.B. Reefer	Jl. 1	£ 7	s. 7	d. 0	19—. Jan. 10.	By Cash .	C.B. 1	£ 7	s. 7	d. 0

1.   BOUGHT JOURNAL

19—. Jan. 1.	V. Good		L.Fo. 1	£ 1	s. 8	d. 6
	Monthly total, say .			£96	5	0

BOUGHT LEDGER

1. *Dr.*   V. Good & Co.   *Cr.*

19—. Jan. 5.	To Cash Discount .	C.B. 1	£ 1	s. 7	d. 9 9	19—. Jan. 1.	By Goods Bt.	J.C. 1	£ 1	s. 8	d. 6

5. *Dr.*   SALES A/c   *Cr.*

	This account will be opened in the Impersonal Ledger.					19—. Jan. 30.	By Sales Journal .	1	£ 156	s. 8	d. 0

6. *Dr.*   PURCHASES A/c   *Cr.*

19—. Jan. 30.	To Sundries	B.Jl. 1	£ 96	s. 5	d. 0						
	Ditto										

CASH BOOK

1.			Discount.	Paid to Bank.			19—.					Discount.	Drawn from Bank.

19—.				£	s	d	19—.				£	s	d
Jan. 1.	Balance b/f.			108	10	6	Jan. 1.	Wages	.	I.L. 8	2	18	6
10.	B. Sharp	. S.L. 1		7	7	0	4.	Self . .	I.L. 9		5	0	0
							5.	V. Good .	B.L. 1	9	1	7	9
							6.	Rent to Dec.					
								Qtr . .	I.L. 7		25	0	0
								Petty Cash .	P.C. 1		5	0	0

---

7.   RENT A/c   7.

19—.				£	s.	d.
Jan. 6.	To Cash	. .	C.B. 1	25	0	0

Impersonal
   Ledger %

---

8.   WAGES A/c.   8.

19—.				£	s.	d.
Jan. 1.	To Cash	. .	C.B. 1	2	18	6

Impersonal
   Ledger %

---

9.   DRAWING A/c   9.

19—				£	s.	d.
Jan. 4.	To Cash	. .	C.B. 1	5	0	0

Impersonal
   Ledger %

---

1.   PETTY CASH BOOK

	Amounts Received.			Total Exp.			Cash Purchases.		General Exp.			Sundries.

19—.	£	s.	d.			£	s.	d.	£	s.	d.	£	s.	d.	
Jan. 6.	5	0	0	Cash Purchase . .			7	6		7	6				
				Boxes for Packing .			10	6					10	6	
				etc.											

Book to have sufficient number of columns for each particular case.

At the end of the financial year, as mentioned earlier in this article, all the balances in the Ledgers should be brought down to form a Trial Balance as follows :

TRIAL BALANCE
(December 31, 19—)

I.L.			£	s.	d.	£	s.	d.
1.	Capital %	. . . . .				492	0	0
5.	Sales % .	. . . .				1,850	10	6
6.	Purchases % .	. . . .	680	9	3			
7.	Rent	. . . . .	100	0	0			
8.	Wages	. . . . .	600	3	6			
9.	Drawing % .	. . . .	260	0	0			
10.	Electric Light .	. . . .	5	10	0			
12.	General Expenses	. . . .	44	10	0			
	Sundry Debtors	. . . .	820	0	0			
	Sundry Creditors	. . . .				440	13	0
	Balance at Bank	. . . .	96	0	0			
	Petty Cash	. . . . .	0	10	9			
	Fixtures and Fittings	. . .	50	0	0			
	Stock (commencing stock figure)	. .	126	0	0			
			£2,783	3	6	£2,783	3	6

When the two sides agree it will be proved that the books are arithmetically correct and Trading and Profit and Loss Accounts and Balance-sheet can be prepared as on page 173.

Some of my readers will no doubt have heard of loose-leaf ledgers, card indexes, etc., and this article would perhaps not be complete without some reference thereto.

The great advantage of loose-leaf ledgers is that only open accounts have to be handled, whereas in bound books closed accounts have to be continually turned over. A further advantage is that the laborious process of opening up a new ledger from time to time when an existing one is full is avoided. If loose-leaf ledgers are used, care should always be exercised by the trader that the leaves are properly locked in their binder, and a serial number should be employed so that each leaf can be traced if necessary. Leaves with closed accounts should be bound up in the same way as those of open accounts in a separate binder.

Card indexes are sometimes used for sales ledger purposes, and they answer a very similar purpose to loose-leaf ledgers, but it is seldom that they are used as a complete bookkeeping system.

It is, however, suggested that every tailor should have a card index of his customers, noting thereon each time an order is placed, alterations in measurements, and, in fact, any informa-

TRADING AND PROFIT AND LOSS A/c

(Year ending December 31, 19—)

	£	s.	d.		£	s.	d.
To Stock Jan. 1, 19—	126	0	0	By Sales . .	1,850	10	6
Purchases . .	680	9	3	Stock at Dec. 31,			
Wages . .	600	3	6	19— . .	150	0	0
Gross Profit .	593	17	9				
	£2,000	10	6		£2,000	10	6

	£	s.	d.		£	s.	d.
To Rent . .	100	0	0	By Gross Profit .	593	17	9
Electric Light .	5	10	0				
General Expenses	44	10	0				
Net Profit . .	443	17	9				
	£593	17	9		£593	17	9

BALANCE SHEET

Liabilities. (as on December 31, 19—) *Assets.*

	£	s.	d.		£	s.	d.
To Sundry Creditors .	440	13	0	By Bank . . .	96	0	0
Capital %—				Cash in hand .		10	9
Balance				Sundry Debtors .	820	0	0
b/f. . £492 0 0				Stock . . .	150	0	0
Profit				Fixtures and Fit-			
b/d. . 443 17 9				tings . .	50	0	0
935 17 9							
Less Draw-							
ing % . 260 0 0							
	675	17	9				
	£1,116	10	9		£1,116	10	9

tion that he may consider useful, as such indexes are very useful indeed, and save quite a lot of time for reference purposes if kept up to date. As a ready means of circularising, they are of course also of great assistance. If such an index is not used, it is suggested that the Order Book should be indexed daily. A customer always appreciates a quick reference to his previous order.

JOURNAL

Up to about fifteen years ago the principal book for recording all commercial transactions in their first stage was the Journal, but its use is now practically confined to recording.

1. Transactions for which there are no subsidiary books of prime entry.

2. Adjusting entries.
3. Opening and closing entries.
4. Transfers.

There are various ways of filing bought invoices, statements, and receipts. It is suggested here that they should be kept in separate files in alphabetical and date order as follows :

1. Unpaid invoices.
2. Paid invoices.
3. Unpaid statements.
4. Receipted statements (and other receipts).

CHAPTER XVI

ADVERTISING FOR TAILORS

By C. B. KEELING

(Ex-President, National Society of Tailors' Cutters)

IN an address delivered before the delegates at a Conference of the National Federation of Foremen Tailors' Societies, the President made the following remark : " Another point that is puzzling is the disinclination of the bespoke tailor to advertise. It has been proved conclusively in all other businesses that publicity is not only necessary but imperative." On the surface this remark might appear out of place at a conference of cutters ; it might seem to be more the concern of the Merchant Tailors. The speaker knew, however, that some of these cutters were Master Tailors, and, having his finger on the pulse of the trade, realised that all was not well with it. He was conscious of its weak points and the necessity for the infusion of modern business methods. He knew as well as I know that the prosperity of the trade is as vital to cutters as to employers, if not more so. There have been numerous instances where competition, especially that of large multiple concerns, has compelled a master, capable of doing his own cutting, reluctantly to dispense with the services of his foreman.

The writer of this article has been for thirty years employed by one of the most successful concerns in the country in the production and marketing direct to the public of medium-class tailoring, both to measure and ready-to-wear. In expressing my views on successful advertising, I would point out that it is essential for the tailor to embrace up-to-date business methods.

Our trade is of such a complex nature that it requires a man of exceptional powers to possess a practical knowledge of sewing and cutting and, at the same time, be able to conduct the financial and organising side of a business. That is why the partnership of the cutter with a qualified salesman invariably makes for success. Each man is an expert conducting his own side of the concern.

The views expressed in this article are not those of an advertising specialist knowing nothing of the practical side of the trade, neither are they those of a tailor ignorant of advertising.

The objects aimed at are to encourage the adoption of advertising as a means to business expansion ; to give ideas and assistance in the preparation of advertisements ; and to point out how the best results may be obtained from outlay. To be successful publicity must not be undertaken in a haphazard manner ; it means time, thought, care, and, most important of all, persistency.

My association with trade organisations has brought me into contact with all classes of tailors. A natural interest in their advertisements makes it apparent that the majority are under the impression that, having booked so many inches in a local paper or some other medium, they have finished, and that the price per inch is the sole expense, whereas they have only paid the ground rent for their building.

The same rule applies in selecting a medium as to one's own trade—the cheapest is not always the best. Circulation is what is wanted, and for that the tailor must be prepared to pay. A good rule is never to advertise in a paper produced solely for the revenue brought by its advertisements.

The tailor's name and address, with the statement that he is practical, does not cut much ice with the public to-day. The probability is that they have not seen, much less read, the advertisement tucked away amongst numerous others. To make advertising pay, both goods and price must be right and the medium selected fit the class of public catered for. If it be a man's trade only, the daily or weekly press should receive first consideration ; then football and cricket programmes and other sporting mediums. It is wise, whenever possible, to secure space on the pages dealing with sport. Bazaar handbook advertising lends itself to high-class displays, as both printing and paper are good. From the point of view of circulation the cost is high. The canvasser is often a customer, which makes it essential that part of the outlay must go in this direction.

The question is often put : " Does the public take the trouble to read these advertisements ? " I should say it all depends on the advertisement ! The tailor should adopt two styles of publicity for newspapers and magazines. One should aim at bringing his name and address, accompanied by some catchy phrase or paragraph appropriate for any time of the year, before the public. If his premises are suitable—and very few are not—a photograph should always appear, if only in miniature, with his name in signature form, the type being foreign to that used on the rest of the page. This means the preparation of blocks, but the cost is not prohibitive, and the results will more than justify the expense entailed, for they create individuality, which should be every tailor's goal.

The second style of advertisement I would term seasonal, that is, dealing with suitable garments at the right time. The tailor who would be modern must adopt advertising, especially as he is gradually being compelled to produce ready-to-wear overcoats of his own manufacture. The return on the capital expended will be found greater in this section than in the Order Department, for it is easier to attract customers for the former than the latter.

The following are examples of general advertisements which can be used at any time, or throughout the year.

1903–1928

TWENTY-FIVE YEARS AGO WE RESOLVED THAT THE PRO-DUCTIONS OF KENNETH BROWN SHOULD BE REPRESENTED BY ALL THAT IS BEST IN THE ART OF TAILORING.

OUR FIRST CONSIDERATION HAS ALWAYS BEEN QUALITY AND NOT CHEAPNESS OF PRODUCTION.

THAT A FIRST-CLASS ARTICLE IS THE BEST INVESTMENT IS FULLY APPRECIATED BY OUR CUSTOMERS AND PROVED BY THEIR NUMEROUS RECOMMENDATIONS.

NAME OF FIRM :......................

ADDRESS :...........................

ABBEY PARK PAVILION

This constitutes one of a series produced by this enterprising firm. It represents a scene in the local park, and each year some inscription is carried out in flowers, the style being known as " carpet bedding." This picture appeared in the local press exactly as reproduced here, with no description or added matter whatever. It is easy to imagine that this firm of tailors was talked about for many a day. In fact, many people were drawn to visit the park to see this unique advertisement, and were somewhat surprised to find it was purely imaginary. Other places of interest were treated in the same manner, as, for example, the Town Hall Square, where a make-believe hoarding was erected, displaying the firm's announcement.

If a tailor would have his name and business talked of, he should select similar sites in his neighbourhood and deal with them in the same manner.

It will be found that the big stores specialise, in their publicity campaigns, on the article in demand at the moment. The old, old story that " Our new season's goods have now arrived and consist of a fine selection of the best Scotch tweeds and worsted suitings " is as dead as mutton. A set of advertisements should be prepared for each season, and I advise every tailor to try to make a hobby of writing them himself, for this may prove full of interest. Of course, if time or confidence should be lacking, he may have them drafted out for him, but this entails expense.

My counsel, once again, is to specialise in the overcoat trade, particularly in the ready-to-wear garment—produced in slack times in one's own workshop, when it is a problem how to keep the hands employed. One overcoat sold in the winter is worth two suits in the summer ; for bad trade during the cold weather considerably reduces the average of net profits and makes it difficult to maintain an adequate staff to cope with summer business.

It is an excellent plan for any tailor to make up his mind that he is going to be THE MAN FOR OVERCOATS in his particular district, and to keep on telling the public until his name is irrefutably connected with them. A slogan like this drives facts home in a convincing manner.

I am including here a sample advertisement illustrating my point. It should be noted that a name has been given to this coat, and that each feature is dealt with in sequence, terminating with the materials from which it is made.

OUR NEWTOWN OVERCOAT

This Coat is the most successful we have ever produced. The easy way it slips on, the comfortable feel about the shoulders, the snug-fitting collar and perfect hanging back are a delight to the wearer, and a credit to the experienced cutter responsible for its production. We make this shape in Fleeces, Naps, Tweeds, and Rainproofs. Call and try one on. We are confident the result will please you.

SEE OUR WINDOWS
Prices £3 3 0 to £5 10 0

HOGGETT & SON
THE PREMIER TAILORS

HIGH STREET   LEICESTER

Dress suits lend themselves to treatment in a similar manner, but for the order trade only. It is a mistake to think that advertising and price-cutting go hand in hand. Even a casual study of the advertisement columns in the daily papers will prove that this is not so. For evening wear, concert and theatre programmes are the best publicity medium. The prevailing styles should be fully described, for the public is keenly interested, although sadly ignorant, on these points. The tailor who sets out to make himself a DRESS CLOTHES SPECIALIST should remember that style details make excellent copy; for example, S.B. or D.B. waistcoat; braided or plain side seams for trousers; barathea, diagonal, or fancy weave material for the coat; facings, linings, etc.

Effective blocks of figures are essential to all advertisements, except those which I term " general "; to my mind they are the chief means of arresting the attention of a prospective customer. No man suddenly decides on a new suit or overcoat. In all probability he has been thinking of it for days, or even weeks, and his wife has been studying advertisements, for the bulk of newspaper advertising is done for the benefit of women.

A good half-tone or line block of a smart overcoat in the local paper will often result in a cash sale, with no fear of alterations the next day, and the first-fruits of an advertising campaign will have been reaped. From my own experience I know that women take a live interest in male attire. A man is frequently accompanied by his wife on a visit to his tailor, and wisdom dictates deference to her judgment.

Another factor in favour of blocks to illustrate advertisements is that the written word makes a much slower appeal than a picture; but if the attention can first be captured the probability is that the text will be read from start to finish.

Fashion blocks are supplied by the leading trade journals at reasonable prices, either in half-tone, for use on art paper, or " line " for newspaper work. The tailor who makes use of this service may be assured of technical correctness, for the figures are generally reproduced from expensive plates.

An arresting headline is another profitable means of securing the attention of prospective buyers. I consider the two following admirable illustrations.

The second appeared in one of Austin Reed's announcements of spring overcoats, and is first-rate in its way. A man contemplating the purchase of a spring overcoat would first be interested in the bold statement that it should be brown, and

PLATE XXIV

HOGGETT & SONS

THE PREMIER
TAILORS

THERE IS
STYLE, CHARACTER
AND
GOOD TASTE
IN ALL OUR
PRODUCTIONS

HIGH STREET and SILVER STREET
Telephone No. 4284   **LEICESTER**

PLATE XXV

THE PAVILION, ABBEY PARK, LEICESTER.

A New Delight in Ladies' Tailored Wear.

IF you want a new experience in wearing a really smart outfit--come along to Addison's. We've a happy way of adding that little extra touch of distinction to everything that leaves our hands. Ladies say that we're adepts at making Coats and Costumes. You'll say so too, once you've tried us !

ADDISON BROS.
5 BELGRAVE GATE
LEICESTER

Your Spring Overcoat
should be brown. But . . .

Though brown *may* be popular, you may have an idea that it isn't your colour.

then intrigued to find that if the shade did not appeal to him new blue-greys, plum tones, etc., were available.

The great bugbear of the tailoring trade, as we all know, is the recurrence of slack periods, usually during January and February and again in August and September. The object of advertising should be to reduce, as much as possible, the length of these two arid seasons. This object has been and can be most successfully obtained at a comparatively small cost by mailing to each customer on the books an imitation type-written letter, pointing out to them the mutual advantage to be gained from the early placing of orders. An advertisement similar to the two which I append, printed on business memo forms, has, in my own experience, proved to be the cheapest and most effective.

Pamphlet advertising should form an effective adjunct to any campaign. A pamphlet should consist of a two- or three-page folder, and both printing and paper should be GOOD. Again my advice is to specialise. Two folders a year should be issued : one in the spring, dealing with lounge suits, sports wear, and spring overcoats, and the second in the autumn illustrating overcoats and dress clothes. To attempt to deal with every garment in a man's wardrobe in one booklet is, in my judgment, a mistake. In the spring it is fifty to one on a new suit ; in the winter perhaps four to one on an overcoat, and the autumn is the only time of year effectively to advertise evening dress.

To repeat what I have already touched on : details of style should be carefully thought out and correctly worded, for the tailor who can put a young man right over his first dress suit is not quickly forgotten.

In conclusion, I would commend to the notice of every tailor

Dear Sir,   In order to induce our customers to place their orders early and thus enable us to give them that amount of attention necessary in the production of High Class Garments, and to avoid the congestion in the busy time, we are offering exceptional value during the next few weeks.   We are making a leading line of a splendid range of superfine Worsted Suitings made from pure botany wool, double twisted yarns and quite pre-war quality, at the low price of £7.7.0 the suit, made and trimmed in our best style.   This is undoubtedly an excellent cloth for wear and appearance.   We have also a very superior range of Tweed Suitings made from pure new wool in all the latest and most effective colourings and designs, which we are offering at £5.5.0 to £6.6.0 the suit.

Indigo blue Serges being as popular as ever, we are offering two special lines at £6.6.0 and £7.7.0 made from pure botany wool, best indigo dye.   We guarantee them to stand sun and sea.   They are of fine texture and of the highest quality.

Owing to the very large sales and the reputation we have gained for "Ready to Wear" Overcoats, we have been encouraged to further extend this department and we have made up the largest and best selection of Spring Overcoats and Raincoats we have ever held. These coats are cut and made on the premises by men that have spent years in specialising in these garments.   We are sure that customers visiting this department will be impressed by the styles, large variety and perfect fitting coats at very moderate prices.

Yours faithfully,

the words of Mr. J. Wallace Black, of the Newcastle Advertising Club, who states :

" There is very little doubt that advertisements are read more by women than by men. The ladies are much more easily interested, and more easily influenced, and it is certain that in the case of goods appealing particularly, or even entirely, to men, the ladies will, nine times out of ten, draw the attention of their menfolk to the advertisements concerning them. The sort of appeal that would carry weight with the ladies would leave the men cold. Men are suspicious as well as conservative animals, and dislike change of any kind. That is why it is worth while to try to secure their business. They are most loyal—so long as they are satisfied. The minute you fail to please them they look around, unwillingly, and a little sadly, maybe, for a successor.

" Men do not like airy generalities, flippant statements, or silly suggestions.

" Men want plain facts and cogent argument. They want to know the reason why they should change their habits. You've got to convince them of the merits of your wares if you desire their custom ; and once you have done so only faithful service, and a rigid keeping up to standard of the goods you sell, will ensure their loyalty. It is a much harder task to sell to men by means of the printed word than to women. Yet it is worth while, men being so slow to change. The ladies, bless their hearts ! are fickle, and flit about from store to store, even as a bee flies from flower to flower, seeking honey where it may. The ladies love and desire change. Variety to them is the spice of life. Men are constant, conservative, slow to change.

" You must have these facts in view when preparing your appeal to men, so that you may put your best and most convincing arguments before them in a plain, common-sensible way, without frills—because you are appealing to very matter-of-fact folk."

CHAPTER XVII

SALESMANSHIP FOR TAILORS

By H. J. CHAPPELL

(Director of Herbert Chappell, Ltd., Gresham Street, London, E.C.)

THE IMPORTANCE OF SALESMANSHIP

IN the past, very little attention has been paid to the selling side of the tailoring trade. It has been left to look after itself ; and while many volumes have been written and thousands of lectures delivered on how a suit should be cut and made, the learned ones of the trade have mostly been silent as to how it should first be sold.

And yet a moment's thought will show how vitally important this selling question is. Unless we can first sell a suit, it can certainly never be cut ; and if a blunder be made in selling no skill with shears or needle can ever put things right.

Careful attention to the art of salesmanship is the most potent weapon with which the vendor of ready-made, mass-produced clothing threatens the genuine bespoke tailor. "Sweet are the uses of advertisement" might well be his motto, and he leaves no stone unturned in his endeavours to lead the public to believe in the value of the goods he offers.

Whether the strong medicine of advertisement should be used is a matter which every bespoke tailor must decide for himself. The question hinges entirely on the type and tastes of his clientèle. While we know many firms of good standing whose skilful use of advertisement is a great source of income, yet in the case of others customers would undoubtedly be offended if the same methods were adopted. The most that can be said is that it is best to feel one's way carefully, rather than rush headlong into advertising schemes involving large sums of money and abrupt changes of policy.

TRAINING THE SALESMAN

There is no royal road to success as a salesman. Proficiency can only be attained by hard work and by carefully watching an experienced man whenever opportunity arises. The first necessity is a good working knowledge of the cloths to be sold. The tyro should learn to distinguish by sight and touch the various types of cloth, and to know the uses for which each is suitable.

An appreciation of the quality of the different grades will come later, together with some acquaintance with dyes. A salesman should learn all he can about the various processes in the manufacture of cloth, and should lose no opportunity of talking to woollen merchants and travellers, whom he will find always ready to give valuable information and advice.

In addition to acquiring a good working knowledge of cloth, the budding salesman should study the prevailing fashions of dress, in order that he may be able to advise his customer as to the correct clothes for any particular occasion. For this purpose a careful study of photographs of well-dressed men in the weekly society papers will well repay the time expended on it, and show the salesman what is being worn by the leaders of fashion.

Thus equipped with learning, the salesman will be enabled to meet his customer with that degree of assurance which inspires confidence. Confidence of the buyer in the salesman is the essential foundation of successful business, and the customer should be made to feel that he can rely on the sound advice of his tailor as to the cloth, style, and colour which will best become him.

OBSERVATION

At the commencement of a sale, the first task of the salesman lies in careful observation, in the process which is sometimes known as " sizing up." He must become a veritable Sherlock Holmes in his endeavour to notice every detail in the customer's appearance and manner which will enable him to deduce his tastes, habits, and financial standing. Much can be learned from the first glance ; his age, his size, his probable occupation, his general tidiness or otherwise. This information must be supplemented by tactful questions and conversation ; and every effort should be made to get the customer to talk about himself. Having learnt all he can about his customer, the salesman is now in a position to decide what will be the most suitable materials to show him.

SELECTION OF MATERIALS

Before considering the best uses of different types of material, it would be as well to utter a word of warning with regard to lengths. Every piece of cloth in a tailor's shop should be marked with the number of yards it contains, and this point must be borne in mind *before the piece is shown to the customer*. It is very annoying, after having spent some time in the selection of a cloth, to be told that there is insufficient for a suit. Similarly it is very uneconomical to sell a suit to a small man from a length of, say, 3¾ yards. Unsuitable lengths, therefore, should be passed over and left in the fixture till a more convenient occasion.

Having decided, in view of the size of the customer, what sort of length he can safely sell, the salesman may now decide on the type of cloth to be recommended. Sometimes the customer has definite ideas of his own on the subject, and then the salesman's task is fairly easy ; and many men are so hidebound in their ideas that suit follows suit of identically the same material. Usually, however, the customer is open to suggestion, and here the tailor's skill comes in. There are certain broad and general rules which may be borne in mind. Stripes in a cloth give a man an appearance of height, while checks and all horizontal lines increase his apparent width. Dark cloths, as a general rule, make a man look small, and again the converse applies. It is typical of human nature that the tall man invariably wants to look shorter and the fat man thinner, while the diminutive individual is generally anxious to be mistaken for Goliath.

With regard to the different cloths, worsteds are generally most suited to the office worker and the professional man, being neat in appearance and retaining their shape in the trousers in spite of constant sitting ; though it should be remembered that whipcords and the less covered worsteds have a tendency to wear shiny.

Tweeds are best worn by the outdoor man and the traveller, builder, and engineer—folk whose work takes them into dirty and dusty places. Tweeds show marks and stains less than other materials, and are very durable, though prone to bag at the knees if used much for office work.

The softer materials, such as Saxonies and flannels, are best kept for holiday wear except for those fortunate individuals who have many changes of raiment and a valet. Such men will often appreciate the beautiful colour and softness of texture to be found in a good Saxony, and they are unlikely to subject it to unfair wear and tear.

Careful attention should be paid to securing the right weight of cloth for a customer's needs. This point will affect his comfort considerably, and there is on record an authentic instance of a man who weighs every suit he receives from his tailor, and if it fails to answer this test the suit becomes a " kill." This is, of course, an extreme case, but it is a good plan to mark each length of cloth with its weight in ounces per yard, and to accustom oneself to the " feel " of the various weights. This enables the salesman to produce a cloth suitable for every season and climate. Generally speaking, heavier weights of cloth are worn in the country than in London, and age as a rule requires a thicker cloth than youth, though some stout and elderly men can bear nothing heavier than the thinnest worsted. As a rule, 15 to 20 ounces are most useful for this country ; 10 to 14 ounces for warm countries such as Egypt or Italy; while worsteds as light as 8 or 9 ounces may be obtained for tropical wear. It used to be necessary to provide suits of very heavy weight for winter wear in Canada and the Northern States of U.S.A., but in these days central heating is almost universally used in America, and thinner suits are worn, aided by a heavy overcoat for out of doors.

SELLING TALK

The demeanour of a salesman towards his customer will materially affect the success of the sale. A cheerful courtesy is absolutely essential, but there is no necessity for the cringing servility which, though apparently common in the past, is now happily more frequent in fiction than in fact. The salesman should adapt his conversation to the needs of his customer, for though some men have plenty of leisure, and enjoy a fairly lengthy exchange of small talk, others may be pressed for time and will wish to confine their remarks strictly to business. A good salesman will explain the merit of his goods, but if he is wise he will refrain from obviously impossible superlatives. " Truth in Advertising " is a slogan which applies equally to the spoken as to the written word, and a sober explanation of the value of the cloth, particularly if backed with a few technical details, will carry much more weight than any vapourings of the " worth double the money " order.

THE WIFE PROBLEM

Tailors are frequently perplexed at the failure of an apparently perfect suit. The customer can find no real fault with it—he " doesn't like the cut " or " can't feel comfortable." The answer, of course, is *cherchez la femme*. More and more of late years wives are beginning to take a greater interest in their husbands' clothes, even to the extent of accompanying them to the tailor and dictating what they shall wear. Curiously enough, this seems to be most frequent in military circles. Let the tailor beware. The lady may be a useful ally, but she will prove a deadly foe, and should he annoy her his customer is as good as lost.

Where husband and wife are agreed the going is fairly easy, and an occasional appeal to the lady's judgment will ensure her friendship and high opinion. But when a clash of wills appears, then the salesman must, like Agag, walk delicately. The difference will often arise from an attempt on the part of the wife to dig her husband from a rut along which he has progressed placidly for years, and force him into something smarter or " younger," and the tailor must use all his tact to avoid falling between two stools. While he may support the lady in reason, particularly with regard to colour, he should not allow himself to be forced into making tight or waisted garments for a man who is used to a very easy fit, and who habitually stuffs his pockets full of luggage of every description.

PLEASE THE CUSTOMER

The salesman must never forget that, above every other consideration, he serves his firm best when he pleases the customer. While there is a great satisfaction in selling a short length to a small man, or in getting rid of a length which has been in stock for some time, yet these advantages must never be allowed to override the ultimate object—the satisfaction of the customer. Only in this way can be built up that intangible asset known as " goodwill " which is the mainstay of every successful business.

> " The friends thou hast, and their adoption tried,
> Grapple them to thy soul with hoops of steel."

CHAPTER XVIII

A GLOSSARY OF TECHNICAL AND TEXTILE TERMS

Compiled by THE EDITOR

A

Albert Cloth.—Reversible, double-faced material, each side a different colour. Used for coats, suits and wraps.

All-Wool.—Any cloth that is composed solely of wool is correctly described as an " all-wool " material. The term is usually applicable to a fabric made of woollen yarn or worsted yarn ; as, for example, an all-wool flannel (woollen goods) or an all-wool serge (worsted goods).

Allpine.—A good, strong and expensive woollen cloth, one time fashionable for men's wear ; made in plain-coloured or speckled effects. While not in vogue at present, it was formerly used by well-to-do folk for coats and breeches, also as a lining for overcoats.

Alpaca.—The woolly hair of the Peruvian llama ; a lustrous cloth woven with weft of alpaca wool over a strong cotton warp ; imitations composed of various proportions of wool, alpaca and cotton ; or wool and cotton, or pure cotton. Alpaca was first introduced into England by Benjamin Outram, of Halifax, who spun a rough yarn with it, which he wove into rugs, shawls and heavy wraps. It was not successfully utilised for the manufacture of cloth until Sir Titus Salt obtained smooth yarns from it, which he wove upon cotton warps. A large industry sprang into existence ; but the fabric gradually lost favour, and cheap imitations made pure alpaca goods unprofitable. Mixed with cotton the material is used for dresses, summer suits or office coats and, in light weights, for linings.

Amazon Cloth.—A fine, lustrous, faced woollen cloth, made in various qualities, the lower ranges being composed of shoddy.

American Shoulders.—Shoulders cut broad and built up, to give the wearer an appearance of massiveness about the shoulder. The type of shoulder favoured in America to-day, it may be said, differs much from this style.

Andalusians.—A cloth woven of Spanish wool ; worsted yarn composed of fine Spanish merino wool.

Angola.—A fabric classed with flannels and other woollen cloths, but really composed of yarns made of mixed cotton and manufactured wools, designed to imitate mohair, or angora.

Angola Yarns (sometimes called Vigogne yarns). These materials are woven into pseudo-woollen shawls, dress goods and suitings. The yarns are produced from cotton or cotton waste mixed with shoddy, mungo, flocks, or extract.

Angora Yarn.—A French yarn used chiefly in the manufacture of sporting goods, and spun from the hair of the Angora rabbit. Fabrics composed of Angora yarn have an electrical property, like that seen in the skin of a cat. As the hair of the Angora rabbit does not pelt, the fabrics made from it can be washed with hot soap and water without shrinkage. Soft and warm, and absorbing moisture, the goods are valued by travellers and sportsmen.

Armozeen.—A stout plain silk, usually black, used for clerical robes, and named from the old French word *armesin*, signifying taffeta.

Armure (Silk).—From the French *armor*, so called because the fabric has a small ridgy or pebbly pattern suggesting chain armour. A stiff, rich-looking silk. Filling yarn is often heavily weighted. Usually black. It is used for dresses, coats, trimmings, facings for dress coats, etc. Weave : fancy, called Barathea.

Armure (Cheviot).—A dress fabric, composed of wool, generally black.

Army Cloth.—Any description of fabric used in the making of military garments.

Artificial or Manufactured Leather Fabrics.—Made by applying a nitro-cellulose coating to a cotton back. The foundation cloth may be firm muslin, or a heavier material napped on the back. Various effects are produced by the weight of cloth and finish on surface. A good grade of manufactured leather is more durable than a poor grade of split leather. It is sold under various trade names, such as Pantasote, Fabrikoid and Leather Wove. Made in various colours, such as brown, green, red, blue, black and tan, it is used, among other things, for millinery and dress trimmings.

Artificial Silk.—An imitation of natural silk, obtained by treating cellulose produced from any form of vegetable matter with various chemicals, so as to form a lustrous gelatinous mass, which is driven through fine nozzles and coagulated in very thin hairs, which are then combined to make yarns.

Artificial silk is easily distinguished from the natural product by the uniform regularity of the component fibres, by burning, and by various chemical tests.

Another definition states that it is called art silk, manufactured silk, or fibre silk, and is coarser, more lustrous, more wiry and less strong than animal or worm silk. It is made by a chemical process from wood pulp (spruce) or from cotton linters (short cotton fibre). There are three processes used, chardonnet, or nitrocellulose and cuprammonium, both of which utilise cotton linters. The newer process, viscose, employs wood pulp.

Art Linen.—A general term applied to a variety of crashes, in either a close or loose weave. It may be unbleached, quarter-bleached, half-bleached, or white. It is used for dresses, skirts and uniforms.

Art Serge.—Any fabric of a serge character in æsthetic colours.

Art Shades.—The intermediate shades of colour, generally paler and more subdued than the ordinary colours.

Astrachan (Astrakan).—Wool or lambs' fur of a curly character, coming from the town of Astrakhan, in Russia.

Astrakan, Imitation (weaving term). The name given to a pile fabric of a coarse texture presenting a curious curly surface. These fabrics are produced in two ways : (1) on the weft principle a shrinkage of the ground texture throwing the pile weft up as a loop ; (2) as a warp mixture, in which a thick curly warp yarn is brought over wires to form the necessary loops.

A 2-and-2 Check would (as the name implies) be formed with two dark, two light, but could only be a check in plain weave, giving the well-known 4-pointed star effect.

A 2-and-2 colouring in common twill would give a stripe and a step diagonal in 6-shaft twill. A tailor might very easily describe the common twill broken stripe effect as a check.

B

Back-and-Fore Stitch.—As its name implies, this is a combination of the back-and-fore, or running stitch; and consists in taking a back- and then a fore-stitch before the needle is removed from the material. The object is to get quickly over the ground. It is a stitch suited for linings and also for pockets; but when used for the latter purpose it ought to be done closely, and with good thread.

Backed Cloth.—A cloth which, in addition to the face fabric, has an under layer of extra weft, extra warp, or another fabric.

Back-stitch.—The back-stitch is the tailor's stitch. It is a sort of lock-stitch, differing from others by covering the whole of the surface between the stitches, with the thread exposed on the face of the material. A perfectly formed back-stitch, pulled home with a proper degree of tightness for the material in which it is placed, gives a perfect line of seam.

Bad Cover.—A defect in cloth caused by setting the warp in the loom too wide for the thickness of the yarns, or by irregular weaving.

Baize.—A coarse open cloth, sometimes frissed on one side. Formerly it was used for clothes, but it is not clear whether baize has deteriorated, or the taste of the weavers has improved. Such cloths were originally dyed a bay or brownish-red colour, hence the name, which is a corruption of the plural form.

Balance Marks.—Balance marks are guides to the workman in sewing the various sections together correctly, and indications to the cutter that such has been done. In trousers they are usually put at knee and hip, on both tops and undersides. By this means the balance of the whole garment is preserved; hence balance marks. In breeches they are varied to help in the location of the fulness.

In coats balance marks may be fixed at various points, such as at side seams, shoulder seams, hindarm and forearm of sleeves.

Balayeuse.—The strip of braid or other hard-wearing material sewn on the inner side of the bottom of a skirt—that is, when skirts were worn long. At the time of writing, when skirts are short, the only danger of them wearing would be that they rubbed against the knee and not the foot.

Bale.—A compressed pack of wool, of a convenient form

for transit. Weights : Crossbred bales (2 packs) 3½ to 4½ cwts. Merino bales (1½ packs) 3½ cwts.

Balmoral.—A broad-crowned Scottish cap, woven or knitted, with a band fitting closely to the head, known earlier as the Kilmarnock, and later as the Tam o'Shanter. A heavy, woollen fabric used for winter petticoats.

Bandana.—A calico cloth in which white or brightly coloured spots are produced upon a red or dark ground, the effect being obtained by knotting the parts to be kept white, etc., thus preventing the deposition of colour when the whole piece is immersed in the dye bath. This mechanical resist method was first employed in India and the Indian Archipelago, where indigo dyeing originated, and is still extensively practised for the production of simple patterns, giving the name to a large range of handkerchiefs known as "bandanas."

Bannockburn Tweed.—A well-known name for a cheviot cloth made with alternate threads of marl twist and solid colour, warp and weft. Originally made in mills at Bannockburn ; now a staple product in all tweed mills.

Baracan.—A kind of stout material, like moleskin cloth. Also a strong thick stuff made of camel's hair, used for garments in towns along the Mediterranean.

Barathea.—A soft-finished worsted cloth, woven in a broken-rib weave effect, in staple colours, such as black and blue, originally a product of the Bradford textile district. It was formerly regarded as a fashionable men's suiting, and for dress suitings is still popular. In Khaki it makes up well for service jackets. The same weave in silk is used to face dress coats.

Baronette Satin.—A trade name for a sports fabric made of fibre silk with a cotton back ; it is used for sports skirts and costumes. Georgette satin is a trade name for a similar fabric.

Barre.—Any pattern produced by stripes or bars extending crosswise of the goods.

Barry.—A fault in fabrics, taking its name from the way in which it shows itself, that is, in bars either lengthways or across the piece. This defect may originate in either the combing, spinning, designing, weaving or finishing operations.

Basket Weave.—A woven effect produced by any kinds of yarns, but more pronounced in a fabric of a solid colour whereby, instead of single threads interlacing in the loom to form a plain (as with the ordinary cotton) weave, two or more threads are laid together, both in the warp and in the weft systems of thread combination, yielding a pattern simulating a plaited cane basket, or an enlarged hopsack or mat appearance.

Baste.—This word is not only used in the sense " to baste a seam," etc., but also to describe a coat prepared for trying-on, because basting is employed in thus getting a garment ready. A full baste is a coat prepared with facings, linings, and wadding basted in ; with collar tacked on, and tabs and buttons ; but the term is also used sometimes when the linings and facings are not included. A forward baste would have the front edges made up, the shoulder, side and back seams basted, and the sleeves basted in ; with the collar padded and tacked on. A shell or skeleton baste is one with canvases tacked in, seams basted, front edges turned in, one sleeve tacked in, and the collar basted on. Sometimes the pockets are put in.

Basting.—Basting may be defined as to sew or " tack " together with long stitches the parts of a piece of work, to hold them in place for the time being.

Batik.—An ancient process of resist printing which originated in Java. It is practised by modern craftsmen and imitated in machine printing.

Batiste.—A very fine fabric of mixed silk and wool, made in Flanders and Picardy ; a class of light-weight, finely finished fabrics, heavier and wider than nainsook, originally made of linen, but now largely woven of cotton. Linen batiste is said to have been invented by a French weaver named Baptiste, in Cambrai, where a statue has been erected to him.

Baudekin.—A very old type of cloth of brocaded or embroidered silk, interwoven with gold or silver threads, for State robes and clerical vestments. It is supposed to be the original of brocade, and in old days was a rich silk woven on a gold warp, and produced in the famous city of Bagdad in its prime. Later Baudekin was a rich crimson silk.

Bayadere.—Stripes in strongly contrasted colours, running across the fabric. The name is derived from the garment worn by dancing girls in India.

Bearers.—Bearers are used both for fly front and fall trousers. They are the sections fastened to the side seams to bear the weight or strain of the trousers, etc., when the fronts are opened, and also to fill up the parts cut away to make the falls. The bearers for whole falls contain the pockets.

Bilston Bearers is a name given to a style of trousers similar to whole falls, but with deeper bearers. Bearers are also used for split falls.

Pocket Bearers are utilised with cross pockets.

French Bearers accompany fly-front trousers, and consist of a continuation of the button catch with two or more holes, buttoning on to a strap which comes from the left-side seam, inside. Often ordered by corpulent men as a support for the abdomen ; should fit a little closer than the actual trousers.

Beaver.—A fine woollen fabric with a napped finish similar to broadcloth. It was originally made in England, to resemble beaver fur, hence the name. The length of the nap varies greatly. A kind of beaver cloth used in millinery is a like fabric somewhat resembling a hatter's plush. The thirty- and thirty-two-ounce beavers used for uniforms and overcoats may be compared with melton. They do not have the hard finish of melton, but always show a nap.

There are several variations of the finishing treatments accorded beaver goods, giving rise to such distinguishing classifications as " patent beaver," " fur beaver," " frosted beaver," " Moscow beaver," " castor beaver," " beaverine," etc.

Bedford Cord.—A substantial cloth made of worsted threads, usually of yarn twists of white and a drab shade, or in solid colours as black and blue, so woven and finished as to produce a well-defined corded face, like corduroy, the ribs running lengthwise of the goods. Such material is chiefly used for overcoatings, riding breeches, and livery garb. In all probability the name comes from the town of Bedford.

Another definition reads : A smooth, corded fabric with cords running lengthwise. One set of filling yarns interlaces with warp and forms the face of the cloth. The other set floats on the back except where it causes the depression between cords. The cords are more pronounced when warp yarns are used for stuffing. They are placed between the face of the cloth and the filling floats on the back. May be worsted, silk, or cotton or combinations.

And yet another : A texture in which the interlacing is so arranged that a warp surface fabric is produced with a rounded cord effect, running warp way, the indented effect being produced by two threads working plain.

Silks and cottons and mixtures are also made up in the same design, and are called Bedford cords.

Beige.—Natural or undyed fabric. The term is sometimes used to describe a material and sometimes a colour. For instance, it is defined by various authorities as a fabric of a twill character, somewhat loose in texture ; and beige serge is spoken of as a cloth woven with wool in the natural colour.

Bengaline.—A bold soft warp-rib silk material.

Bird's Eye.—A weave effect, in staple worsted suiting cloths ; the clear finish given the fabric emphasising the minute indentations of the weave structure suggesting birds' eyes, hence the name. It is also spoken of as a diaper weave.

Black, Superfine.—The highest grade of heavy woollen cloths, formerly woven in the West of England, heavily felted or milled, raised, cropped or shorn, brushed, steamed and pressed, to make it firm yet soft to handle, with a smooth and lustrous face. The trade in this cloth is now very small.

Bleached Calico.—The common cotton cloth which has been passed through a bleaching process, similar in quality to grey calico, but different in appearance.

Bluff Edges.—Edges made up in the usual way, but finished outside without stitching.

Body.—A term applied to textiles, suggesting compactness, solidity, and richness of handle in the raw, semi-manufactured, or manufactured state.

Bolivia.—A woollen or worsted weft pile fabric, soft and velvety to feel. The tufts of pile usually appear in diagonal or vertical rows. Yarn or piece-dyed. In good grades it wears well, and is made up in ladies' coats and costumes.

Bolt.—An entire length of cloth from the loom, rolled or folded. Bolts vary in length.

Bombazine.—A fine stuff woven in an open twill with worsted weft on a silk warp. It is a fabric of ancient origin, originally of silk and known to the Romans as Bombycinum. In more recent days it has undergone a number of changes in its fibrous composition and weave structure, and to-day is produced as above, with cheap imitations in cotton. At one time summer " dusters," popular for carriage driving, were made from yellow or grey bombazine, while black was in demand for mourning attire.

Botany.—Originally merino wool grown near Botany Bay, Australia ; at the present time a term applied to all classes of fine wools, and also applied to all fine worsteds.

Botany Twill.—A twilled mixture, the warp and weft of which are made from Botany wool.

Boucle.—A novelty yarn and finish effect produced on cloths, like staple worsted cheviots, whereby very small drawn-out, curly loops in the individual threads appear on the surface of the goods. The name is from the French *bouclé*, meaning a buckle or ringlet. The knots or loops on the surface are frequently in imitation of astrachan.

Bound Edges.—Edges finished with braid, etc.

Box Cloth.—A heavy and thoroughly milled, or fulled, woollen cloth like melton ; it is, in reality, a heavy melton, used for overcoats. Its compactness and impenetrable quality, due to much fulling in the process of manufacture, make it specially valuable for wear in cold and stormy seasons, or where there is much exposure. In the old days of mail-coaching it was the ideal material for greatcoats, and received its name because it was used by driver and passengers exposed to the elements on the box of a stage coach. It is still used for livery greatcoats for coachmen, footmen, and grooms, etc. Another name for the cloth is Devon, from the county of its origin.

Breech.—The term used by military tailors for the seat.

Bridle.—A bridle is actually controlling gear ; and therefore the term is aptly used for the piece of linen or other material which is padded on to the canvas along the crease or roll of lapel, to hold or control it.

Broad Cloth.—A fine woollen cloth, usually woven plain, finely dyed, dressed, and finished. The original style was undoubtedly set very wide in the loom to allow for a considerable shrinkage, hence the name. As late as twenty-five or thirty years ago broad cloth was being made up for dress clothes. It was the usual custom with coat and waistcoat (either frock or dress) of broad cloth, to have the trousers of doeskin, the latter being heavier and more fitted for the purpose.

A hundred years ago, when the dress coat was worn for day as well as evening wear, broad cloths of bright colours, such as blue, green, plum, claret, brown, etc., were the vogue. The term "broad cloth" distinguished it from narrower and inferior fabrics.

Brocade.—A fabric with decorative figures or patterns, usually floral, woven in. It is made on a Jacquard loom. Originally it was heavy silk with a pattern in gold and silver threads. Brocaded satin may show the pattern by the difference in reflection of light on the weave.

Broken Twill.—A design or plan in which the effect is that of an ordinary twill arranged in a broken or non-continuous order. In this variation of the regular twill weave the direction of the twill is reversed, giving a zigzag effect, to which the term "herringbone " is applied.

Brilliantine.—Wiry silk-wool fabric, like alpaca, but usually of higher lustre; made from Angora-goat hair. Used in the same way as alpaca.

Buckram.—A coarse cloth made of linen and stiffened with size or glue. Another definition gives it as a stout material made of hemp or low-grade flax yarns, woven loosely and stiffened with gum, used as a stiffening in dresses, for making hat shapes and for binding books. It is known mainly to tailors as a stiffening for " stand " collars for military uniforms. There have been various suggestions as to the origin of the word. It has been said that its resistance ingeniously suggested the combined strength of a buck and a ram. Another fanciful assumption is that it was coined from two words " buck," meaning to bleach or boil a cloth in lye or suds, and " ram," meaning to fill and make compact by force.

These explanations appear fantastic, and I favour the theory that it was named after Bokhara, the Tartar city, where a similar material was once made in a fine and costly form. Silks and woollens and other fabrics have, from time immemorial, been manufactured in that eastern city, and its bazaars gorged with the richest wares of Europe and Asia. It may also be said that the Bokhara district is notable for its hemp and other fibres employed in textile manufacture.

Buckskin.—A thick, heavily milled woollen cloth, usually woven in white or buff tint. Its high gloss finish gives it an appearance somewhat resembling kerseymere cloth, a distinguishing difference being that its twill pattern is discernible on the face. Its firm and serviceable texture, chiefly due to the prolonged fulling treatment given in finishing, likens it to a buck's hide, which is responsible for its name. It is used for riding breeches and livery breeches, and at one time four-in-hand coaching overcoats were made from it.

A technical description is : A cloth of a fine warp surface, sateen twill texture ; originally made of fine woollen yarns.

Buckskin Weave.—An eight-end twill pattern, largely used in the weaving of fine woollen cloths, indicating the appearance of the leather of that name. Another description is: A point-paper plan usually based upon the 8-warp sateen, to which a dot is added, thus producing an upright warp twill effect.

Buggy.—The strip of lining across back neck, which gives a finish at that part of the coat, when the back is otherwise unlined. In the wholesale trade when the lining comes 4" or · 5" below the scye, it is still called a buggy ; but in the bespoke it would probably be referred to as " half-lined."

Burat.—A light woollen fabric, generally used for making priests', barristers', and college dons' robes.

Burling.—Originally the operation of removing burrs from cloths made of wool, but now synonymous with inspection of cloths. The cloth is hung over the top roller of a frame placed in a good light, and drawn over yard by yard, the burler marking the faults in weaving or colour, or picking out the burrs with his iron.

Butcher's Linen.—A kind of bleached crash which was originally used for butchers' aprons. It is said to have been almost replaced by art crashes and Indian Head.

Butternut.—Descriptive of a colour (brown) applied to a coarse woollen homespun fabric, extensively worn in the country districts of the Southern States of America before and during the Civil War. It took its name, which was a sort of badge of economy, from the fact that the cloth was dyed with the bark of the butternut or walnut tree.

C

Cadet Cloth.—The regulation bluish-grey woollen cloth of standard colour, composition, structure, and weight provided for uniforms for cadets at the United States Military Academy, and adopted also by other public and private military schools, etc. The shade of colour is attained by a corded mixture of definite percentages of indigo-dyed wool and bleached white wool, spun into woollen yarn and woven and finished like a heavy flannel.

Calamanco.—A woollen cloth woven with a variegated warp which shows checks on one side of the cloth, formerly manufactured almost exclusively in the Netherlands, but now made at Roubaix and other European towns, as well as in England.

Calendering.—The operation by which textile fabrics are pressed smooth and made lustrous. The calendering machine consists of rollers, technically termed bowls, placed above each other, in contact, the pressure of which is regulated so that the cloths passed through may be pressed as required.

Calico.—The name is derived from Calicut, India, where cloth was first printed with wood blocks by hand. It was originally a fine printed cotton fabric, but has become an inferior material. Narrow and coarse, it is made from cheap grade cotton and highly sized.

Cambric.—A fine muslin cloth made of fine flax or cotton. The texture of linen cambric is regular, clear and fine, with a thready feel. To obtain the same result in cotton the warp must be hard and fine, and is composed, as a rule, of Egyptian cotton. The material is used for handkerchiefs and fine underclothing and certain makes are said to have a limited use as a tailor's trimming. Originally made at Cambrai.

Cambric (lining).—A thin, narrow, stiff, glazed cotton fabric made from poorer yarns than underwear cambric. May be white or piece-dyed. It is always sized, and has a high polish, on the right side. Does not launder. It is used for linings, pattern modelling, and fancy dress costumes.

Camel's Hair.—A fabric with a hairy surface made entirely or partly of camel's hair. In cheaper grades, cow hair is used, when the material is called camel's hair back. Used for coats, overcoats, and horse blankets.

Camlet.—The generic term for goods composed of camel's hair, or imitations of such fabrics. Some of the kinds are :

Camblet : a thin stuff originally made of camel's hair, but now of wool and silk, or goat's hair and wool or silk. Camelot : a low-grade quality of cloth, woven of flat hair or hairy wool. Camoca : a cloak or mantle fabric consisting of camel's hair and silk.

Campbell Twill.—An 8-thread weave of the irregular sateen derivative class—also termed Mayo, or Campbell coating. According to an authority on the subject, in 1887 Campbell and Corkscrew twills were mostly worn for " best," but are not often seen now. It is also known as " Scotch " twill, probably because it originated in Scotland ; but Mayo or Campbell is correct.

Cangette.—Small serge twill : said to have been manufactured first at Caen, whence the name is derived.

Cannelle.—A cloth with a ribbed weft effect ; also called rep.

Canton Crêpe.—Same as crêpe de chine, only heavier and richer-looking.

Canton Finish.—A dull mangle finish, imparting to cotton fabrics a firm feel, but without harshness.

Canton Flannel.—A cotton flannel, having a twill weave face to the cloth, with a soft downy nap on the back, available in unbleached, bleached, or plain colours. Used for pocketings, linings, undergarments, and bath robes. It is not strictly a flannel, but converted cotton goods. The name is derived from Canton, China, which city did a flourishing business in such stuff.

Canton Linen.—Commonly called grass cloth, Chinese grass cloth, or grass linen. A fine, translucent fabric which looks like linen. Made of ramie fibre (china grass). It wrinkles like linen, but has a distinctive, clear, oiled appearance due to the lustre of ramie fibres when not twisted. It is much worn in China in the stiff (or natural gum) unbleached state. Mostly hand-woven. Cool and durable. Bleached, or dyed blue.

Cantoon.—A kind of stout fustian, with a cord effect on one side.

Canvas.—Originally a cloth made with hemp yarns, and named from the word *cannabis*, signifying hemp ; but the term has come to be applied to rough, heavy fabric woven of flax and cotton, and sometimes jute. The lowest grades of canvas, made of jute or rough hemp, are used for outside coverings of packages ; better grades, mostly made of flax or linen, range from the gum-stiffened material used for inside linings or heavy garments, softer makes also for interlinings, up to finer cloths for making good-class towels. The linen make is probably the best for interlining coats.

Caracul.—An imitation of astrachan fur, woven with a lustrous wool pile on a plain ground.

Carding.—A process in which the staples and fibres of material are thoroughly disentangled and subsequently blended together so as to produce a film or sliver of material of a uniform character.

Casement Cloth.—A linen fabric, used for light summer dresses ; a fabric, either linen or cotton, woven twill, herringbone or plain, and worn by ladies ; a plain linen used as curtains for casement windows. Mohair, alpaca, lustre, and all-cotton fabrics, on occasion, are known by this name.

Cashan.—A heavy twill cotton cloth, resembling silesia, but heavier.

Cashmere.—A fine, light texture, warp of cotton or wool ; weft always of a fine Botany yarn ; weave 2/1 weft twill. The warp is set fairly close, but a great number of picks per $\frac{1}{4}''$ are inserted, thus giving what is known as the " Cashmere Twill," or " Plain-back." Other definitions are : A light-weight dress fabric, originally made from the fine soft wool of the Cashmere goat, but now (both in England and America) from soft, native wools. It is similar to Henrietta, but not so closely woven or highly polished. And : A material in solid staple colours for overcoats and in fancy effects for vests, made of fine-quality woollen yarn, and given a very soft finish to resemble its proto-type, an Asiatic cloth made from the downy hair of the wild Kashmir goats of Indian and Chinese Thibet.

Cashmerette.—A soft, lustrous fabric made in imitation of real cashmere cloth, composed entirely of cotton.

Cassimere.—A 4-end twill weave, " two-and-two " in technical phrase, and the pattern most frequently employed in the manufacture of woollen goods. The exact meaning of the term has been lost, probably because of a confusion between " kerseymere " and " Cashmere," the former being an open sort of coarse woollen cloth. At any rate, cassimere is now very loosely applied to various grades of woollen and worsted cloths woven 2-end two-and-two twill.

Another definition reads : General name for a class of cloths in fancy effects, made of hard twisted woollen yarn, usually woven with a twill and finished with the face side closely sheared ; used principally for men's suits.

Castor.—A heavy quilted all-wool face-finished fabric suitable for overcoats ; it is heavier than kersey, but a little lighter than beaver. The word is also used to describe a ladies' glove made of beaver skin, a silk hat, and a tall hat made of beaver.

Celtic Twill.—A weave with a sateen base, otherwise spoken of as twilled hopsack.

Chain-stitch.—This is exclusively used for ornamentation, and is in reality an elongated loop-stitch, formed in precisely the same manner, except that the needle is put forward instead of sideways, and begun from the right instead of the left.

Chain Weave.—A cloth weave that attained popularity some years ago, the face effect on clear finished staple worsted goods being that of a succession of small cable-chain links in a narrow diagonal twill throughout the fabric. Johann Erckens Söhne, cloth manufacturer, Burtscheid, Prussia, brought out this design, with the result that the " Erckens " chain weave, like the well-known " Clay " diagonal, had many imitators.

A simpler definition is of a chain twill : A twilled fabric of a chain character or appearance, obtained by a combination of weave and material.

Challis, Challie, or Chally.—Light-weight woollen material in smooth weave. Has beautiful plain and printed colour combinations ; wears satisfactorily, and is easily cleaned. An excellent material for dresses and négligés.

Chamois.—While not actually a cloth, chamois is a serviceable tailor's trimming material ; it is used for pocketing, for lining ladies' riding breeches, and in cold countries for interlining coats. Real chamois is the dressed skin of the small antelope or chamois living on the ridges of the Alps. Imitation chamois is made from the split hides of young bulls, or the skins of sheep.

Charmeuse.—A light-weight, rich-looking soft satin with a dull back. It is sometimes described as a very soft satin with a subdued lustre, due to the twist in warp. It drapes well. Crêpe charmeuse is clinging and has a dull finish.

Cheese Cloth.—A coarse muslin originally used for wrapping cheese ; sometimes used for trimming or pattern modelling.

Check.—The term given to the square appearance produced on a fabric by employing a special weave or two or more colours of warp and weft specially arranged to give this appearance. Another definition reads : A rectangular pattern formed by crossing warp and weft of different colours upon each other, or by changing the weave so as to form squares on the width and length of the cloth. A check may be formed very simply by weaving so many ends twill and so many plain, and reversing on the repeat, the warp ends woven twill in the first instance being woven plain in the second.

Cheviot.—A rough woollen fabric, either of staple or fancy character, and made in various weaves, but usually with a twill predominating ; used for suits and overcoats. The name refers to the Cheviot Hills of Scotland, the sheep of that region yielding rough, shaggy wool. By a system of napping in worsted cloth finishing, by which the fibres of the yarns comprising the material are raised to form a rough nap, " worsted cheviots " are produced.

To give another definition : The kind of woollen cloth woven on the Scottish Border with the wool of the Cheviot sheep, and formerly the name given to that class of goods as distinguished from Saxonys, the finer class of woollens. The term is still applied to all kinds of rough tweeds, though Cheviot wool is not now extensively used, and a large proportion of those fabrics are woven with shoddy yarns.

A succinct definition is : All woollens of coarser grade than 56's quality.

Chiffon.—A thin gauze-like fabric with soft or sometimes a stiff finish. Chiffon cloth is heavier in weight than chiffon, and more durable. As a descriptive term, it indicates light weight and soft finish, as chiffon velvet or taffeta.

Chinchilla.—A soft-bodied woollen cloth used for winter overcoats, the face side of which is covered with small nibs or tightly twisted tufts. These nibs are treated in the cloth-finishing operation, whereby the fabric is run through a specially constructed machine provided with a flat metal plate covered with strong corduroy or corrugated rubber. This plate is lowered upon the cloth (a downy nap having previously been raised on the goods), and when the said plate is given a circular motion, the nibs are rubbed upon the intended face side of the material. The name is taken from Chinchilla, a village in Spain, where such a kind of cloth was first made.

The fur named Chinchilla is of a pearly grey shade, obtained from a small animal of the rodent species, native to Chile, South America, and used for muffs, stoles, scarfs, and other fur articles of wear. It is very costly.

Clay Worsted.—A fabric with a twill similar to serge, but with the diagonal lines lying so flat to the surface as to be almost imperceptible. This particular weave owes its name to its long association with the mill products of J. T. Clay, of Rastrick, Yorkshire. " Clay " weaves, or " Clay " diagonals, have come to mean a special weave formation rather than the output of a certain cloth manufacturer.

Closing.—Sewing the centre of back seam and felling the lining at the same place.

Cloud Yarn.—A term given to yarns of irregular twist obtained by alternately holding one of the component threads while the other—being delivered quickly—is twisted round it, and then reversing the position of the two threads, thus producing alternate clouds of the two colours. This effect may also be produced by the action of the bar on the twisting frame coming in between the two threads to be twisted.

Coating.—Worsted in weights suitable for men's wear.

Cobourg.—A cloth made from cotton warp and Botany weft, with an interlacing of the 2/1 or cashmere weave.

College Cloth.—A soft make of thin woollen cloth, something like Russell cord.

Combination Twill.—A twill produced by combining two simple twills together, thread and thread, or two threads and one thread, etc. ; or pick and pick ; or two picks and one pick, etc.

Corduroy.—The word is the anglicising of a French phrase, *corde du Roi*, meaning " cord of the king," and so called because it was originally made and exclusively used for clothes for the huntsmen of a certain Bourbon King of France. The material is technically classified as a " pile " fabric, being a strong corded velveteen made of cotton, with the ribs in regular repeat on the face of the goods running lengthwise in the piece. The back is finished plain. Colours are staple and solid, including, besides black and white, blues, browns, greens, greys, and their various shades ; also in mottled effects known as partridge cord. The pile is made of mercerised yarns formed by an extra filling or weft in the loom. A special cutting machine secures the round effect on the pile. The size of the rib gives it distinctive names, thus : Thickset : the narrowest rib made ; 9-shaft, ribs 9 to the inch ; 8-shaft, ribs 8 to the inch. Constitution : very wide ribs.

Corkscrew.—This has nothing in common with a certain spiral steel instrument looked upon by prohibitionists as a symbol, for the old-time weave of cloth thus named has no circular or spiral pattern, but is, in reality, a ribbed twill. How it got its name I have never been able to find out. In its loom construction only the warp-threads of the fabric are made to appear on the face, and the design is limited to clear finished staple worsted suitings. Very few corkscrews are used to-day, but thirty or forty years ago they were made up for morning coats, dress suits, etc.

A technical description of a corkscrew cloth is : A closely set fabric usually made from fine worsted yarns, and presenting the appearance of a warp rib running almost in the weft direction ; and of a corkscrew weave : A twilled warp rib running at a low angle.

Cotton-back.—A double or extra warp cloth, the upper side or face being of worsted or woollen yarns, while the underside, or back, is constructed of cotton yarns. If a double fabric, the face and the back are usually of different weaves, both ingeniously interstitched together in the process of manufacture.

Cotton-warp.—A cloth in which the warp system is of cotton yarns and the weft of worsted or woollen yarns. Cotton being a comparatively stronger fibre than wool, it is thus used for the warp rather than for the weft, to withstand the strain and friction of the threads incidental to weaving ; hence such a self-descriptive name for the fabric.

Cotton Worsted.—Imitation worsted cloths, either of fancy or staple character, but more often in fancy colour and weave effects, woven from combed cotton yarns and given a hard "worsted" finish. Made for the very cheap clothing trade.

Cottonade.—A fabric made in imitation of fancy cassimere for men's wear ; sometimes simply a cotton material imitating something else.

Covert Coating.—A medium-weight cloth of woollen or worsted yarns. The warp is formed of two-ply yarns, one of which is white (slightly twisted). This gives a specked effect in colour. Colours : castor, tan green, grey, or drab. It wears well, and is used for overcoats, riding habits, suits, etc. The term is sometimes applied to fabrics that have an appearance akin to the standard fabric. The original use of such material for shooting dress favours the assumption that the name came from the thicket or covert in which the pursued game took refuge.

Crash.—A rough texture in linen or cotton, or a combination of the two. Various effects are produced by close or open weaves, and by rough or smoothly spun yarns. Colour : natural, bleached, half-bleached, or dyed. Among other uses it is made up in dresses and suits. From the Latin *crassus*, meaning coarse.

Cravenette.—A showerproof cloth, named after Craven, the inventor.

Crêpe.—One kind of crêpe is a thin, crimped black gauze made of silk or cotton ; used as a mourning accessory material. Crêpe, used by tailors for clergymen's and elderly men's garments, is a soft, lustre-finished worsted cloth, with the weave on the face of the fabric presenting the appearance of minute wrinkles, and dyed black.

Crêpe de Chine.—A fabric produced from a fine silk warp and a right and left (open band and cross band) tightly twisted worsted weft, this latter during the finishing operation disturbing the straightness of both itself and the warp, and thus producing a crêpe effect.

Crêpe Weave.—An interlacing of threads and picks in a more or less mixed or indiscriminate order to produce an appearance of a finely broken character, usually associated with crêpe cloths.

Crepoline.—A fabric of a warp rib character, in which the regular order of the weave is so broken as to give it a " rib-crêpe " effect.

Crêpon.—A structure, as the name implies, of a crêpe-like character, this being obtainable in at least five ways : (a) By combination of materials ; (b) by combination of weaves ; (c) by combination of (a) and (b) ; (d) by mechanical arrangement during weaving ; (e) by subjecting fabrics specially constructed to a special chemical process during finishing.

Crinoline.—Originally a stiff fabric composed of horsehair and cotton for holding out a lady's dress, and later a petticoat expanded with hoops of whalebone or steel ; but now applied to a kind of hat frame made of horsehair, or imitation of it, stiffened and shaped. There is a make of haircloth used for interlinings, called crinoline.

Cross-bred.—A term applied to wools obtained from sheep of mixed breed. The bulk of the wool used in manufacture is cross-bred ; it is strong and useful, but lacks fineness and high quality.

Cross-stitch.—This is used for ornamentation, or as a substitute for felling in thin and washing materials, or those liable to fray on the edge. The formation of the stitch begins on the left and consists in passing the needle alternately on and off the edge, slightly through the material and in advance of the last stitch. A development of the cross-stitch producing two distinct appearances is also occasionally used for ornamental purposes.

Crow Twill.—The 3/1 twill ; the simplest form of four-end twill, used in producing swansdown and other twilled goods.

Crutch, or Crotch.—A fork ; the angle formed by the parting of two legs or branches. It is used sometimes for the fork of trousers.

A Crutch Lining is that which is placed at fork to cover the junction of the four seams.

A Crutch Piece is a piece sewn on to the undersides at fork, when the material is not wide enough.

Curtains.—A term used to describe the pieces of material, usually of same fabric as waistband linings, put across the top of undersides from side seam to seat seam.

Curved Twill.—A waved pattern produced by a graduated variation in the twill weave.

D

Damask.—Originally a figured silk fabric, introduced from Damascus, in Syria, the silk variety now being known as satin damask. Cotton, linen, and worsted are now used in its manufacture. The figuring is produced by varying the prominence of the weft and the warp, making, for instance, the figures by warp satin, and the ground weft satin. Linen damasks are produced on the same principle, the figures being warp-flushed satin and the ground weft-flushed satin. For this reason all damasks are reversible, the figures on the back being formed by the weft and the ground by the warp. Linen damask is sometimes called Dammasse.

Dam-brod.—A black and white check in squares, resembling the figures on a draught-board.

Dandy Canvas.—A rather heavy make of flax material, used to interline coats.

Delaine.—A light all-wool cloth of plain weave. It is usually printed in various designs and colours. The term probably has its origin in " Mousselaine delaine," signifying wool muslin.

Denim.—A coarse cotton drilling or twill, usually made with coloured warp threads of blue and the weft of white threads, giving a blue and white weave effect. Its use for clothing is limited to such things as workmen's overalls. The word comes from the French town of Nîmes, " serges de Nîmes."

Derby Tweed.—A hard make of woollen cloth finished in a twill pattern.

Devon.—A very heavy make of woollen cloth finished with a bright smooth surface. Mostly made up for livery overcoats ; same as Box-cloth.

Dhoti.—An Indian cotton garment piece worn by the men round the waist and over the thighs ; worn 2 to 7 yards in length, and 2' to 4' in width, with a figured pattern at one end always and occasionally at both ends ; the plain-woven striped cotton fabric manufactured in Lancashire to supply Dhotis to the lower-grade natives of India ; also Dhooti, Dhuti, Dhooty, and Dhotee.

Diagonal.—A weave formation, produced by any kind of yarn, in which the cloth design, instead of describing perpendicular or horizontal lines, has straight oblique welts at some angular degree, in regular repeat through the fabric ; in other words, a twill. When a " Diagonal " is spoken of in the trade it is understood to mean a hard-finished staple worsted cloth with a well-defined right-hand twill face, as the Clay Diamond, or a standard serge.

Diamond Twill.—A lozenge pattern, produced by reversing the weave of warp and weft in a common twill.

Diaper.—A fabric on which small square figures are woven. Formerly diaper was a silk fabric, but at present the name is chiefly associated with linens having a small diamond-shaped pattern or figure in a square, though the fabric is also imitated in cotton.

Dice.—Small squares of different colours. Diced patterns are used for edgings of dresses, stockings, etc., and as tartan for the bands of Highland bonnets.

Dimity.—A stout cotton cloth similar to a fustian, but not usually so thick in texture, being frequently figured with raised stripes. In the seventeenth century, we are told, Manchester imported cotton from Cyprus and Smyrna, and worked it into fustian, vermilions, and dimities. It is said, however, that dimity was originally brought from India.

Doeskin.—A closely woven, face-finished woollen cloth, generally a warp-faced twill, heavily felted, and cropped to a fine, smooth surface so as to resemble the skin of an animal. Another definition : A fine woollen cloth made from the best Botany wool, finely spun and finely set in the loom, with the five-sateen warp interlacing being employed.

This fine black cloth of compact weave and finish was at one time made into dress trousers to wear with coat and waistcoat of broadcloth. It is still used for livery trousers.

Domett.—A flannel cloth with a cotton warp, napped on both sides, and used extensively for warm linings, shirts, and such purposes. If a tailor had to define this material he would probably do so in these terms : A soft make of woollen material, very loose and spongy, used mostly for padding, and especially to fill out the fronts of a dress coat under the silk facing.

Double Cloth.—A cloth woven with two warps and one filling, one warp and two fillings, two fillings and two warps, or with a fifth set of bindery yarns to unite the two cloths. Both sides may be alike, or show a pattern reversed in colour or design.

Drab.—A thick, woollen fabric, generally of a reddish-brown colour.

Drabette.—A twill cotton material of rather hard finish, usually drab in colour.

Draft.—A draft (or draught) is a sketch, drawing, or plan. To chalk a garment out by system is to make a draft. The instruction " to draft " means to draw.

Drap d'Alma.—Soft, double-diagonal twill. A good fabric for dresses and suits.

Drap d'Été.—A worsted fabric, used principally for religious garments, very fine twill, and closely woven.

Drawing.—This is a stitch sewn on the surface for the purpose of joining two double edges together, so as to give it the appearance of being seamed in the ordinary way, as in the case of collar ends. It consists in alternately passing the needle through each double edge, and drawing the thread moderately tight, so as to pull the two edges close together. Another form of drawing is a stitch substituted in the case of thick materials, to join two edges together in place of serging. The stitch is formed by passing the needle alternately under and over each edge of the cloth.

Drawing-in.—It may be described as a running stitch drawn tight so as to gather the material more or less upon itself ; but in this form it is seldom used by the tailor, except for basting purposes. There is another form of drawing-in, used for the production of piping in various descriptions of robes, as in the gowns of barristers, etc. These are made of thin material, the backs and sleeves being gathered, in the form of piping, on to a shoulder-piece.

Dress.—To take the " dress " from a pair of trousers is to cut a section from the right side at fork, to make it fit as closely as the left.

Drill, or Drilling.—A stout twilled cotton material, bleached, unbleached or piece-dyed ; usually unbleached. A light drill is called jean, or middy twill. A khaki-coloured drill is called khaki.

Duck.—A heavy canvas-like cotton fabric used for tents. Usually two warp yarns are treated as one in weaving. Bleached, unbleached, dyed or printed. In lighter weights it is used for men's and women's suits and middies. It is so called because it sheds water.

Duffel.—A thick woollen frieze cloth having a thick nap ; a cloth woven with cotton warp and an open-spun woollen weft, used for warm loose robes and dressing-gowns. This is said to be one of the historic names connected with the industry, and probably derived from the town of same name in Brabant (Flanders).

Dungaree.—A coarse cotton fabric, usually dyed blue, worn originally by Indian coolies, but now in general use among firemen and engineers.

Duvetyn.—A soft velvety material, first made from spun silk. It may be wool or silk, or a combination. Fine soft woollen yarns on face. Fine downy nap raised with an emery cylinder. It is of continental origin and is known under a variety of names, such as " velours," " mouse-skin," etc.

E

Ecru Silk.—Silk from which only a small amount of natural gum has been removed.

Eider-down Cloth.—A warm, light, elastic cloth with heavy nap on one or both sides. The surface is napped to give a light, fluffy feel.

Elongated Twills.—A class of twills in which the angle is greater than 45 degrees.

Elysian.—Heavy woollen cloth, napped in a wave-like pattern. Used for overcoats.

Eolienne.—Similar to poplin, but lighter in weight. Usually silk warp with cotton or worsted filling. From the Greek, Æolus, God of the Winds.

Épingle.—Fine rib effect running cross-wise of cloth. A variety of fabrics are referred to as épingles.

Éponge.—French, meaning sponge. A soft, loose fabric similar to ratine, cotton, wool, or silk. The warp is usually hard-twisted, with nubby or looped filling yarns. Made into dresses and suits.

Estamene.—A cloth made from cross-bred yarn, usually employing the 2/2 or 3/3 twill. It is given a raised rough finish.

Étamine.—Soft, light-weight woollen in plain open weave. Used for shirred and pleated dresses.

Extra Warp or Weft.—The term given to warp or weft threads which are added to a single cloth with the object of (*a*) increasing the weight of the cloth ; (*b*) figuring the cloth ; (*c*) both increasing the weight and figuring at one and the same time.

F

Fabric.—Any kind of article made by a combination of textile yarns ; it is the most comprehensive term that can be used in the textile trade. Cloth, which ranks next to fabric in comprehensiveness, cannot be used to denote lace, net, carpet, and knitted goods ; but all these are fabrics—that is, materials made with textile fibres or yarns.

Face.—The right or upper side of a cloth ; the front of a backed or double cloth.

Face Finish.—The finish given to woollen and worsted cloths to cover the face with a soft and regular nap.

Faced Cloths.—Those cloths which have a different weave or finish on the front, or face, from the back.

Falls.—Falls are of two kinds ; one is a whole or full fall, and the other is a split fall. The former opens or has the vents at each side, and buttons across the top on to the bearers horizontally, serving the same purpose as a fly. The split fall does not button all the way across, and was so named because the half width of each topside was cut or split vertically down the fronts. Split falls nowadays are only placed in riding breeches.

The Fall Seam is an expression which is dying out, except in country trades. It is the same as the fly line, but instead of an opening there is a seam ; it was termed " fall seam " because the old style of trousers was finished with a fall.

Fancies.—Vari-coloured woollen cloths, or wool cloths woven other than plain ; ribbons and silks with coloured patterns.

Fastness of Colour, or Dye.—Property of dye to retain its colour when exposed to sun or washing. The term "fastness" is a comparative one, as a dye might be extremely fast to light and only moderately fast to washing. No colour is absolutely fast to all conditions.

Fearnaught.—A heavy woollen cloth, with a shaggy nap, used for making overcoats. It has also been described as a name for heavy woollen cheviot cloths in the Batley trade.

Felling.—In its simplest form felling consists of sewing one piece of material, by its edge, upon another, the sewn edge being either raw or turned in according to the material, or the purpose to be accomplished.

There are three methods of applying this form of sewing.

In very fine and delicate work, such as felling silk linings and facing, sewing on braids, etc., a form of side-stitch is utilised. In this method the needle is put close to the side of the thread, where it leaves the upper material ; but just under its edge a sufficiently firm hold is taken of the under material to prevent breaking away, and the point of the needle is brought up to catch the extreme edge of the top layer. The hand is drawn out so as to allow the stitch to be pulled home lightly. This is the ordinary application of the felling-stitch.

Another method of applying it is similar to the hemming-stitch used by women, and is employed by the tailor when raw edge cloth is to be felled.

Still a third form of stitch is prick-felling, which is used in connection with tacking, the needle being inserted alternately from the top and underside.

Felting.—The process of making felt ; the operation by which woollen cloths are shrunk and compacted, the fibres in the cloths being pressed and kneaded under beaters, or rollers, so as to draw them closer and cause them to adhere.

Fents.—Short damaged lengths of cloths, or short lengths cut from piece ends.

Fine Drawing.—This is a process by which two edges are joined together without the sewing being visible ; in practice it is used for mending tears. A very fine needle must be used, and one strand of the finest twist. Then the needle is passed backwards and forwards across the edges to be joined, and just under the surface of the material ; but, at each insertion of the needle, the length of the stitch must be varied, so as to prevent the appearance of a ridge at the ends of the sewing.

Fish.—A fish is a cut or dart, taken from the waist of various garments, to give a closer fit at waist and to throw round or ease at breast or seat. It owes its name to its rough resemblance to a fish, being wider in the middle than at either end.

Five-end Twill.—A twill which is completed on five warp ends, the regular pattern flushing four warp threads, or four weft picks every shot, the remaining thread in each case being the binder. Five-end satin, however, is a broken twill in which the binding stitches, instead of being in regular succession, are distributed as widely as possible over the figure.

Firette.—A light woollen or cotton cloth, woven diagonal twill, and made at Troyes ; it is mostly used for linings.

Flannel.—A soft woollen fabric of open texture with a fine nap, generally woven plain, but may be twilled ; it is used for warm undergarments, suits and costumes, and thick linings.

Flannelette.—A structure made of cotton from soft mule-spin yarns, the fabric being subsequently raised to give an imitation of the true wool flannel.

Flap.—A flap is a covering for the pocket mouth.

Flecked.—A spotted appearance on either yarns or fabrics due to some distinctive colour or material thrown in some way or other on to the ground texture or colour.

Flocks.—Very short wool fibres thrown off by different processes in woollen and worsted manufacture, such as shearing. Used for increasing the body of woollens by pressing in after weaving.

Florentine.—A kind of twilled silk used in making fancy waistcoats, and for covering cloth buttons; 4-shaft cotton drill.

Florentine Twill.—A weave suitable for lustre fabrics on eight threads and eight picks.

Fly.—An inner flap on trousers, overcoat, etc., to conceal a row of buttons. In trousers the fly is on the opening in front on the left side, and is stitched on to conceal the method of fastening. It is made up and has buttonholes worked in it before being fastened to the left topside.

The **Fly Line** is the line up the centre of front from the fork to the top of the waistband.

The **Fly Catch,** or button catch, is the counterpart of the fly, and is seamed on to the right topside. The buttons on the fly catch fasten to the fly, to keep the trousers closed in front.

A **Blind Fly** is one that is fastened down instead of being left open between the buttons.

Fork.—In trousers the fork has two meanings. It is used to describe the point at which the legs join ; and also means the small sections on both topsides and undersides which extend beyond the fly line. The latter is more correctly termed " fork quantity."

Foulard.—A fabric which has a coloured pattern produced by first padding the cloth through the dye and then discharging either to a white, or substituting another colour by mixing it with the discharge paste.

Foule.—An all-Botany wool cloth which receives a severely milled finish, thus hiding the weave structure.

Four-end Twill.—A twill weave containing four warp ends in the repeat ; it is used to distinguish the common twill of that size from the cassimere twill, which is written 2/2 instead of 3/1 in the designer's plan.

French Merino.—A fine worsted dress cloth, originally

made in France, but now manufactured in this country, though the quality of the goods has been greatly reduced.

Frieze.—A heavy woollen overcoating having a nap on the face. Similar to chinchilla, but a lower-grade fabric. The nap is heavy and shaggy, without balls, as in chinchilla. Woollen yarns of coarse-quality wool. Shoddy is often employed in the modern fabric, and mixed colours are used. I have always heard that frieze was originally made in Ireland, but recently read that it was first produced in the Province of Friesland, Holland. However this may be, the Irish make has a reputation second to none.

Frog Pocket.—A triangular-shaped pocket in trousers, opening about 4½″ across the waistband, and about 4½″ down the side seam from the waistband seam ; fastened in the corner with a hole and button.

Fulling.—An operation through which wool cloth is passed to increase it in thickness, density, and solidity, and also to improve it in handle.

Fustian.—A class of stout double-weft cotton fabrics, those woven satin twill, and with the face weft cut to form a pile, being variously named velveteen, beaverteen, or corduroy, according to the sett of the twill and the manner in which the pile is cut and finished ; other fustians are cantoon, moleskin, etc. It is said that the original fustian, a coarse-twilled stuff, was made at El Fustat (Cairo) Egypt, where it was given the low Latin name of Fustaneum.

G

Gabardine, or Gaberdine.—A firm material similar to whipcord. Also made in cotton. Worsted yarns. May be hard, smooth finish like worsted, or dull, soft finish, like woollens. The word is a striking instance of how the meaning and value of a term may gradually change. Originally it was used to describe a coarse outer garment or cloak. Shylock, it will be recalled, in his diatribe, cried : " You spit upon my Jewish gaberdine." The second stage was for gabardine to be used as a description of raincoats. Finally it was adopted as a name for cloths suitable for raincoats.

Galloon.—A silk, woollen, or union tape used for binding and braiding ; embroidered trimming made in narrow width of silk or cotton ; a narrow lace made of gold, silver, or other metal threads, employed in edging and trimming uniforms.

Gambroon.—A rather heavy twilled linen cloth used for linings.

Gauntlet Cuffs.—Cuffs with the ends pointed to project beyond the hindarm.

Gauze.—A weave in which the warp yarns, instead of lying parallel, twist about each other and are held by the filling so as to make an open lacy effect. When combined with a plain weave it is called leno. It was originally brought from Gaza as a silk fabric, but gauze is now commonly made of cotton.

Georgette.—A thin, sheer silk fabric, dull in texture, with a " crêpy " effect, due to right and left twist in both warp and filling yarns.

Gigging.—The process of producing a nap or raised surface on cloths by passing them through the gig.

Gimp.—A narrow flat-braiding made of silk twisted over cord or wire. The gimp thread is suitable for making raised edges round buttonholes, or flat embroidery designs.

Gimp Yarn.—A thin, tightly twisted Botany worsted thread and a thick, soft thread of fine wool twisted together, the latter being wound spirally on the former, which forms the core of the yarn ; a combination of chain and screw twist, composed of four yarns, and made, as a rule, of mohair.

Gingham.—A plaided or checked cotton fabric suitable for dress goods. The word is said to be of Malay origin.

Glacé Silk.—A silk cloth which has been specially dressed for the purpose of obtaining a smooth and lustrous surface. It is sometimes of a figured character made from a fine cotton warp, with a comparatively thick mohair weft, which is made to do all the binding.

Glen Urquhart Check.—Briefly, a " Glen check." It is a compound colouring effect, the simplest example of which is two dark, two light, for a number of repeats, say twenty-four threads ; and four dark, four light, for the same number and wefted as warp.

Gloria.—Diagonal twilled weave of wool, silk, and cotton ; strong and durable ; sometimes called Zanella cloth.

Glossing.—The operation of steaming and stretching silk yarns to give them a glossy appearance ; sometimes calendering is described by the term.

Gordon Cord.—The name applied to a weave of a twilled cord character.

Grandelle, or Granderelle.—A fancy yarn produced by twisting two, three, or more threads of different colours into one, all the threads being delivered at equal tension, and therefore twisted equally ; a kind of shirting largely woven with granderelle yarns, generally twofold ; also grandrills, etc.

Granite Cloth.—A hard finished, pebbly cloth, its roughness suggesting the surface of granite.

Granite Weave.—A wide twill, giving a variegated effect.

Grenadine.—Usually silk or cotton, sometimes of worsted yarn. An open gauze-like fabric similar to marquisette, except that the latter has two warp yarns twisted about two filling yarns. Grenadine has two warps twisted around one filling. It is commonly known as marquisette. The term grenadine as now used covers many lace-like effects in weave. Some are two fabrics ; that is, a combination of plain and gauze weaves, which form window-like patterns in the cloth. These open spaces are not always produced by gauze weave, but by other contrivances for spacing warp and filling yarns.

Gros Grain.—A firm, stiff, closely woven, corded or grained fabric. Ribs vary from fifty to seventy per inch. Filling may be of cotton, but usually weighted silk. Cords are heavier and closer than those in poplin, more round than those in Faille.

Gun Club Check.—A simple check with three or four colours, thus : Six blue, six slate, six brown, six slate ; weft as warp. This gives the appearance of a check within a check.

Gypsy Cloth.—A heavily napped cotton fabric used in making tennis, boating, and cricket suits.

H

Hair Cloth.—A stiff, wiry fabric made of a cotton, worsted, or linen warp (usually cotton) and filling of horsehair. Hair is from the horse's mane. The fabric is as wide as the length of a hair. A single hair forms one pick of the filling. The forerunner of the present-day hair cloth, and similarly used, was a stuff made entirely of coarse hair and known as " lasting."

Hairline.—Strictly speaking, these stripes should be formed on the true hairline principle, which is, that for the stripe in the warp direction each colour of warp must be covered by its own colour of weft, and for the weft direction that each colour of weft should be covered by its own colour of warp.

The old West of England hairlines were so called because of their fine stripes. This cloth has become intimately associated with juvenile wear for trousers to accompany an Eton jacket.

Half-back Stitch.—This is much preferable to the back-and-fore stitch for the sewing of unimportant portions of a garment. It is formed by taking an incomplete back-stitch ; which is a thinly made stitch which locks behind at each application of the needle and thread, which the back-and-fore stitch does not.

Harlequin Check.—A plaid effect of a somewhat striking character in three or more distinct colours.

Heather Mixture.—The combination of woollen or worsted yarns of bright colours to produce a rich but subdued effect in both woven and knitted fabrics.

Heavy Goods.—Woollen and worsted cloths weighing over fourteen ounces to the yard.

Henrietta.—A term originally used to designate a fabric resembling cashmere, having a silk warp and wool filling or weft, but later employed to distinguish German from French cashmere. At present Henrietta is a fabric with a twill face and a smooth back, composed of different kinds of yarns, according to the grade of quality designed. When a silk warp is required, spun silk is used. A technical description reads : A cloth usually made from silk warp and from fine Botany weft, with a 2/1 weft twill heavily wefted. It was named in honour of Henrietta Maria, French Queen of England in 1624, wife of Charles I.

Herringbone.—A pattern very popular in tweeds and

worsted cloths, showing sharply zigzagged lines, and produced by reversing the draft of the warp in the repeat of a common twill, or by reversing the order in which the healds are lifted. It is also called a broken twill.

Holland.—A linen cloth of fine texture, either bleached or unbleached, and with a glazed or dull-faced finish ; used as a tailor's trimming material. Originally made in Holland.

Homespun.—Rough, loose, strong woollen cloth woven on hand looms. The term has been extensively used to define all coarse fabrics of a tweed character. The Law Courts, however, have declared that this description could only be applied to cloth the wool of which was hand-spun and woven on hand looms at home.

Honeycomb.—A pattern designed to form fitted squares on the surface of the fabric resembling the cells of the honeycomb.

Hopsack, or Matt Weave.—A weave which is produced by dividing the warp into two sheds only, a 2/2 hopsack being produced by two threads and two picks working together ; the 3/3 hopsack by three threads and three picks working together. Another definition is : A pattern in cloth produced by repeating in both warp and weft the plain weave on as many picks and ends as the figure requires, the effect being a series of small squares or mats.

Hunter's Pink.—A standard colour (vivid scarlet) that Melton cloths, intended for frock and dress (or clawhammer) coats for riding to hounds, are dyed.

I

Inauguration Cloth.—A heavyweight, superfine black, unfinished twill worsted fabric for double-breasted frock and morning coats, introduced by American textile mills as a timely creation ; and given such a distinguishing name in honour of President McKinley's induction into office.

India Linen.—A material slightly heavier than batiste, finished on a special calender to give it the appearance of linen.

Indian Head.—A heavy cotton fabric with much the same texture as butcher's linen. Made with soft or hard finish, white or colours. Among other things it is used for uniforms and shirts.

India Linon (cotton).—French for lawn. Fine, closely woven, white fabric. Generally firmer and more durable than lawn. It is used, *inter alia*, for dresses and lingerie.

Indigo.—The vegetable substance from which the most brilliant and durable blue dyes are obtained by various processes. The dyestuff is extracted from the leaves and stems of certain tropical and semi-tropical plants, and sold in cakes as commercial or impure indigo, which is afterwards purified into indigotin. It is the latter substance which is reduced to indigo white, and imparted to fabrics.

Indigo Dyeing.—The name given to the different methods of impregnating fabrics with indigo. Indigo-dyeing processes are numerous, but most of them, if not all, employ the principle of reducing the indigotin to indigo white in a solvent condition, and reconverting the substance into indigotin after dyeing, by exposure to the oxygen of the atmosphere.

Ingrain.—Originally a fabric dyed crimson, scarlet, or purple, with Kermes, known as scarlet grains ; later applied to fabrics made with wool yarns spun from dyed wools, as distinct from the same fabric printed. At present the term applies to fabrics dyed in the fibre or yarn before weaving.

Inlays.—Inlays are sometimes called outlets, and consist of the extra width left beyond what is required for seams, so that if any mistake has been made they can be utilised for enlargement.

Irish Duck.—A stout linen cloth used for overalls.

Irish Tweed.—A fancy tweed cloth woven with homespun yarns.

Italian Cloth.—A strong, lustrous lining, generally made of cotton and mohair or cotton and wool. A technical definition is : A cloth made of cotton warp and fine Botany or cotton weft, the weave being five-sateen weft face, and the balance of the cloth a greater number of picks to comparatively few threads. These fabrics are usually woven from black warp and grey weft, being piece-dyed. Italian cloth is sometimes called " farmer's satin." Italy being the original source of this material, it is said to have been largely used there for the garb of priests.

J

Jacconettes.—Tanjibs, Mulls, Cambrics, and Nainsooks are all varieties of plain cloth differing in width, length, counts of yarn, reed, and picks. These goods areall woven in the grey.

Jacquard.—The loom-mounting named after its inventor, Joseph Marie Jacquard, who was born at Lyons in 1752 and died in 1834. The Jacquard is the appliance almost universally employed for the purpose of producing very elaborate patterns in fabrics of all kinds. Jacquards are used in the production of fancy cloths, brocades, brocatelles, figured muslins, lace, knitted goods, etc.

Japanese Silk.—A silk fabric with a weft face and having a linen warp.

Jasper.—A fabric constructed of black warp and white weft, or white warp and black weft, to form grey or gun-metal shades.

Jean.—A heavy twilled cotton fabric like drilling, only a little finer and bleached ; also called middy twill. White, plain colours or stripes. In heavy grades it is used for suitings, corsets, pockets, etc. ; and in lighter makes for linings, underwear and children's clothes. A technical definition is : A cotton term for a three-shaft twill 2/1 made with weft predominating.

The name has undoubtedly some reference to Genoa, either as the place of its first manufacture or chief market. It has been suggested that perhaps the adoption of the term came about in Genoa through the merchants charging a Jane (a small silver coin) for so much of the goods. " Kentucky Jean," for clothing made of low woollen and cotton stock, in dark mixtures, with a coarse " satin " weave, is an American product.

Jeanette.—A similar fabric to jean, in which the warp predominates.

Jean Satin.—A smooth-faced, heavy twilled cotton.

Jersey Cloth.—Woollen or silk mixed stockinette weave. Used chiefly for undergarments and petticoats in the old days, but now a fashionable item of women's sports wear.

Jetting.—A beading or piping of cloth or other material at pockets, etc. A facing is sewn to the lower section of a pocket mouth, and, in turning it over, it is allowed to show instead of being turned underneath. Jettings may be placed at top as well as bottom of the pocket mouth. In the past edges were occasionally made up jetted. The dictionary gives the following meanings to the verb " jet " : to throw out, shoot forth, to encroach : and that is, with little doubt, the derivation of the tailor's term "jetting."

Jigger Button.—A name given by tailors to the button placed inside the left forepart of a man's double-breasted coat, or waistcoat, or the right side of a lady's, to keep the underneath forepart in position.

K

Kelt.—The Scottish name for cloth made of natural black and white wool mixed and spun together.

Kendal.—A green woollen cloth, originally made at Kendal, Westmorland.

Kersey.—A thick woollen cloth similar to Melton, but finished differently. It may contain cotton warp with wool filling, or have cotton mixed with yarn in wool, but usually has all woollen yarns. Felted, napped, and finished dull. Much like a heavy broadcloth without polish. Nap is not laid down.

Kerseymere.—Usually considered a corruption of cassimere.

Khaki.—An East Indian word meaning earth colour, or, as some say, dung, hence the appropriateness of this term in connection with the well-known shade in which field service military clothes of cotton or wool are dyed.

Kink.—A snarl or curl produced by a hard twisted thread receding upon itself.

Knickerbocker Yarns.—Yarns which are spotted or striped often in several colours. They may be produced in several ways, but the true knickerbocker yarn is produced by flecking the spotting material on to the carder.

Knop Yarn.— A kind of fancy yarn in which small knobs of fibre are gathered at intervals for effect ; a kind of doubled fancy wool yarn, generally vari-coloured, in which one of the yarns is gathered in spirals.

Knot.—A fault in a cloth, caused by the joining of broken warp or weft ; a looped tie.

L

Ladies' Cloth.—A dress flannel with a broadcloth finish. Lighter weight, less fulled and napped than broadcloth, but similar in appearance.

Lahore Cloth.—A name given to cloth made with cashmere wool.

La Jerz.—A heavy soft silk material resembling closely knitted fabric. Usually white, or with coloured stripes. It is used for blouses and shirts.

Lamb's-wool.—A fine yarn composed of the fine wool shorn from the young sheep in the first year ; the wool used for making very fine cloths.

Lansdowne.—A light-weight fabric with silk warp and fine worsted filling. Piece-dyed. Black, white and colours. It isused for dresses, etc.

Lasting.—A fine durable fabric made from strong wool or cotton, somewhat hard to handle but smooth in appearance.

Laventine.—A very thin silk fabric, chiefly suitable for linings of sleeves.

Lawn.—Takes its name from Laon, France, where it was originally made of linen. A light, thin cotton material, usually sized and highly polished. Also called India Linon. May have a soft or stiff finish. Fine lawns may take the place of organdies. Coarse grade called " lining lawn." Another definition is : A very fine fabric made of linen or cotton yarns of counts ranging from 75's to 83's warp and weft, the warp being of finer quality than the weft.

Left-hand Twill.—Designation for a twill weave where the diagonal inclines to the left (running from bottom to top), as distinguished from a twill inclining in a right-hand direction. Occasionally, to meet a demand for variety, dress worsteds or other kinds of staple fabric are woven in such reverse order of diagonal.

Leicester Wool.—A quality of wool finer than Lincoln (that is, about 40's to 44's), fairly long, most lustrous, and of light staple. Weight of fleece 7 to 9 lb., used for lustre fabrics, such as Sicilians, linings, etc.

Leno.—A kind of fine, open gauze, the warp threads of which are crossed upon each other, and held by the weft.

Levantine.—A stout twilled silk cloth, originally obtained form the Levant.

Lincoln Green.—A stout woollen cloth formerly woven and dyed at Lincoln.

Lincoln Wool.—Long and lustrous and thick, staple of 36's to 40's average quality. The weight of the fleece is 8 to 12 lb. It is used for lustre fabrics, such as Sicilians, linings, etc.

Line.—The twelfth part of an inch, used as a standard for measuring buttons and other articles ; the longer fibres of the raw flax, which is divided by hackling into line and tow.

Linen.—The fabrics made of flax fibres.

Linen Cambric.—A plain, fine, smooth white linen fabric.

Linen Goods.—Hessian, canvas, sail-cloth, French canvas, roughs, packsheet, holland, sheeting, twill sheeting, towelling, apron cloths, casement cloth, tea-cloth, grass cloth, huckaback, diaper, lawn, cambric, damask, etc.

Linsey Woolsey.—A strong fabric of coarse texture, made with a linen or cotton warp, and a wool or wool-and-cotton weft.

List.—The edge or selvedge of a piece.

Listed.—A defect which occurs on the list or edge of a piece such as the edge being torn away, stained, or otherwise damaged.

Livery Cloths.—General classification for fabrics of various character, such as buckskin, dress refine, Bedford cord, corduroy, velvet, Box cloth, striped Valencia vesting, etc., used for making distinctive garb for coachmen, footmen, grooms, butlers, chauffeurs, etc. Livery tweeds is a term to describe hard-wearing tweeds for coachmen and grooms, for undress—also called stable tweeds.

Llama.—A cloth made, with an admixture of fine wool, from the soft, furry hair of the South American Llama, a mountain animal somewhat resembling the camel, but smaller. Its luxurious character limits the use of such material, either the genuine or near imitations, to such apparel as frock coats, morning coats, and overcoats for formal wear.

London Shrunk.—A fabric fully shrunk, from which the mill finish has been removed to meet the preferences of tailors.

Loop-stitch.—This stitch has an affinity with the cross-stitch ; and in one of its forms, under the designation of " post-and-rail," it is used for overcasting edges when it is not desirable to increase their thickness by either binding or turning over and felling.

M

Mackinaw.—Typical mackinaw cloth, for the topcoat or belted jacket of the same name, popular among the "lumber-jacks" of North-west America. It is a heavy-weight, well-fulled, coarse-quality fabric with a large, bold check pattern of fancy colours, the lustrous and hairy features of its woollen composition being reflected in the finished goods.

Making Up.—A process which finished goods are put through, such as rolling, ticketing, papering, etc., in preparation for the market. Different markets require goods to be made up in special ways.

Manchester Goods.—A department in drapery devoted to the various kinds of cotton piece goods, specially calicoes, longcloths, sheetings, flannels, fustians, and similar stuffs.

Manchester Velvet.—A kind of cotton velvet.

Marabou.—A special kind of white silk which can be dyed without being degummed or boiled off.

Marcella.—A cotton material, usually having a diamond pattern ; used for waistcoats, shirts, etc.

Marcelline.—A light, thin, diaphanous silk fabric, largely used in millinery and for lining ladies' dresses.

Marl.—A term applied to a particular kind of coloured two-fold or single yarn. In the former (the 2-fold) one or both threads making the two-fold yarn are spun from two rovings of different colours, causing the single thread to have a twist-like appearance. Or the process may be begun earlier, by the two colours being run together in the thick roving, thus producing a twist-like effect in the smaller roving immediately preceding the spinning. These single twist-looking threads are usually folded with a solid colour, frequently black. If folded with each other they are called " double marls." A single-yarn marl is this yarn without the folding ; it is sometimes used as a weft for fine twist effects.

Marseilles.—Originally made in Marseilles, France. A heavy, double-faced white cotton cloth with a raised woven pattern. Also a vesting made of cotton, in fancy weave, in all white or with coloured figure, and starch-finished.

Mat Braid.—A closely woven thick braid used for binding or trimming.

Matelasse.—French, meaning to cushion or pad, hence a quilted surface produced on the loom. A type of fabric usually produced from a cotton warp interwoven with flush weaves of mohair weft ; or it may be produced from mohair or silk warp or cotton, or low-quality weft. The true Matelasse should have wadding material introduced to give a more or less raised appearance.

Mat-weave.—Weaves of the hopsack type which give to fabrics an appearance similar to closely interwoven mats.

Mayo, or Campbell Twill.—An irregular 8-sateen derivative weave, no doubt in the first instance employed for Scottish tartans, but now largely employed in all types of fabrics.

Melton.—A heavily milled woollen in which the fibres have been caused to stand straight up, and then the piece cut bare to obtain the typical melton. Both light and heavy meltons are made with cotton warp and woollen weft. Named from the town of Melton Mowbray, it is said, and eventually shortened.

Mercerised.—A chemical process used on cotton. Cotton yarns are held under tension to prevent shrinking, and are treated with caustic soda. The process is also applied to woven goods. Mercerised cotton becomes more lustrous, stronger, and absorbs dye more readily. The process was the accidental discovery, more than half a century ago, of a Lancashire cotton printer, John Mercer, whose name has become inseparably associated with the method. Mercerising is not resorted to with intent to deceive, but holds a legitimate place in the textile industry.

Merino.—In the hosiery trade, yarn or knitted goods composed of blended wool and cotton. In the dress goods trade, an all-wool fabric, twilled alike on back and face, and made from single yarn. In the waste trade, a name for waste produced by pulling rags of merino quality.

Merino Wool.—The best of all wool, giving 60's and 80's quality. It is also the softest and whitest.

Merveilleux.—A word from the French, meaning marvellous or wonderful ; descriptive of the fine-twilled silk fabric to which the name has been given. The material somewhat resembles Surah, and in black and blue solid colours is used for coat and overcoat lining.

Mestizo Wool.—This is commonly known on the wool market as River Plate. It is obtained from the sheep produced by crossing the Spanish merino with the native South American sheep, the Criolla. The wool is of high quality, but has the defect of being infested with what are called " screw " burrs, very difficult to extract, resisting the drastic carbonising process of burring to such a degree that a special machine has to be employed in addition, if the wool is to be properly cleaned.

Milled.—Woollen cloths after weaving are rendered compact by the moisture, heat, and frictional treatment they receive in the fulling mill during the finishing process. " Single," " double," and " treble " milled are relative terms, expressing the progressive degree of shrinking given certain fabrics made of woollen yarns to produce, with proper thickness or ply of weave, the prescribed weight per yard of goods. A treble-milled melton, for instance, is an extra heavy and firm material, approximately when finished 32 ounces per yard double width.

Mistral.—Twisted warp-and-woof threads woven to give a crêpe effect. Used for dresses.

Mixture Cloth.—A cloth produced from mixture yarn or blended fibres of different colour. Sometimes denotes absence of any regular design in contradistinction to striped or checked goods.

Mixture Yarns.—Wool yarns made up of different colours, generally greys, composed of varying quantities of black and white wools ; yarns composed of a blend of cotton and wool.

Mock Leno.—A cotton fabric woven so as to show the gauze effect of true leno. The warp threads are sleyed in groups of three or four, one group to a dent, with an open dent between the groups. Similarly, in order to produce the same effect with the weft, the take-up on the beam is regulated so that openings may show between the picks. The texture of the fabric is not so clear as that of real leno, and does not wear so well. As a cheap substitute, however, mock leno has its uses.

Another definition reads : A type of fabric which, although woven in ordinary healds, has the appearance of a gauze or leno. Six-end variety consists of two threads plain cloth, and one thread 3/3 warp cord.

Mohair.—The fine, soft, silky hair of the Angora goat, native to the vilayet of that name in Asia Minor, now extensively raised in Cape Colony, South Africa ; fabrics made of Angora goat hair, characterised by their strength, lightness, and lustre ; stuffs composed of wool and cotton, woven to imitate mohair, but easily detected by the expert, because, while wool and cotton combine closely, and cling, the fibres of mohair are clearly separable.

Mohair Braid.—A binding made of mohair, very strong, lustrous, and durable.

Mohair Lustre.—A black dress material, closely resembling alpaca, woven of mohair weft, and cotton warp. It is generally made in three qualities, known by different names, viz. lustre, brilliantine, and Sicilian. Brilliantine is woven close, and has the most lustrous surface ; Sicilian is heavier, and more durable than the other two fabrics.

Moiré.—French, meaning wave. Watered or clouded effect on silk. Taffeta may be used, but generally a ribbed type, as poplin, is finished in this way ; produced by the flattening at intervals of the corded surface, the original roundness remaining in other places. Also, on plain or satin weaves by means of engraved rollers with heat and pressure. Moiré antique, a richer material, is produced by folding the fabric lengthwise, face in. The selvedges are stitched together, the fabric is dampened and passed between hot cylinders. This gives a watered moiré effect which is lasting, and shows more pronounced and irregular markings than by the former method.

Moiré Français.—A moiré effect in stripes.

Moiré à Pois.—A watered effect with small satin spots well distributed over the face of the fabric. (French, pois = pea.)

Moiré Impérial.—An indefinite watered effect extended over the face of the fabric.

Moirette.—A fabric similar to the moreen, but of lighter make.

Moleskin.—A strong twilled fabric resembling in touch and appearance the skin of a mole. Dyed slate or tan colour, its uses are limited to such garments as labourers' trousers and some kinds of breeches. It is said that college football players' breeches in America are made from it ; this may mean shorts.

Montagnac.—A superfine, thick-bodied overcoating cloth for winter wear, having a tufted face somewhat like an astrakhan cloth, manufactured by Montagnac et Fils of Sedan, France. Imitated by other mills and marketed under the same name ; not with intent to deceive, but as an identifying term for a fabric of distinctive structure and finish.

Moreen.—A plain weave fabric composed of fine warp and thick weft, so constructed that upon the fabric being pressed with itself it develops an excellent moiré effect.

Mousseline-de-Laine.—A very light worsted fabric.

Mull.—A thin, soft, cotton muslin, finished without stiffening of any sort, and used for light summer dresses or clothing in tropical countries. China mull is a light, plain fabric, made of varying proportions of silk and cotton, according to grade.

Mummy, or Momie, Cloth.—From the French Momie,

puckered or shrivelled. An irregular weave, producing a pebbly surface similar to granite cloth in wool.

Mungo.—The waste produced by grinding up the more felted worsteds and woollens ; usually fine and very short.

Muslin.—A very fine cotton fabric, the original name of which was Mousseline, because first known to Europeans from Moussoul, or Mosul, a town in Kurdistan. Muslins are of various kinds, and may be plain, twill, figured, or gauze woven. The chief varieties are : book, mull, jaconet, lawn, organdie, saccharilla, nainsook, leno, swiss, anglo-swiss, etc., etc.

N

Nail.—An old cloth measure, equal to $2\frac{1}{4}''$.

Nankeen.—A cotton cloth of dull yellowish colour, the natural hue of the cotton of which it is made. Much of the nankeen cloth sold is made in Lancashire with ordinary cotton, and dyed the same shade as the ancient nankeen fabric.

Nap.—A somewhat heavy woollen cloth raised and rubbed in the finishing operations to give it the nap from which it derives its name.

Natural Coloured Wool.—The wool used to form a fabric without either bleaching or dyeing. It is sometimes necessary to distinguish natural from dyed wool. Unless the tint is so faint as to appear colourless under the microscope, dyed wool shows uniformity of colouring throughout. The natural colour in wool, on the other hand, appears in definitely restricted areas in the cortex, lines and irregular groups of dots standing out clearly distinguishable.

Navy Twilled Flannel.—A heavy wool flannel, commonly dyed indigo blue, and used in making overshirts worn by firemen, sailors, and other workers.

Neps.—Wool fibres curled into little lumps mainly on the carding engine by the action of rollers. Neps are usually an indication of bad setting.

Niggerhead.—A kind of woollen suiting like an astrakhan fabric, having the face of the cloth covered with kinking curls.

Noil.—The short fibre extracted from the long in combing worsted and silk waste.

Novelty Suiting.—Originally of plain homespun weave with rough, irregular filling of different colours ; but the name is frequently applied to all weaves, especially brocaded or Jacquard effects. Used for skirts and suits.

Nun's Veiling.—Soft, light-weight fabric, in plain weave. Sometimes called wool batiste ; coarser weaves called nun's cloth. Very satisfactory for shirred dresses, as it drapes well.

O

Oatmeal Effect.—A style of granite interlacing which gives to the fabric an appearance something like oatmeal.

Oilskin.—A cloth thoroughly impregnated with a drying oil, forming a smooth surface, and used as a waterproof covering ; it is worn by sailors, watermen, and others exposed to the elements.

Oldham.—A rough worsted cloth, originally made at Oldham, in the county of Norfolk, but in later times the seat of manufacture was Norwich.

Olive Drab.—A standard shade of colour, self-descriptive, adopted by the United States Army, and in vogue for service uniforms and overcoats made of worsted or woollen cloths. Commonly abbreviated to O.D.

Ombré.—A shaded effect produced by dressing the warp of a fabric in tones shading from light to dark, any number of hues between twelve to thirty being employed.

Openness and Closeness.—The open style of cut, in trousers, gives a greater angle from the fork to the bottom of side seam, and consequently greater ease ; the close cut infuses less angle from the fork to bottom of side seam, and less ease. The close cut would tend to give a smarter fit. Openness and closeness in coats are concerned with the amount added over the breast measure from centre of back to centre of front, or from top of back to neck-point.

Organdie.—A fine cotton fabric of gauzy texture, woven plain white usually, though sometimes in checked and striped patterns, in widths ranging from 18″ to 60″, and heavily dressed and glazed, the thick dressing filling up all the openings between the threads, so as to present a closer, glossy appearance. Washing destroys the gloss on organdie. The fabric is sometimes printed with small floral designs, and then bleached for the printer, the dressing being put on afterwards. Organdie is coarser than muslin, for which it is substituted as a material for light dress goods.

Orleans.—Dress goods and linings, plain and figured, the ground of a plain weave, composed of cotton warp and lustre-wool or worsted filling ; first made at Orleans in 1837. These fabrics are generally cross-dyed, and are frequently sold as imitation alpacas and mohairs.

Ottoman Cloth.—A dress fabric of a warp rib structure, usually made from hard crisp yarns.

Outing Cloths.—An American general classification for fabrics, including white, striped, and fancy-coloured flannels, plain, white, and cream serges, and the like ; used for tennis, cricket, and outdoor clothes for recreation.

Overcheck and Overplaid.—A check introduced over and above a ground check.

A pattern effect in colours employed in many fancy woollen suitings, consisting of a block figure superimposed upon another of smaller design, or upon a checked ground. Typical examples are found in most of the tartans of the various Scottish clans.

Overlaid Seams.—Where the seam is sewn in the ordinary way and turned over and stitched again ; sometimes called a raised seam. Double-sewn overlaid seams are the same as above, but stitched twice.

Oxford Grey.—A fabric composed of mixed black-and-white wools, the proportions ranging from 85 to 95 per cent. black to 15 and 5 per cent. white. Previous to mixing, the black wools are dyed.

An Oxford mixture has been defined as a solid, dark grey shade of colour imparted to semi-staple woollen and worsted fabrics of various character, effected by blending certain properties of bleached white and black dyed wools in the carding or combing operation preliminary to spinning into yarn. A lighter grey has been given the name of Cambridge Mixture, by way of distinguishing it from the other ; suggested by the fact that the " University colours " of Cambridge are light (blue), while those of Oxford are dark (blue).

Ozenbrigs.—An old-fashioned sort of linen cloth, in various plain colours, used as a jacket, breeches, and shirt material for servants' wear. Originally made at Osnabrück, Prussia.

P

Padding.—A stitch used for giving a fixed shape to parts of a garment, principally the collars and lapels of coats. In padding there must be at least two pieces of material to sew together ; one laid over the other, and both lying in an elliptical form over the finger of the sewer—the upper piece being gathered more or less upon the under one. So little of the thread is intended to be shown on the right side that it used to be the boast of some men that they could pad a collar or lapel with white cotton.

Paisley.—Refers to designs printed or woven which imitate patterns in Paisley shawls. The Paisley pattern is the Persian pine-cone pattern, finely elaborated, and developed in the Scottish town of Paisley, in the manufacture of the famous Paisley shawls, woven on the harness loom, and since used in prints and other fabrics.

Palm Beach Cloth.—So named because it was originally made for wear at Palm Beach resorts. A light-weight, cool fabric, yarn-dyed, often striped.

Panama Cloth.—A piece-dyed worsted fabric of any colour woven plain.

Panne.—A worsted plush made in France ; sometimes applied to satin-faced velvet, or silk fabrics having a high lustre.

Paramatta.—A thin fabric composed of a cotton warp and a Botany weft interlaced 2 and 1 weft twill. This cloth is used for water-proofing purposes. It probably owes its name to the fact that the fine wools with which it was first made were obtained from Paramatta, a township in New South Wales.

Partridge Cord.—A corduroy of mottled colours ; so called because of its resemblance to the features of a partridge, or quail.

Peau de Mouton.—A woollen cloth with a heavy and rough nap, resembling sheepskin, used for making ladies' cloaks.

Peau de Soie.—A heavy dress silk, interwoven with a double satin weave, self-coloured and dull-finished, with a somewhat grainy appearance.

Peau de Suède.—A woollen cloth, with a velvet pile, used for ladies' wear.

Pencil Stripe.—An effect on cloths, particularly fancy worsted suitings, produced by the introduction in weaving of a series of coloured threads at regular intervals, across the piece, running lengthwise of the goods, fancifully suggesting that such lines or stripes might have been drawn by a pencil, and ordinarily understood to be a heavier marking than a hairline.

Penistone.—A rough woollen cloth, heavily milled, named after the town of Penistone, where it was manufactured.

Pepper-and-Salt.—The mixed effect produced in woollen and worsted cloths by the use of doubled and twisted yarns, composed of black and white threads of unequal thickness, the black or white being the heavier yarn, according to the lightness or darkness of the effect desired. The cloth may be woven of the black and white yarns, both warp and weft; but more commonly the body of the cloth is one colour, and the two-colour yarns introduced one in three or four. Another pattern is produced by weaving a marled warp with a black weft, or a spot effect may be produced by alternation in the weave.

Percale.—A cotton fabric, of firm weave structure, finished with a light dressing, without gloss. In coloured stripe effects used as a tailor's trimming for sleeve linings, etc. The term is French, but the material itself probably is of East Indian origin.

Persian Cord.—A cloth made from cotton warp and worsted weft, employing the plain weave, but with the warp-threads working in two's, thus giving a rib effect.

Petanelle.—A material composed of peat fibres incorporated with wool, having certain antiseptic properties, made into various articles of clothing.

Petersham.—A very heavy woollen cloth, with the nap formed into small nops, or curls, used in the making of heavy overcoats; the heavy greatcoat made of the cloth, named after Lord Petersham, who set the example of wearing it; a kind of fancy webbing used for waist-bands.

Pick.—A single strand of weft reaching once across a piece. This term is also used to express the action of throwing or picking a shuttle in a loom.

Pick and Pick.—This implies the throwing of single picks of different colours into a fabric.

Piece-dyed.—A term denoting that cloths have been woven with yarn in the natural colour, and have been dyed after weaving. The opposite term is " yarn-dyed," which usually implies superior quality, the yarns having been dyed before weaving, and therefore most deeply imbued with the colour. Close examination reveals the difference, the yarns in piece-dyed cloths showing that the dye has not completely impregnated them, while the yarns of the yarn-dyed cloth are covered all over with the dye. The test is seldom required, because nearly all cloths of one colour are now piece-dyed.

Pile.—A fabric having a surface made of upright ends, as in fur. Pile may be made of extra yarns, as in velvets and plushes, or of extra filling yarns, as in velveteens and corduroys. Pile may be uncut as in Brussels carpet. Warp pile may cause loops on both sides, as in terry (Turkish towelling).

Pilot Cloth.—A stout woollen cloth with a nap surface, generally dyed blue ; used for overcoats, etc., such as are worn by seamen, pilots, etc.

Pin Check.—An effect on fancy worsted suitings, notably in grey and white, where the small checks of the pattern approach the size of pinheads.

Piqué.—A stout cotton fabric having a raised surface of cords or welts from selvedge to selvedge. It is made with two sets of warps ; one slack and containing twice as many yarns as the tightly drawn warp. The fine slack warp yarns interweave with the single filling to form the plain face of the goods. The tightly drawn back warp interweaves with the face of the goods only at those intervals where the goods are to be drawn in to produce the cord effect, like the rows of stitching in quilting. Cords or welts vary in width and depth. Unlike Bedford cords, where the welts run lengthwise. Bedford cord in cotton is sometimes inaccurately termed piqué.

Plaid.—The long, rectangular piece of cloth which formed, in ancient times, the main clothing of the Scottish Highlanders ; but later the garment became divided into the kilt, covering the lower body and limbs ; and the plaid, wrapped over the shoulders and across the breast. The long or belted plaid is thick and heavy, and worn in winter ; the dress plaid is short and light, being suitable for ceremonial occasions. Plaid patterns, sometimes simply called plaids, are checks and lines forming longer checks, defined by variation in colour, usually termed tartans. The tartans are divided into three large divisions : (1) Highland clan and family tartans ; (2) Royal and fancy tartans ; (3) Regimental tartans.

Plaid Back, or Check Back.—A heavy woollen overcoating made as a double cloth, the two being woven together, or stitched together ; the face side is of some subdued colour, generally given a soft finish, while the back is of a bold fancy check or plaid, clear-finished. Such fancy backing, in making up the material into topcoats and cloaks, serves as a substitute for a body lining for the garment.

Plain Cloth.—The simplest form of a woven texture, both

warp and weft being over one and under one. By changes in materials, sizes of yarns, and balance of structure, many of the best recognised styles of fabrics are produced with this interlacing.

Plain Back.—A double or pile-faced fabric which is woven plain at the back or in the ground.

Plugging.—The name given to the process of fastening on buttons with metal shanks, which are not for actual use. For instance, in military and livery coats there are certain buttons which, although ornamental, are never fastened into a button-hole. If sewn on in the usual way these buttons would not be flat on the garment. To obviate this, plugging is resorted to. It consists in making a hole in the cloth, forcing the shank through, and fastening it on the other side with a plug of linen, silesia, or other material.

Plush.—A fabric composed of a ground texture and a pile texture, the latter standing up more or less straight. There are two classes : (1) weft piles, and (2) warp piles. In weft piles the pile weft during weaving is simply floated on the top of the ground texture, to be subsequently cut in the finishing operation. In the warp piles, the pile is formed by warp threads. which are either looped over wires to form the pile, or two ground textures are woven with a small space in between, across which the pile warp threads pass from one cloth to the other, and the two cloths are cut apart in finishing.

Ply.—A term indicating the number of units of which either a yarn or fabric is composed. Thus : 2-ply yarn indicates a yarn composed of two single strands. Three-ply cloth refers to a cloth which is really composed of three single cloths solidly bound together.

Pockets.—Everyone knows what a pocket is, but it is not easy to define. Probably the best description is : A small bag inserted in a garment to carry various articles. In coats there are the breast pockets (inside and out) ; ticket pocket (inside or out) ; side pockets with flaps, jettings or else welted ; and such additions as game pockets, which are also used for commercial purposes.

For trousers, a side pocket is one placed in the side seam ; a cross pocket starts at the side seam and runs forward and up in front. There are also hip, fob, cash, and rule pockets. In connection with the last, a pocket for a 12″ rule would be placed in side seam below the side pocket ; one for a 6″ rule would go on the hip.

Poiret Twill.—A fine worsted material with a soft or hard finish. It is similar to gabardine, only finer and smoother.

Polo Cloth.—A heavy fabric for sports garments, similar to old-fashioned golf cloth. Usually white. Two sides may differ in colour and pattern. Yarn-dyed. Fulled, napped, and sometimes rubbed to give chinchilla effect.

Pompadour.—A small and dainty floral pattern, printed or woven. Named from Madame Pompadour.

Pongée.—A strong, somewhat rough silk in the natural colour, a light tan. It is made from cocoons of wild silkworms, which feed on oak leaves, and produce a coarser silk than the mulberry or cultivated silkworm. Because of the inequality in the output of wild silkworms, pongée varies greatly in colour and texture. In drapery fabrics made of wild silk, spun silk yarns are often used, giving a rougher surface. Pongée originated in China, and is now made mostly in Shantung province ; hence the name Shantung for a grade of pongée. In China every family has its own loom, and pongée is hand-woven. Much modern pongée is, however, woven by machinery. Tussah, a Hindu word for a species of worm natural to India, also refers to a wild silkworm in China ; sometimes loosely used as a fabric name for a grade of pongée.

Poplin.—A fabric with a cord effect across the cloth, which may be combined with damask twill, brocade, and other fancy weaves. Originally the fabric was woven with a fine silk warp and a worsted weft, the latter being so much heavier than the former as to produce the rep effect. The manufacture of poplin was introduced into Ireland by a colony of Huguenots, fugitives from France, in 1683, who settled in Dublin and practised the industry there.

Latterly the term " poplin " has become more applicable to the structure than the substance of the fabric, cotton poplins being largely produced and sold.

President.—A weft-backed woollen cloth, 2 picks of face to 1 pick of back. Face weave 5 weft sateen, backing tied in 5 sateen order. A cotton warp is usually employed with a wool and mungo blend face weft, and a long, fibrous—say alpaca, or mohair waste—backing weft.

Prick-stitch.—This stitch is employed to give either strength or appearance, and consists in alternately passing the needle straight up and down through the material, the stitch itself being either a back or a side-stitch. In nearly all cases of strapping, pricking must be resorted to in consequence of the thickness of material ; and in lapped seams of heavy beavers, Devons, etc.

Prunella.—A firm stuff, somewhat like lasting, or haircloth, made of wool and hair. The name was applied from the prevailing colour of the material, it being plum-coloured.

Prunella Twill.—The 2 and 1 warp twill, taking its name from the possibilities of producing by this weave a bird's-eye effect.

Pyjamas.—Sleeping clothes. The word, said to come from the Persian, means " leg clothing."

Q

Quilting.—This is of two descriptions, the one consisting of rows of side-stitching crossing each other so as to show a diamond pattern. Then there is quilting which is preceded by the use of an iron to crease the material to the pattern to be represented ; after which it is basted on the under-lining, and sewn with a side-stitch at each corner only.

R

Raising.—A process applied to heavy woollen goods and some few lighter-weight goods, whereby fibres are raised out of the body of the cloth on to the surface. In the case of worsted and dress goods, brushing takes the place of raising.

Rantering.—This is a process for the purpose of concealing the presence of a seam. The seam to be rantered must first be lightly and evenly seamed by the back stitch. After sewing the seam, both edges must be doubled back on the right side, being worked with the finger and thumb as close down to the sewing as possible. The needle must then be passed backwards and forwards through both edges, taking the smallest possible grip of the material, the hand being pulled just tight enough to sink the stitch ; the stitch itself being a side-stitch set slightly forward. The seam must then be turned over on to the wrong side, into the same position as when being sewn, and rubbed along between the fingers and thumbs of both hands. It must then be turned over on to the right side, and the wool stretched over the ranter with a stout needle.

Rateen.—A weft-pile wool fabric, used for overcoatings, cloakings, and heavy wraps, sometimes made with a cotton warp ; a kind of chinchilla imitation in which the velvet pile is worked into small round knobs on the chinchilla machine, instead of being formed into ridges as for ordinary chinchilla finish ; also ratine, ratteen, and rattinet.

Ratteen.—A thick twilled or quilled (fluted) woollen cloth of similar appearance to, and used as, drugget ; at one time popular for men's garments. A thinner material was known as rattinet.

Raw Edges.—A raw edge is, as the name implies, an edge not turned in ; the edge of forepart and facing lie one on the other and are stitched through. Such a finish is only possible in Meltons, box-cloths, and materials which do not fray or ravel. The bottoms of coats are sometimes left raw.

Regatta Stripe.—A trade term for a class of light-weight worsted or woollen suiting with a neat fancy stripe effect, as in some flannels.

Repp.—A term usually applied to fabrics of the warp ribbed class, in which the rib, or repp, runs weft-way. It is sometimes, however, applied to the weft rib also. Also an unequal mat weave.

Another definition is : A corded pattern produced by weaving a thick weft into a thin warp, or several shoots of weft together, and therefore showing the cord effect across the width of the cloth, not lengthwise, as in the pattern commonly designated " cord."

Rib Weave.—A descriptive term for a class of fabrics, of staple character, wherein the weave formation produces prominent longitudinal ridges, or ribs, repeated regularly, on the face side of the material ; such as in Bedford cords.

Running Stitch.—This consists in passing the needle straight forward in front of the thread through the material being sewn, leaving the stitches the same length on the top and undersides. This stitch, in its primitive form, is seldom used by tailors ; but it was, in other days, often used instead of rows of side-stitching in the stands of collars.

Russell Cord.—A cloth made from cotton warp and worsted weft, employing the plain weave, but with the warp woven double ends instead of single to give a rib or cord effect.

Russet.—A coarse homespun cloth ; a cloth dyed with bark to a dark brown, and generally of rough texture ; a country dress.

S

Saggathy.—A name of Roman origin, still applied in particular localities to four-shaft twill woollens.

Sarcenet.—A very fine and soft silk fabric, woven plain or twill, used principally for linings, but sometimes made into light dresses. Also Sarsenet.

Sateen.—A large class of goods, the distinguishing feature of which is the broken twill or satin weave by which they are fabricated. Originally sateen was simply an imitation of satin in wool or cotton, but in time the fabric became recognised as a valuable and useful class of goods.

Satin.—A warp or weft surface cloth in which the intersections of warp and weft are so arranged as to be imperceptible, the fabric thus possessing the smoothness for which satins are noticeable.

The true satin is made entirely of silk, or with a fine silk warp and a cotton weft, and is specially noted for its lustre.

Satinet.—An imitation of the true satin in mercerised cotton or pure yarns.

Satin Soleil.—A smooth crosswise weave in satin finish. Used considerably for dresses and light-weight suits.

Saxony.—More particularly in the Scottish woollen trade, " Saxony " signifies Botany or merino quality, in corded yarns. Used in contradistinction to " Cheviot," which latter name is applied generically to goods of Cheviot and crossbred, or other than merino wool. Merino wool from Saxony was at one time an important article of commerce.

Since the introduction of Australasian wools, generically named " Botany," the term has lost its definite significance. There are still, however, three uses for the term : (1) A high-grade wool, produced from the merino sheep bred in Saxony ; (2) the yarns spun from Saxony wool ; (3) a fine worsted cloth woven with the Saxony yarns.

Scales.—Scales may be termed relative dimensions, ratios of reduction or enlargement, etc. In coat and waistcoat cutting one-half of the breast measure, two-thirds of the middle shoulder, etc., are used as scales to cut by ; with trousers one-half of the seat usually gives the scale. For making diagrams, garments are drawn to scale, such as one-sixth, one-fourth, etc.

Seam.—A seam is a line of junction between two edges—especially of cloth. As a rule the width of a seam is $\frac{1}{4}''$; but this varies.

Seat Allowance.—Seat allowance must not be confused with seat angle ; it is a quantity (generally from 2" to 3" for trousers, more for breeches, etc.) allowed for the expansion of seat when the wearer is seated ; whereas seat angle is an allowance for increased length.

Seat Angle.—A term used to define the amount of ease given to the undersides of trousers ; it is also called straightness and crookedness. When a large amount of seat angle is given a crooked cut is produced, but a small amount gives a straight or closer fit.

Seat-piece.—A seat-piece is a section of material sometimes sewn across the top of undersides of trousers when the material is not long enough to cut them without a join.

Self-figured.—A cloth wherein the figure or pattern is produced by the weave, the goods being of one solid colour as, for instance, fancy weave worsted piece dyes.

Selvedge.—A narrow strip woven on both sides of a cloth to prevent fraying and to strengthen the edges. As a rule, selvedges are made by a weave different from that of the body of the cloth ; but if the cloth is a plain weave, the selvedges are composed of coarser and harder warp yarns, so as to make a tighter and stronger fabric. This involves some difficulty of adjustment, and to avoid it the selvedge warp threads are sometimes merely twined upon each other and interwoven with the weft to connect them with the body of the fabric. When two cloths are woven together in one width of the loom, centre selvedges are required. These are seldom satisfactory, but the best are made by what is practically a separate little web with healding and wefting plan of its own. The quality of a selvedge affects the value of a cloth, and buyers should examine them closely. Some authorities use the term "Selvage." Selvedge is, of course, synonymous with "list."

Semi-staple.—A generic term for a cloth of weave, colour, or finish midway between the severity or plainness of a staple fabric such as broadcloth, and a clay diagonal, or a black or blue serge on the one hand and a pronounced fancy suiting or overcoating on the other. Mixture serges, covert coatings, and the like are typical semi-staples.

Serge.—A term applied to fabrics of a twill character and of a rough make, as distinct from the finer make of worsteds ; the weave is usually two and two twill, and the yarns woollen or cross-bred. The term was originally applied to a twill silk, which was reversible.

Serge (cotton lining).—A mercerised lining used for lining coats.

Serge, French.—Very fine, soft weave ; easily tailored ; wears well, but produces a shine more readily than other serges. Used for dresses, skirts, and suits.

Serge (mohair).—A lining fabric for men's overcoats. May be all wool or cotton warp with mohair filling.

Serge, Storm.—Hard, fine weave with nap.

Serge, Wide Wale.—Pronounced diagonal weave. Used for dress skirts and suits.

Serging.—A stitch which casts the thread over a material ; generally done with the uncovered seams of washing and ravelling materials—both to prevent the ravelling which would weaken the seam and the appearance of long, unsightly threads.

Serging is also used for joining two edges together in cases where it is necessary that the pieces joined should be flat, as in the serging of a cuff to the sleeve.

Shading Effects.—Effects produced by different colours or qualities of materials, or by weave, the result being a gradual change of appearance from one colour, or structure, to another.

Shadow Weave.—A term describing an effect on certain cloths of staple character, such as worsted suitings, either clear-finished or unfinished, whereby part of the weave is presented in, say, a medium shade of blue yarn and the remainder in a darker shade of blue yarn, giving the appearance in combination of reflected shadows over the goods. Another kind of shadow weave is produced on self-figured staple worsteds, as those of herringbone or diamond pattern, by having the yarns used in certain parts of the woven design twisted in a reverse direction, so that by contrast with the yarns of regular twist a sort of shadow pattern effect results.

Shepherd's Plaid, or Check.—A check pattern of black and white, originally used for Scottish shepherds' plaids (which are now of a coloured pattern). It is woven on the plain loom, the checks being formed by alternate stripes of black and white warp, and a similar alternation in the weft.

Shoddy.—The worked-up waste of woollen or other worsted goods, in which the initial material has been of the long-fibred class, as against the short-fibred class, which is worked up into mungo.

Shot.—(1) Scotch term for " pick." (2) Changeable effect, as in silk produced by use of filling in different colours from warp.

Sicilian.—A cloth made from a fine cotton warp and a thick mohair weft, employing the plain weave.

Side-edges.—Slips of cloth inserted in back pleats, as in a livery coat.

Side-stitch.—This stitch is used for sewing two pieces of material together, leaving an impression merely without showing the thread. In fancy stitching, such as facings or the stand of a collar, the stitch is formed by placing the needle close by the side of the silk; but in stitching an edge of a coat, in forming the stitch, the needle is put slightly in the front of the thread, and the hand drawn carefully tight.

Silesia.—A coarse linen cloth woven on a wide setting; a cotton imitation of the linen cloth used for linings.

The origin of the name is said to be as follows: Joseph Ferguson, founder of Ferguson Brothers, of Carlisle, originated the idea of beetling cotton goods. By this process he was enabled to obtain a soft silky finish, and his cotton goods quickly won wide renown as " Silesias," a Polish name suggested by his wife through their mutually sympathetic interest in the efforts of the Poles to avert the partition of their country by Germany, Austria, and Russia.

Silk.—The finest, strongest, and most beautiful of textile fabrics.

Silk Cocoons.—The form in which the silk is obtained by stifling the enclosed chrysalis. Silk yarns are produced by reeling the fine filaments, three to five in a yarn, from the cocoons; but both cocoons and yarns are imported by silk manufacturers. The principal countries of production are China, Japan, India, France, and Italy.

Silk Conditioning.—The process of degumming and otherwise preparing raw silks for textile uses.

Silk Cotton.—The silk fibre of short staple produced by the Indian cotton-tree, Bombax, used for making a coarse kind of cloth.

Silk Goods.—Those goods which are wholly or mostly composed of silk yarns. There is little or no exact standardisation, and the custom of the trade has to be depended upon for classification. As a broad division the fabrics may be ranged under three headings, viz.: pure silks, all-silks, and silks.

(1) Pure silks are materials composed of silk yarns, free from extraneous matters, such as tannic acid, sugar of lead, tin salts, or any other chemical or vegetable ingredients. Both warp and weft must be free from any admixture of cotton, wool, or artificial silk; but they may be of any kind of silk,

bombax, or tussore, or even spun silk : in the last instance notification of the fact is advisable, the difference between the textile strength if spun and any kind of thrown silk being considerable.

(2) All-silks should contain no other textile fibres or yarns, such as cotton, wool, ramie, or artificial silks ; but all-silk fabrics are almost universally weighted in dyeing or finishing, chiefly by means of weighted dyes. The limit of adulteration commonly sent in dyeing is a return of 24 oz. in warp and 32 oz. in weft. That is to say, the dyer receives so many pounds of silk, 16 oz. to the pound, and returns each pound of warp with 8 oz. added, and each pound of weft with 16 oz. added. It is customary to reckon this as adding 50 per cent. to the warp and 100 per cent. to the weft ; but actually the percentage in relation to the pure silk is much higher. In the process of boiling off, before dyeing, and necessary for the production of soft silks, the weight of the silk is reduced by about 25 per cent. on the average. A pound of silk after the boiling off is only 12 oz. in weight, and if a return of 24 oz. is required in warp, the adulteration amounts to 100 per cent. In the case of the weft the added weight reaches 167 per cent. Black silks are commonly weighted in warp up to 30 oz. return, and in weft to 48 oz. return. Goods made up of hard unboiled silk, however, are not considered as being adulterated, and restoration of the 25 per cent. lost in boiling off is accepted as legitimate.

(3) Silks : The term "silk goods" may be taken to describe fabrics composed of a mixture of cotton or wool with silk.

Single Cloth.—This term describes a fabric that has been constructed of but one system of weave—that is to say, one set of warp threads and one set of weft threads, as distinguished from a backed or double cloth. Such character of material, as seen in practically all fancy suitings or summer weights, and for the most part winter weight suitings, is also called a " through-and-through " cloth.

Sizing.—Finishing process. Yarns and cloth treated with stiffening substance to give strength, stiffness, and smoothness. Size may contain starch (potato, wheat, corn, sago), glue, casein, gelatin, gluten, minerals, wax, gum, paraffin, and antiseptic substances.

Slated Seams.—Slated or overlaid seams are not so much heard of nowadays as a generation ago. This kind of seam, as will be understood by the name, has one section laid upon the other, after the manner of slates upon a roof. It is only suitable for heavy materials which have a firm edge, such as meltons, beavers, box cloths, and friezes. Usually these seams are double-sewn, i.e. one sewing quite on the edge, with a second row at any desired distance, to match the edges.

Snob's Thumb.—A piece of cloth, circular in shape, about 1″ in diameter, to cover the plugged buttons on skirts, etc.

Soleil.—An all-wool fabric with a highly reflecting warp surface of a broken rib character.

Sponge Cloth.—A heavy, soft cotton fabric with a loop-pile face, made in a wide range of qualities, and used as a ladies' dress cloth.

Staple.—Generic term for a cloth of conservative weave and colour, such as dress worsteds, black and blue serges, diagonals, whipcords, corkscrews, kerseys, meltons, etc. ; in contradistinction to a semi-staple, or fancy suiting, or overcoating.

Stays.—These are small strips of linen, etc., put at the back to stay or strengthen buttons, pocket-tacks, etc.

Stockinette.—Elastic fabric, flat or tubular, made on a knitting machine.

Stoting.—This is an operation by which two edges are sewn together by means of a stitch taken through and over at the same time. Its object is to secure thinness, and that the join may be less prominent than a seam ; indeed, the notion is to take such care as to avoid observation. It is generally used where seams are not supposed to be, either on the inside or outside of a garment—in piecing facings inside, cuts under rolls, etc. At one time it was not uncommon for edges to be stoted.

Stripe.—A term applied to patterns running longitudinally with the warp in textile fabrics, produced by employing a special weave or two, or more colours of warp specially arranged.

Suiting.—A general term which applies to a variety of weaves and finishes. Many novelties are introduced from time to time.

Superfine.—A high-grade West of England cloth, usually black in colour, at one time fashionable for dress-coats, frock-coats, etc.

Swansdown.—A heavy twilled cotton fabric ; the simplest of twill weaves, plushing all but one of the warp ends, the 4-end plushing three ends ; the 5-end plushing four ends, and so on.

Swatch.—A strip of cloth used as a sample.

Swiss.—So called because first made in Switzerland. A fine, sheer, cotton fabric which may be plain or embroidered (lappet weave) in dots or figures. Design may be introduced by swivel weaving, which produces shaggy surface on one side. Composition dot or figure may be applied chemically.

Sword-slash.—A piece of cloth sewn on the skirt of livery coats, vandyked at back, with three buttons.

T

Tabby.—A term largely employed in the plush districts for plain cloth. Named after a suburb of Bagdad ; a rich silk stuff with a wavy surface, the effect being produced by heavy calendering with engraved rollers ; a very high-grade velvet ; the plain weave.

Taffeta.—A fine cloth made from silk warp and Botany weft, employing the plain weave ; a plain, closely woven, very smooth silk fabric, the warp and filling of the same or nearly the same count. It may have a small figure introduced on plain background. Skein, or piece-dyed. It is apt to be heavily weighted. Tends to split badly. Chiffon taffeta is softer than plain taffeta. The derivation of the word is from the Persian Taftan—to spin.

Tammy.—An old form of cloth woven of wool, formerly called Coventry ware ; it is now known as a stout woollen stuff.

Tarlatan.—A thin, very open cotton fabric, highly sized and polished. About as coarse as thin cheese-cloth, only very wiry and transparent. It has a square mesh. White or coloured. It will not launder, and is very perishable. Among other purposes it is used for pageant costumes.

Tartan.—An old name for plain woollen surviving in Army use ; the type of pattern composed of checks and crossed lines adopted as distinctive by the Highland clans of Scotland, each clan, sept, and family having its own special pattern or patterns. There are about two hundred distinct clan tartans, and in addition there are regimental and numerous fancy tartans designed on the same principle.

Tartan Velvet.—A velvet with a short pile, woven in a tartan pattern.

Tartarine.—A silk fabric, so named because it was said to˙ come from Tartary.

Taunton.—A broadcloth, giving about 11 oz. to the narrow yard, made at Taunton, Somerset.

Tavistock.—A broadcloth, formerly made at Tavistock, Devon, which was called Western Dozens.

Tennis Cloth.—A cloth usually of a lightish texture and colour, soft to handle, and usually made from wool.

Tentering (otherwise Stentering).—A finishing process in which goods are widened out or tentered by being hooked on to chains, which expand to the width required, then carry the cloth through a heated chamber or over gas jets, so that the cloth is dried in this position.

Terry.—A velvet with the loop pile uncut ; a shaggy towelling, with a loop pile.

Terry Poplin.—A fabric composed of silk warp and wool weft, in which alternate warp threads are looped up to form a fine pile on the surface of the cloth.

Top.—The longer wool fibres which are separated from the short ones (noils) by combing—used for worsted yarns.

Trimmings.—The accessories required for the making and ornamenting of any article of dress, for curtains, hangings, or drapery. " Trimmings " is a term of wide application, taking in haberdashery on the one hand and the Manchester goods department on the other. To the tailor, trimmings are canvas, linings, buttons, twist, silk, etc. ; to the dressmaker, linings, braids, buttons, hooks and eyes, tapes, frills, flounces, yokes. ribbons, and other accessories ; for the milliner, ribbons, feathers, flowers, etc., are trimmings.

Tropical Whipcord.—A shower-proofed material woven with a thatched surface weave, used for overcoatings.

Trouserings.—Cloths recognised as suitable for making into trousers, generally with striped patterns of ¾ width.

Tulle.—A fine net fabric, made of silk, and one of the first forms of machine-made net, illusion, spotted, grenadine, and other nets of the same kind being variants. Tulle is possibly the most generally useful of lace nets, being made into robes, veils, frills, and trimmings of many kinds.

Tussah (Tussore).—Silk of a brown colour : the produce of the wild silkworm, which feeds on oak-leaves.

Tweed.—The woollen goods woven with dyed yarns, vari-coloured, plain or twilled, felted and rough-finished, made into suits for men and boys, and skirts, jackets and over-garments, etc., for ladies. Tweeds were originally twilled cloths woven of cheviot wool, with a heavy nap ; but the name has been applied to woollen cloths of a light make almost indiscriminately, so that now there are Harris tweeds, Donegal, Irish, and other hand-woven plain tweeds, fancy tweeds, and an almost endless variety of patterns. The word is said to derive from " twirls "—a happy mistake due to careless or indifferent handwriting.

Twill.—A fundamental weave admitting of many varia-tions. Found in serge, denim, Canton flannel, etc. Intersection of yarns form lines running to the right or left diagonally across the fabric.

Twist.—The turns inserted into a yarn to bind its fibres together, and thereby to add more strength for manipulation and weaving. The amount of twist applied varies according to the material process, means employed for its application, and ultimate requirements.

Two-ply.—A doubled woollen or worsted·yarn.

U

Unbleached Cloths.—Goods made up in the grey state for sale.

Union.—Fabrics are " union " when composed of two materials otherwise than by blending. Union worsted has a cotton warp and worsted weft, or vice versa. Other compositions include linen and wool, linen and cotton, etc.

In the Morley (Yorkshire) trade a " union " is a cotton warp cloth of boiled and teazled finish, superficially resembling the ancestral broadcloth.

Upland Cotton.—A distinct type of cotton comprising the great bulk of cotton produced in the United States, and belonging to a species distinct from the sea-island and Egyptian cotton.

Upturn.—Upturn, or turn-up, is the inlay at the bottom of sleeves, coat, trousers, etc.

V

Valenciennes.—A kind of lace formed in a six-sided mesh, and ornamented with figures, named after the French town where it was hand-made for centuries. Valenciennes net was the first lace to be imitated by a fabric made upon an adapted knitting-frame, and the bulk of the goods now sold as Valenciennes lace is machine-made.

Valentia.—A fabric composed of woollen, worsted, cotton, and silk yarns, specially designed for livery waistcoats.

Velour.—A general term for pile fabrics. Used for draperies. Usually a short pile. Mercerised cotton pile most common. Mohair and silk are used. Typical velour is a durable material and rich-looking.

Velour (wool).—So called because of its velvety texture. A soft woollen fabric with a nap raised and sheared to absorb light like dull velvet. The quality depends upon the quality of the woollen yarns used. A good velour wears well; but the cheaper grades " wear off " badly and wrinkle.

Velvet.—A fabric with a surface of close pile formed by a special warp woven into the ground cloth or backing. Velvets vary, and are woven in different ways. Silk velvet of the highest class is woven with a backing of silk, and the silk pile warp is formed into a row of loops after each pick of weft by the insertion of long wires, which are withdrawn after the pile warp has been bound down into the ground fabric by the crossing of the warp and weft, leaving a row of loops. For terry or looped-pile velvet, the pile is allowed to remain in that condition, but for ordinary velvet the loops are cut, forming a close, upstanding pile. In inferior qualities of silk velvet, the backing is wool or cotton. Cheap, power-woven velvets are often woven like a double cloth, the pile being formed between the two cloths ; a knife is passed through between the cloths, cutting the pile in halves, and leaving a smooth pile face on such fabrics.

Velvet Finish.—A finish in which a fairly dense pile of a velvet description is produced upon a woollen fabric by wet-raising in various directions, and then cropping just to level the pile, but not to leave the fabric bare.

Velveteen.—A short, pile fabric of cotton made in imitation of silk velvet. Pile made by extra set of filling yarns, while in velvet pile is made by extra set of warp yarns. Pile is highly mercerised in better grades. Wide velveteen or heavy make is called costume velvet. Good qualities are very durable.

Venetian.—A fabric of an upright warp twill character, produced by a sateen warp weave with a dot added. The term was originally applied to a dress face woollen cloth, but later worsted dress venetians have been made, and, later still, cotton venetians.

Verona Serge.—A mixture fabric, woven in various colours, with mohair or worsted and cotton.

Vicuna.—The long, silky hair of the South American goat, inhabiting the higher regions of Bolivia and Chile ; the hair is of the highest textile quality, and when first introduced was made into a fine broadcloth, at once light and strong and comfortable ; but the fibre has become so valuable that real vicuna cloth is very costly, and the fabrics sold as vicuna are mostly woollen imitations.

Vicuna Cloth.—The cloth with the wool from the vicuna ; the imitation cloth made with fine wools and felted, shorn, and napped to give the appearance of real vicuna.

Viyella.—A light cloth largely made from cotton and wool scrubbled together ; principally used for underclothing.

Voile.—An open cloth of a canvas type, made with plain weave interlining, and hard-twist cotton or worsted yarn.

W

Wadding.—A sheet of carded cotton sized on one side, and used as padding in the make-up of various garments, or for surgical purposes.

Wadding Pick.—A thick pick, usually of low quality, which is inserted often without interlacings between the two fabrics in double cloths, and between the two warps in a warp-backed structure. This gives weight to the fabric, and a certain degree of solidarity, without the pick being seen, or without its being detrimental to the fabric in any other respects.

Wadmol.—A stout, coarse woollen cloth.

Waistband.—This denotes a piece cut separately and seamed on at the hollow of waist, all round the top and undersides of trousers.

Wale.—Refers to raised line or ridge in twill, as " wide-wale serge."

Warp.—The series of threads placed longitudinally in the loom and spread over any desired width.

Warp Rib.—A warp-surface weave, in which the weft picks, being thicker or grouped together in greater numbers, lie straight, causing the warp threads to bind round them.

Washing Goods.—Those fabrics which are easily washed, and do not lose colour or quality in the process.

Watering.—A finishing process by which watered patterns are produced on plain woven fabrics. The principle of this operation is that two fabrics of precisely similar build when pressed together naturally " water " one another, owing to the coincidence or non-coincidence of the threads or picks causing flatness or ribbedness of a sufficiently marked character under conditions of heat and pressure.

Waterproof Fabrics.—Cloth rendered impervious to water.

Waterproofing.—Any process of rendering fabrics waterproof or moisture-repellent. There are three methods of making goods waterproof. The first is by watering the surface over with a material through which water cannot pass. Oils and compositions of various kinds have been used, but the thin coating of vulcanised rubber, invented by Mackintosh, has almost superseded all others for clothing purposes. To be effective, however, the coating of rubber must be so thick as to obscure, and almost obliterate, the woven pattern of the fabric ; and this has been a drawback to its use. Fabrics thus treated with rubber are also airproof, and therefore unhygienic.

The second plan, which in some of its most efficient forms is a modification of the Mackintosh method, is to fill up the interstices between the threads of a cloth with a water-resisting substance. Soaps and resins are the agents generally used; but effective waterproofing on that principle renders fabrics stiff and unhygienic, while lighter applications are not effectively waterproof.

The third method, and probably the oldest, is the utilisation of agents which are water-repelling. Oils repel water, but are not suitable for clothing materials. Alumina is the substance most commonly and effectively employed. The cloths are impregnated with alumina and dried. This agent, by being colourless, modifies but little the pattern, and adheres closely to the fibres. For clothing materials the water-repelling principle has been found the most suitable, and most of the systems now employed are based upon it.

Waved Warp.—An effect in fabrics produced by changing the direction of the warp threads with every pick.

Waves.—Woollen cloths with a long nap, which is disposed in a kind of undulating pattern by means of oscillating rollers.

Weave.—The interlacing of warp and weft with one another to form a suitable cloth.

Web.—The cloth being woven in the loom; the whole piece which has been woven at one time.

Weft.—The series of threads—technically termed picks or shoots—thrown into a cloth at right angles to the warp by means of the shuttle. Weft yarns, as a rule, are softer spun, and consequently weaker than warp yarns.

Weighting.—Process of adding any substance to increase the natural weight of a fabric. Cotton may be weighted by the addition of size. Silk may be weighted, or " loaded," with vegetable substances, as sugar solution or rice powder (pongée). Mineral weighting is most commonly used. This method employs salts of metals, as chlorides or sulphate of iron, tin, aluminium, or magnesium.

Welsh Wool Fabrics.—A class of goods made with the wool of the sheep native to Wales, characterised by a fine, hairy quality, weaving into dense flannelly goods.

Welt.—That which, being sewn or otherwise fastened to an edge, pocket, or border, serves to guard, strengthen, or adorn it. Outside breast pockets and waistcoat pockets are usually finished in this style. Top welts are strips of cloth sewn on trousers at topsides only, when material is short, or when pleats at waist are wanted.

West of England Cloths.—Certain high qualities of serges and woollen goods woven in the Stroud and Gloucester districts.

Wheel-piece.—A piece, triangular in shape, added to the end of the skirt, from the pleat round—when the material is insufficient in width.

Whip.—An extra warp used for making cords or patterns on the face of a fabric.

Whipcord.—A cloth having a corded surface, the lines being clearly defined.

White Goods.—The large class of fabrics which are colourless or bleached, generally formed into a department in a large drapery store. White goods are commonly of linen and cotton, in piece and make-up.

Wigan.—A cotton fabric woven with a wide reed, and dressed with a gummy substance, used as a stiffening in ladies' dresses. A special grade of calico and sheeting made at Wigan, in Lancashire.

Wincey.—A cloth composed of a cotton warp and a woollen weft of a fairly heavy type.

Wings.—Thin pads of wadding, covered, to reach from the sidebody round back scye to shoulder ; used for an unlined coat.

Witney.—A woollen nap cloth napped in a particular pattern.

Woof.—A term sometimes applied to the bar-trees (Scottish term " stakes ") upon which warps are made, but more frequently a term (now almost obsolete) synonymous with weft or filling.

Woollen Fabric.—Cloth constructed from corded woollen material ; not necessarily synonymous with all-wool.

Woollen Yarn.—Yarns spun from wool in which anything but a parallel position of the fibres is noticeable—as distinct from worsted yarn, in which the wool fibres are markedly parallelised.

Worsted Fabric.—The typical worsted is a clear, smooth-handling fabric, in which the structure and colour are clearly defined, owing to the clearness and smoothness of both the yarns and the interlacing.

Worsted Yarn.—Yarns spun from wool in which the fibres are markedly parallelised—as distinct from woollen yarns in which anything but a parallel position of the fibres is noticeable.

Y

Yarn-dyed.—Dyed in the yarn, not in the piece, the slubbing, or the wool state.

Z

Zephyr.—A fine, light cotton fabric, generally woven with dyed yarns in a variety of fancy patterns ; printed imitations.

Zibeline.—A dress fabric made in cross-bred yarns, strangely coloured, usually in stripe form, and in finishing partly raised, with fibre laid in one direction.

END OF VOL. II

Lightning Source UK Ltd.
Milton Keynes UK
10 August 2010

158177UK00001B/99/P